Indian Detours

Sidestone Press

Mededelingen van het Rijksmuseum voor Volkenkunde N°. 45

ISBN 978-90-8890-336-6

Published by Sidestone Press, Leiden
www.sidestone.com

Published in Cooperation with the National Museum of Ethnology, Leiden
www.volkenkunde.nl
Head of Publications Committee: Fanny Wonu Veys

Lay-out & cover design: Sidestone Press

Photograph cover: Hopi dancers at the Grand Canyon, Arizona, 1928; photo by Ludolf Gratama (Drents Archief, nr. DA 680).

Also available as:
e-book (PDF): ISBN 978-90-8890-335-9

Contents

In memory of Dennison Nash, 1924-2012

Preface

Pieter Hovens and Mette van der Hooft

"Communication" was the core topic of the 2014 (European) American Indian Workshop, held in Leiden, the Netherlands, from May 21-25. The conference was hosted by the University of Leiden and the National Museum of Ethnology (Rijksmuseum voor Volkenkunde; now: National Museum of World Cultures) and attracted almost 200 academics from Europe and North America. Because of ongoing research at the museum into "Indian tourism," one double workshop of the conference was devoted to the presentation of papers on this type of intercultural communication. The outcome is this volume of studies, published in collaboration between the museum and Sidestone Press, a Leiden company specializing in books on archaeology and anthropology (www.sidestone.com).

Most of the papers presented during the tourism sessions at the 2014 AIW-conference have been developed into articles for this volume. Several contributors to the conference were unable to do so. Instead, one article has been included of an author who planned but was unable to attend the conference. Hovens used the opportunity to unite initially two separate articles into a long essay.

While most of the papers for the 2014 AIW Conference addressed the topic of communication implicitly or explicitly, there was sufficient space within the program for papers on other topics of ongoing research. This approach has over the years resulted in varied conference programs that draw colleagues annually to major academic centers across Europe. The other strength of the program is its interdisciplinary nature, and usually presentations are given by specialists in anthropology, sociology, psychology, political science, economics, archaeology, art history, history, linguistics, literary science, media studies, education, law, etc.

The contributions to this volume address the subject of Indian tourism from various perspectives and focus on different aspects of this multi-faceted phenomenon. Because the American Southwest is the area where natural wonders and Native American attractions are concentrated and draw by far the largest numbers of tourists, it is no surprise that this region is the focus of no less than five contributions.

Pieter Hovens provides a narrative historical overview of the involvement of Dutch individuals in Southwestern tourism between 1870 and 2014. They played a variety of roles, as researchers and adventurers, lecturers and authors, artists and collectors, travelers and tourists. Their impact hovers between the intimately personal and private on one end of the spectrum to the broad public realm on the other. The exploits of the twin sisters Constance and Peronne Arntzenius take central stage as they undertook the most extensive journeys across the country over a period of many years. The author takes a somewhat different approach to authenticity in the tourist arena than usual.

Mette van der Hooft presents the only known example of an individual Grand Tour undertaken by Dutch involving Native North America. The Gratamas published the narrative of their trip pertaining to the Pacific, but their manuscript regarding the North American part of their journey was only recently discovered. It is rare to find such first-person unpublished narratives as well as the original photographs from the itinerary. From the manuscript those paragraphs have been selected about travel conditions, encounters and experiences with Native Americans, and several other highlights of their journey.

Eloïse Gaillard focuses on the beginning of tourism and collecting in the Southwest, and the production of Indian curios for an emerging collectors and tourist market, encouraged by white traders. She highlights the group of clay Pueblo figures aggregated by Frenchman Alphonse Pinart, now curated at the Musée du quai Branly in Paris. It is just one example of many collections in European museums offering opportunities for research.

The development of the Indian casino industry and the opportunities it provides for self-representation by Native communities to travelers and tourists in New Mexico is presented by Suzanne Berthier-Foglar. She discusses the increasing trend in Indian-owned casinos to represent Native traditions in architecture and interior decoration, and the trend towards more luxurious accommodations for gambling, entertainment, and hospitality. In addition, the tension between the economic necessity of tapping into the tourist economy on the one hand while maintaining cultural privacy on the other is addressed.

The perspective of the hosts is central to the discussion by Bruce Bernstein on standards of authenticity of arts and crafts as viewed by Native artists and craftspeople themselves. His contribution documents that this standard is not only contested among academics and collectors, but also within source communities. He shows how Indian identities are (re)produced and defended in the marketplace, with the annual Indian Market in Santa Fe as an ideal case study. Such studies of internal discourse within source communities add significantly to the scientific analysis and understanding of authenticity.

Moving beyond the Southwest Markus Lindner presents the results of his fieldwork into the development of tourism on the Standing Rock Indian Reservation straddling the central border between South and North Dakota. Studies of the role of tourism in Plains Indian communities are rare, and his contribution is therefore of particular interest. Tribal tourism policy, involvement of the local communities, and the production and sale of arts and crafts are his focus.

Maaike de Jong and Alexander Grit address the visitors' gaze on exhibitions showing Native North American peoples and cultures, notably "The Plains Indians: Artists of Earth and Sky" as presented at the Musée du quai Branly in Paris. As a major destination of leisure travel the show was visited and viewed by large numbers of tourists from across Europe and the wider world. It induced criticism from anthropologists and Native peoples for the way it was co-curated and exhibited sacred objects.

The contribution of Birgit Däwes explores aspects of what might be regarded as the mirror image of classic Indian tourism as it has been predominantly perceived. She discusses visits of several Native individuals from North America to Europe between 1710 and 1860. Although their primary purpose of travel was politics or business, they spent leisure time visiting palaces, churches, theatres, and other cultural attractions in Europe. Two Native visitors, Samson Occom and Peter Jones, left written records of their experiences. These provide an opportunity for juxtaposition of traveler and tourist views of "the Other" from both sides of the Atlantic. This line of historical inquiry reveals new potential for tourism studies, and can be extended to the present. One recent example is the visit by Native Canadian veteran soldiers to Europe and the Netherlands in 2014 and 2015 to commemorate the 70th anniversaries of D-Day in France and Operation Market Garden in The Netherlands, and the end of the Second World War.

This volume is dedicated to the memory of Dennison Nash who visited Leiden in the early 1990s and expressed great interest in the discussion within the then National Museum of Ethnology to focus on tourism as a major subject of research. Although a communal endeavor did not materialize, several curators took up the topic in various ways (*cf.* Van Beek & Schmidt 2012; Hovens & Van der Hooft 2010). With tourism as the largest sector in the global marketplace, the subject will only attract more attention of museum researchers in the near future.[1]

Leiden: February, 2016

References

Walter van Beek & Annette Schmidt, eds. (2012), *African Hosts and Their Guests: Cultural Dyamics of Touris*m. Woodbridge, UK, and Rochester, NY: James Currey.

Pieter Hovens & Mette van der Hooft (2010), Van Drenthe naar het Wilde Westen: de Grand Tour van Ludolf Gratama en Johanna Schultz van Haegen door Indiaans Amerika (1928); in: *Drenthse Volksalmanak* 2010:1-27.

---

1 The editors wish to acknowledge the effective assistance of museum librarian Paul van Dongen in the preparation of the digital illustrations.

Communicating across the Red Atlantic

Early Native American Tourism and the Question of Agency

Birgit Däwes

Red Atlantic, Blue Ravens

In Gerald Vizenor's most recent historical novel, *Blue Ravens* (2014), two Anishinaabe soldiers decide to return to France after serving on the European frontlines in World War I. The fictitious veterans, Aloysius and Basile Hudon Beaulieu, an artist and a writer, become successful members of the modernist avant-garde in Europe; creating, as the narrator phrases it, "our native sense of presence with imagination and a sense of chance, and not with the sorrow of lost traditions. Yes, we were exiles on a federal reservation but not as soldiers, and we were never exiles in Paris" (Vizenor 2014:256). To them, in short, Europe becomes a welcome escape from the legacy of colonial oppression.

By the early 1920s, Native Americans "were already old hands at oceanic travel" (Weaver 2011:423): from the first sixteen captives that Columbus brought to Spain in 1493 (*cf.* Foreman 1943:20) to the Lakota performers in Buffalo Bill's Wild West Show, tens of thousands of Native North Americans had crossed the Atlantic for various purposes, as slaves, guides, or interpreters, as expert sailors on whaling ships, as performers and 'show Indians,' or as diplomats, fundraisers, and official political delegates. In a pioneer study from 1943, Carolyn Foreman outlines various transatlantic encounters in great historical detail; and various other historians, including Jack D. Forbes and Alden Vaughan, have followed suit (see also: Bellin 2009; Feest 1989; Flint 2009; and Fulford 2012).[1] Very few of them, however, chose to communicate their own stories. As Christian Feest deplores, "the absence of a sufficient body of Native American personal documents that is unimpeachable" results in perceptions of "Native American-European contacts [which are] based almost exclusively on notions existing in the minds of the Europeans" (1989:621). By merging well-researched historical characters (including Vizenor's own relatives, as well as famous writers and artists of the Lost Generation in Paris) with two fictional Native artists, Gerald Vizenor fills this gap and gives a voice to the experience of indigenous travelers: "Paris meant more to us," the narrator states, "than a luminous tourist destination of

1 In light of this long neglected traffic route, Tim Fulford and Kevin Hutchings argue, in 2009, for a terminological and conceptual move toward the "Indian Atlantic" as a larger geopolitical structure which places indigenous people in direct relation to "a capitalized transatlantic commerce" (2009:2): "[T]here was a 'Red Atlantic' just as deserving of our attention as the 'Black Atlantic'" (2009:18).

culture and liberation. The city had become our vision of art and literature, and a chance of recognition as native artists" (Vizenor 2014:144). By successfully "evad[ing] the romance of the primitive and sentiments of victimry" (Vizenor 2014:156), these fictitious characters communicate a firm sense of presence across what Jace Weaver terms "the Red Atlantic": that "multilane highway that American indigenes traveled back and forth in surprising numbers" (2011:15).

Departing from Paul Gilroy's seminal concept of the Black Atlantic, Weaver argues in a brand new study that "Indians, far from being marginal to the Atlantic experience, were, in fact, as central as Africans" (Weaver 2014:17) and substantiates this claim with numerous examples. I would like to add to this revisionist move by setting into relation four encounters from the periphery of the Red Atlantic from the early eighteenth to the early nineteenth century. Obviously, these encounters were not touristic in a classic sense, if one defines tourism as either a social practice exclusively linked to leisure or as an "industry" (Lickorish & Jenkins 1997:1). More recently, however, tourism studies have moved toward a diversification of concepts and understood tourism as "a serious individual engagement with the changing (and fluid) conditions of modernity with implications for nation formation and citizenship, the rise of consumerism, cosmopolitanism, the natural world, and globalization" (Franklin 2003:2). John Urry has influentially emphasized the importance of seeing as a mode of both communication and performance (1990; 2011), and other critics have taken up his argument to demonstrate that this is always a complex, multilateral process, in which agency is not necessarily one-sided: "if tourism is spectacle, then surely there are multiple parties involved in the creation of this spectacle" (Knudsen *et al.* 2008:4). If tourism is thus "a central component of modern social identity formation and engagement" (Franklin 2003:2), also including forms of business travel "as a work-oriented form of tourism" (Hall *et al.* 2004:5), then a historical perspective on intercultural encounters helps us to shed more light on the complex processes of identity construction that are located within, and contribute to the construction of, the Red Atlantic.

In this paper, I will use this wider understanding of tourism as a site of complex encounters, intercultural performance, and transnational communication to expand the notion of the Red Atlantic. Specifically, by comparing two non-indigenous depictions of Native North Americans with journals and travelogues by Samson Occom and Peter Jones, my purpose is threefold: first, to address the intersections of communication, presence, and agency in less dichotomous terms; second, to explore specific visual and textual perforations of the dominant "romance of the primitive" (Vizenor 2014:156), and third, to expand and refine the "Red Atlantic", in Weaver's sense as "part of a larger story of globalization and the worldwide movement of Western Hemisphere indigenes and their technologies, ideas, and material goods" (2014:32), into a multilateral cartography of Vizenorian "survivance," which helps us to navigate new waters of transnationalism, travel writing, tourism studies, and American literary history at large.

Unusual Travels

To begin, the juxtaposition of two encounters with indigenous Americans in the early eighteenth century, one in Connecticut, and one in London, is useful in order to illustrate a few topoi of alterity and exoticism at the time, as well as to show how the textual and visual discourses that establish these concepts simultaneously invite their own deconstruction. In 1704, Sarah Kemble Knight, a Puritan businesswoman from Boston, undertook a journey to New Haven in order to settle the estate of her brother-in-law. Her trip, as a woman traveling by herself, had been unprecedented and has been read by critics as a case of early feminism, an example of early American humor, or as a picaresque American Odyssey (Stephens 1964; *cf.* also Derounian-Stodola 1992, and Stanford 1984). Scott Michaelsen convincingly shows how the text departs from the tradition of providential narrative (*cf.* 1994: 36-37); and Julia Stern argues that Knight's *Journal* "marks the shift from Puritan to Yankee world view" much more clearly than Benjamin Franklin's *Autobiography* (Stern 1997:2). During this journey, Knight also comes across a few Native Americans and describes them as follows: "There are everywhere in the Towns as I passed, a Number of Indians the Natives of the Country, and are the most salvage [sic] of all the salvages of that kind that I had ever Seen: little or no care taken (as I heard upon enquiry) to make them otherwise" (Knight 1920:39). With apparent ethnographic interest, she notes some of their social and legal conventions: "they marry many wives and at pleasure put them away, and on the least dislike or fickle humour, on either side, saying *stand away* to one another is a sufficient Divorce. And indeed those uncomely *Stand aways* are too much in Vogue among the English in this (Indulgent Colony) as their Records plentifully prove [...]" (Knight 1920:39). While at first glance, this description seems to tie in neatly with common Puritan stereotypes of Native people, as savages who are emotionally and socially inconsistent and thus incapable of maintaining functional communities, a closer look reveals the subtle shift of responsibility in the first quote, and the rather explicit one in the second: the "uncomely *Stand aways*" may have been an indigenous convention, but it is the English settlers in Connecticut who have brought this practice of divorce to full fruition. Likewise, the Natives are "the most salvage of all the salvages *of that kind*", which implies yet another kind, and this is precisely the kind who fails to treat them appropriately: the local administrators of English descent. Knight draws this connection even more distinctly a few pages later: "We may Observe here the great necessity and bennifitt both of Education and Conversation; for these people have as Large a portion of mother witt, and sometimes a Larger, than those who have bin brought up in Citties; But for want of emprovements, Render themselves almost Ridiculos[sic], as above" (Knight 1920:43-44). By the "ridiculous" people, however, she refers not to Native people, but to the rural population of New England. In colonial Connecticut in 1704, at least from the point of view of an upper-class Bostonian, it is no longer certain who the savages actually are.

Six years later, in 1710, in the middle of Queen Anne's War (the second of the French and Indian Wars), and only 17 years after Cotton Mather wrote about indigenous America as "the devil's territories" where, according to Mather the Salem Witchcraft Trials showcased Satan's attempts to revolt against the Christians,[2] three Mohawks and one Mahican traveled to London on a diplomatic visit to the British Queen. They came with a purpose: worried by the increasing dominance of the French in their homeland, they requested British assistance to reduce the influence of Jesuit missionaries on their cultural sovereignty, their hunting rights and trading routes. Their foreign policy proved successful: they were "received as royalty on a state visit" (Weaver 2014:154), visited the Tower and St. Paul's Cathedral, attended a performance of Shakespeare's *Macbeth,* and were painted, at the request of Queen Anne, by Jan Verelst, the court's renowned portrait artist from Holland (*cf.* Pratt 2013:44-45), as well as by British artists, including John Faber and Bernard Lens (*cf.* Bond 1952:66-67; Vaughan 2006:113-36).[3]

Like Knight's journal, these images were authored by non-indigenous artists, and thus document the European construction of the *indian*[4] rather than the visitors themselves, but this construction is intricately interlaced with traces of agency, as well. In Lens's image, the "Four Indian Kings" are framed within insignia of European monarchy, which remarkably invests the visitors with political status and power. In Verelst's version, Tee Yee Neen Ho Ga Row, or Hendrick Peters is even advertised as the "Emperour of the Six Nations," and, in contrast to more common exoticist projections of the time, depicted in English buckled shoes, a black frock coat, and a red, gold-rimmed velvet cloak. Historically, these epithets are, of course, far from accurate: first of all, until the Tuscarora joined the Iroquois Confederacy in 1722, there had been only five nations (Mohawk, Seneca, Onondaga, Oneida, Cayuga). Peter Schuyler, who was in charge of the venture, used "Six Nations" to include the Mahicans, but

---

2 "I believe there were never more satanical devices," Mather writes in "The Wonders of the Invisible World in 1693, "used for the unsettling of any people under the sun, than what have been employed for the extirpation of the vine which God has here planted, casting out the heathen, and preparing a room before it, and causing it to take deep root, and fill the land [...]" (2012:329).

3 As with Pocahontas a century earlier, who came to London with her husband John Rolfe, no first-hand account exists. Peter Schuyler, the mayor of Albany, NY, who accompanied the Natives to England, notes down that Hendrick Peters addressed the Queen with the following words: "We were mightily rejoyed when we heard by *Anadagarjaux* [Colonel Nicholson], that our Great Queen had resolved to send an Army to reduce *Canada;* from whose Mouth we readily embraced our Great Queen's Instructions; an in Token of our Friendship, we hung up the *Kettle,* and took up the *Hatchet* [...]. The Reduction of *Canada* is of such Weight, that after the effecting thereof, We should have *Free Hunting* and a great Trade with our *Great Queen's* Children; and as a Token of the Sincerity of the Six Nations, We do here, in the Name of All, present our *Great Queen* with these *BELTS of WAMPUM*" (quoted in Pratt 2013:44, and Vaughan 2006:120 [emphases original]). Beyond these reports, however, we do not have any sources that could give us the Haudenosaunee perspective.

4 Following Gerald Vizenor, I am using the lower-case, italicized spelling of *Indian* for the stereotypical simulation which "has no real referent, no actual native ancestors" (Vizenor 2003:169), whereas Native American or First Nation refers to historical people.

"[w]hether this was Schuyler's ploy or an honest mistake by the English press is unclear" (Vaughan 2006:299n). Second, the delegate was neither an emperor nor any other official political leader: he had been hand-picked, along with the others, by the English colonists who also sought British support against the French (*cf.* Vaughan 2006:116-17). Most importantly, far from an Empire, the Iroquois Confederacy relied on democratic structures and elections and is, in fact, the oldest living participatory democracy on the planet. These misconceptions shape the intercultural encounters of the time; and they necessitate careful practices of reading and translation, especially in those cases in which Native Americans left no written documents that recorded their impressions of Europe.

By choosing, as a setting for his portrait of Tee Yee Neen Ho Ga Row, not the studio in London, but a fabricated forest scenery, Jan Verelst calls attention to what Mary Louise Pratt defines as the "contact zone": "the space of colonial encounters, the space in which peoples geographically and historically separated come into contact with each other and establish ongoing relations, usually involving conditions of coercion, radical inequality, and intractable conflict" (Pratt 1992:6). This contact zone is traditionally located on the American continent; it is the frontier that translates dichotomous differences into a geographical signifier. By moving this contact zone back to the old world, and by overwriting it with visual signifiers of bilateralism, if not equality, these documents substantially de-hierarchize the contact zone, allowing us "to foreground the interactive, improvisational dimensions of colonial encounters so easily ignored or suppressed by diffusionist accounts of conquest and domination" (Pratt 1992:7).

"What the Iroquois thought of all this," Richmond Bond writes about their attendance of *Macbeth,* "of the audience, [...] of Shakespeare in general, and the Haymarket in particular [...] – this there is of course no way to know" (Bond 1952:5). At the same time, these images also yield what Gerald Vizenor calls "traces of Native survivance" (2009:9). In Verelst's depictions of Sagayenwaraton (or simply Brant) and Tee Yee Neen Ho Ga Row, the contact zone is quite obviously visualized, and verbalized, by the visitors' Mohawk and English names –in terms of what Homi Bhabha terms "hybridity – "the sign of the productivity of colonial power, its shifting forces and fixities" (1985:1175).

Hybridity is not merely the mixing of two cultures, but it exposes, in its semiotic processes of repetition and imitation, the very power structures that colonial discourse tries to conceal. If we look closely, the Mohawks in this painting have literally put on an English guise: the realm of cultural authenticity is replaced by the self-reflexive visual gesture of simulation. Hybridity, according to Bhabha, "intervenes in the exercise of authority not merely to indicate the impossibility of its identity, but to represent the unpredictability of its presence. The book [as a signifier of Christianity] retains its presence, but it is no longer a representation of an essence; it is now a partial presence, a (strategic) device in a specific colonial engagement, and appurtenance of authority" (1985:1177).

The intercultural communication involved in these visits, in other words, is potentially subversive, even if we lack an explicit Native voice. "Native imagination, experience, and remembrance are the real landscapes of liberty in the literature of this continent," Gerald Vizenor asserts: "discoveries and dominance are silence, absence, want, and cultural nostalgia" (2009:7). Thus, just like the Natives from Connecticut in Knight's journal, these Haudenosaunee delegates are inscribed into the contact zone as presences, rewriting what Jace Weaver terms "Atlantic exceptionalism" (2014:9) from an indigenous angle.

"What Great Difference There Is": Samson Occom's Fundraising Tour

Samson Occom, a Mohegan missionary from Connecticut, the first Native American autobiographer, and, according to Bernd Peyer, "the father of North American Indian literature" (1997:61), went to London half a century after the Five Nations delegates who met with Queen Anne. His purpose was fundraising: he was sent by Eleazar Wheelock, whose mission school Occom had attended himself (between 1743 and 1747), and whose educational project he embodied, supported, and advertised. Occom left his family behind and, together with another Reverend, Nathaniel Whitaker, embarked for England in December 1765. The tour was greatly successful: traveling across England, Scotland, and Ireland, the Mohegan Reverend enjoyed enormous popularity, presented several hundreds of sermons, and collected some 12,000 pounds for the Indian Charity School (*cf.* Peyer 1997:76; Vaughan 2006:191).[5] It is notable that, even though his fundraising works very well, and he becomes a highly esteemed public speaker, the Reverend himself does not spend any ink on the details of his successes. While, as Bernd Peyer outlines, "in most places, he was kindly received by leading religious and political personalities of the day" (1997:75), Occom often restricts himself to summarily noting that people "made a collection for us" (2006:273), without any numbers or details. Upon his return, however, Occom turns to more detailed words when he finds out that his family had not been aptly supported by Wheelock. Outraged by the betrayal, he writes the famous "Short Narrative of My Life," in which he bitterly accuses his employers of exploiting him.

It is important to mention that Occom did not write a travelogue for the public. His journals and letters, however, document all the more reliably his impressions of the foreign country. His conflicting loyalties shine through his reports from the very beginning, when he writes to Wheelock about his doubts before the journey: "I have a Struggle in my Mind At times, knowing not where I am going, I don't know but I am Looking for a Spot of Ground where my

5 Ruth Rosenberg notes in detail that "he raised £ 9,497 from 2,169 people in 305 churches in England; and in Scotland, where he displayed the Oneida wampum belt, he raised an additional £ 2,529" (1997:205).

Bones must be Buried, and never to See my Poor Family again, but I verely believe I am Calld of god by Strange Providence and that is Enough" (Occom 2006:74). Throughout his journey, his Montauk wife Mary Fowler, and his family at home plays a major role for him, and he notes down often that he sent packages abroad, with "Presents from Bristol" (2006:78) or clothing for his children (see also: Peyer 1997:66).

In the same way that American travel writing, an excessively popular genre at the time, works as "constitutive" discourse, "a tool of self- and national fashioning that constructs its object even as it describes it" (Hamera & Bendixen 2009:1), Occom's private notes, his journals and letters depict and design both English society and his own position as a cultural broker. He notes down the people he dines with, the places he visits, and the appointments he fulfills, as well as various impediments to his health (such as a mild case of smallpox: After "a Cold I have" (2006:269), Occom is inoculated, which is a kind of early vaccination against smallpox, in which the patient was cut and subcutaneously exposed to smallpox scabs in order to obtain immunity. He suffers from a mild case for weeks, writing to his wife that "this after-Noon, I was Inoculated by Mr. Whitaker, and you will Soon hear whether I am well of it or Dead with it" (2006:76).

Occom is neither impressed by the British weather, complaining for instance about the "Tedious Cold rainy Day" (2006:267) or that it "rain'd very hard" (2006:273), nor by the conventional sights of London. He mentions Westminster Abbey and the Tower only in passing, but is more attentive toward the landscape, which, as he repeatedly states, "is like one Continued Garden" (2006:266,273). What is particularly interesting in analyzing Samson Occom's "contact zone" is the fact that the lines of cultural difference do not run between Native Americans and Europeans for him. He focuses instead rather critically on London's internal social divides: "Saw such Confusion as I never Dreamt of – there was Some at Churches Singing & Preaching, in the Streets some Cursing, Swaring & Damning one another, [...]& Coaches and footmen passing and repassing, Crossing and Cross-Crossing, and the poor Begars Praying, Crying, and Beging upon their knees" (2006:266-67).

Occom's diagnosis of class differences and of poverty and crime in England is contrasted with the charity work of George Whitefield (who, in the spirit of Methodism, ran an orphanage) and other "good people [who] live in this place" (2006:272). As in Sarah Kemble Knight's journal, the diagnosis of difference goes beyond the usual suspects here; reversing the exotic gaze and disseminating its construction of the Other, in Derrida's sense of the word, as "the impossible return to any rejoined, readjusted unity of meaning" (Derrida 2004:268, 299). This dissemination culminates contrastively in the description of King George III, who is "quite a Comly [handsome] man," according to Occom: "his Crown is Richly adorn'd with Diamonds, how grand and Dazling is it to our Eyes, – if an Earthly Crown is So grand – How great and glorious must the

Crown of the glorious Redeemer be, at the right hand of the majesty on High – tho' he was once Crown'd with Thorns" (2006:268).

From the very beginning of intercultural contact, as Carolyn Foreman reminds us, "English rulers lost no opportunity to exhibit their armies" (1943:13) in order to underline their military, political, and economic power. While King George, too, takes great care to display the insignia of his earthly power to his visitor in 1766, Occom, in turn, never fails to emphasize the relativity of such materialism in light of spiritual salvation. As little as he has to say about the pompous cathedrals and palaces of London, Occom here turns verbose, and almost redundant, in his counterbalancing of the royal spectacle. Secular possession is not explicitly rejected, but by comparing the King's adornment with that of Jesus Christ, he implicitly charges the sovereign of England with hubris.

The same holds true for the aristocrats of London, who also present themselves to him in all their glory: "we Saw some of the Nobility In their Shining Robes and a throng of People all around, – the Sight of the Nobility put me in mind of Dives and the Rich Gluton, and the poor reminded me of Lazarus – what great Difference there is Between the Rich and the Poor – and What Diference [sic] there is and will be, Between Gods poor and the Devils Rich, &c -" (2006:268).

Without spending too many words on the actual outfits or jewelry, Occom turns straight to simile, this time rather explicitly drawing an analogy between the paraders and Satan. "O Lord God Amighty," he adds, "let not my Eyes be Dazled with the glitering Toys of this World but let m be fixt and my Soul Long after Jx [Jesus Christ] Who is the only Pearl of great Price" (2006:268). If the assorted possessions and garments of the European aristocracy serve as tokens of power and civilization, Occom effectively voids them by reference to higher powers. Without openly criticizing the King and his nobility, he nevertheless puts them in their place, both ethically and politically. In light of the economic injustice he encounters in the contact zone, the Mohegan missionary thus simply overwrites the social structure of the British Empire with an indictment of devilish greed, and a vision of global equality in Christ.

"Saw Everything That Was To Be Seen": Kah-Ke-Wa-Quo-Na-By (Peter Jones)

Sixty-five years after Samson Occom, another Native North American missionary visited England for a fund-raising tour. Kah-Ke-Wa-Quo-Na-By, or Peter Jones, was "the first Aboriginal Methodist minister in Canada" (Smith 2013:18), with both Mississauga (Anishinaabe) and English heritage. Born and raised on the western shore of Lake Ontario, he was educated at a log-cabin school, and, at the age of twenty-one, converted to the Methodist faith (Smith 1987:41; see also: Smith 2003). On his first trip to England Jones spent a little over a year in England, traveling around the country for fundraising, "to make appeals to the benevolent people of England, in order to support the Missions and schools" in Upper Canada (Jones 1860:299), and noting down his impressions. His journal is far more extensive than Occom's, and he documents some of his encounters in great detail. It is all the more surprising that there is no mention of a rather crucial experience of his trip: as his biographer outlines, Jones fell in love with an upper-class Englishwoman named Eliza Field, whom he probably met in the fall of 1831 (*cf.* Smith 1987:130-49), and whom he convinced to return to Canada with him. They were married in New York in 1833.

Like the Haudenosaunee delegates and Occom before him, Jones too was received by the Royals, in his case William IV and his wife. In contrast to Occom, however, Jones seems clearly impressed by the splendor and prosperity of the royal procession do not fail to impress Jones. When he first sees the King, William IV, in his palace, he notices that "the old King [...] appeared to be in good health and good spirits" (1860:325); and the Reverend seems impressed by "the magnificence of the rooms" (1860:325), but he also notices that "[t] heir Majesties bowed their heads when we bowed to them. They were standing when we entered the room, and stood the whole time while we remained with them" (1860:342). These details go beyond mere interest in royal protocol: by foregrounding that they were literally on an equal footing, Jones, as a representative of his nation, assumes a position of similar dignity and power. This lack of difference in rank is also underlined by the verbatim documentation of their dialogue: "I told him that I belong'd to the Chippeway nation, residing in Upper Canada. He then asked how many of us there were in the nation. I told him about 40 or 50,000. He asked me how old I was. I replied thirty-one. When I was baptized ? I told him about nine or ten years ago. What my name was? I replied, Kahkewaquonaby, in the Indian–Peter Jones in the English" (1860:342).

The Mississauga visitor gets to have not only the answers, but also the last word, his name, before he presents King William with his Anishinaabe translation of the Gospel of St. John. At dinner a bit later, Jones repeats a toast of praise in honor of the royals: "Long may they live to be a blessing to their nation and people! May God direct them in the good and right path of righteousness! God bless the King and Queen!" (1860:344). Again, as in Occom's journal, there is no explicit criticism, but the reference to God's necessary direction and guidance relativizes the sovereign's earthly power once more. In the journal, Jones is a little more explicit when he describes, a few months earlier, the tomb of John Wesley, "the Father of the Methodists": "It is right that good and holy men should be honoured and esteemed, but never to be worshipped, as God is the only proper object of worship" (1860:312). Similarly, he expresses his disapproval of a Catholic service, where he "saw the superstitions of the people, in going through their several maneuvers, all to make a show, and attract the poor deluded multitude, who are fools enough to bow to the priests" (1860:322). His criticism of class differences and materialism, however, is most pointed in a letter to his brother, which A. LaVonne Brown Ruoff quotes: "their motto seems to be 'Money, money; get money, get rich, and be a gentleman.' With this sentiment they fly about in every direction, like a swarm of bees, in search of the treasure which lies so near their hearts" (quoted in Ruoff 2001:209). This critique of materialist excess and the preoccupation with class differences are common elements in many Native Americans' nineteenth-century impressions of Europe, and they stem from both the Protestant denominations of these travelers and a sense of social solidarity that had been shaped by their lives in indigenous communities.

The encounter between Peter Jones and the English king and queen is even more significant when read in relation to a visit of Westminster Abbey two months previously. Again, if the display of royal wealth is to impress the Native visitors and demonstrate British power to them, this symbolic act fails in Jones's case, as well: he notably refrains from using upbeat adjectives or linguistic decorum, adding instead a tongue-in-cheek performance of his own: "After breakfast, I went through Westminister Abbey [sic], and saw everything that was to be seen in it. The statues, monuments, tombs, vaults, &c., of the kings, queens, and great men, were numerous. I also saw the place where the Kings of England are crowned, and the royal chairs that they sit on when they are thus crowned. I took the liberty to seat myself down upon them as we passed by, so that I can now say that I, a poor Indian from the woods of Canada, sat in the king's and queen's great crowning chairs" (1860:328).

In contrast to the monotony by which he refers to "everything that was to be seen," his adoption of the royal pose marks a shift in tone and clearly turns into what Gerald Vizenor calls an "imagic moment" (*cf.* Vizenor 2003), one of those moments of resistance in which "Native storiers create, at their best, a singular sense of presence by natural reason, customary words, perceptive tropes, observant irony, and imagic scenes. That authorial sense of presence is the premise of a distinctive aesthetics of survivance" (2009:1). This "sense of presence" is visible throughout Peter Jones's account, a set of "imagic scenes" by a traveler who skillfully moved across different registers and expectations.

Conclusion

When Gerald Vizenor's Anishinaabe narrator returns from World War I, he emphasizes the power of cultural belonging: "The stories that heal must have an origin, a mark or notice, and a native sense of natural motion and presence. A story must create a new sense of presence with every new version of the story" (2014:193). This origin, however, cannot remain in the past: it lives on, just like the travelogues of Samson Occom and Peter Jones, in new versions and new encounters.

According to Jace Weaver, the aim of reconceptualizing the Red Atlantic is to "restor[e] Indians as actors in the transoceanic story. In helping create the Red Atlantic, they were integrated into – and integrated themselves into – the nascent world economy. Not merely slaves and victims (though they were that, too), they were self-determined and not simply selves-determined" (2011:456).

As Samson Occom and Peter Jones demonstrate, together with many travelers after them, such as George Henry, George Copway or Emily Pauline Johnson, Vizenorian "imagic moments" abound in the European contact zone. Through strategies of selection, omission, simile, metaphor, semantic relocation, and irony, these travel accounts rewrite the contact zone as a site of encounter among equals, and within the terminological frameworks of "tourism." Far from the exoticist grip of *Indian* stereotypes, they develop positions of Native American authority, sovereignty, and knowledge. If travel writing is indeed, as Judith Hamera and Alfred Bendixen suggest, intimately linked to the formation of American identity, then Native American impressions of Europe rewrite this very identity in crucial ways.[6]

Furthermore, like all travel writing, these texts serve as mirrors for those who read them, negotiating the boundaries between self and other, and redrawing the lines between home and abroad. From the fictional narrative of an Oglala Wild West Show performer in James Welch's *The Heartsong of Charging Elk* to Vizenor's Anishinaabe soldiers, the Red Atlantic is therefore not only "about more than the movement of human bodies around and across the Atlantic" (Weaver 2014:268), but its impact also clearly goes beyond first-hand communication. Whereas Tim Fulford writes that "The Indian Atlantic died, as a personal and political reality" after 1783 (2012:121), and Weaver sees its closure in 1927 (2014:267), I believe that it continues as an important tool in reconsidering the cartographies of imperialism far beyond the outlines of historical travels. Like the "new version[s] of the story" in *Blue Ravens,* this multilateral web of communication involves an ongoing ethics of cultural exchange, of Native sovereignty, agency, and presence. If the Red Atlantic continues to be shaped in variants of literary and cultural survivance as we speak, the task remains pertinent to follow its traces, and to prevent it from becoming just another rhetorical tool in the deceptive colonialist narrative of closure.

6 American travel writing, as Judith Hamera & Alfred Bendixen remind us, "simultaneously exposes inter- and intra-cultural contradictions and contains them. It creates American 'selves' and American landscapes through affirmation, exclusion, and negation of others, and interpellates readers into these selves and landscapes through specific rhetorical and genre conventions" (2009:1).

References

Bellin, Joshua David (2009), The Savage Tour: Indian Performance Across the Atlantic; in: Tim Fulford & Kevin Hutchings (eds.), *Native Americans and Anglo-American Culture, 1750-1850*: 241-255. Cambridge: Cambridge University Press.

Bendixen, Alfred (2009), American Travel Books about Europe before the Civil War; in: Alfred Bendixen & Judith Hamera (eds.), *The Cambridge Companion to American Travel Writing*, 103-126. Cambridge: Cambridge University Press.

Bhabha, Homi (1985/2004), Signs Taken for Wonders; in: Julie Rivkin & Michael Ryan (eds.), *Literary Theory: An Anthology* (2nd ed.): 1167-1184. Malden, MA: Blackwell.

Bond, Richmond P. (1952), *Queen Anne's American Kings.* Oxford: Clarendon Press.

Derounian-Stodola, Kathryn Zabelle. (1992), The New England Frontier and the Picaresque in Sarah Kemble Knight's Journal; in: Kathryn ZabelleDerounian-Stodola (ed.), *Early American Literature and Culture: Essays Honoring Harrison T. Meserole*: 122-131. Newark: University of Delaware Press.

Derrida, Jacques (2004), *Dissemination.* New York: Bloomsbury Academic.

Feest, Christian F. (1989), Indians and Europe? Editor's Postscript; in: Christian F. Feest (ed.), *Indians and Europe: An Interdisciplinary Collection of Essays*: 609-628. Lincoln, NE: University of Nebraska Press.

Flint, Kate (2009), *The Transatlantic Indian, 1776-1930.* Princeton, NJ: Princeton University Press.

Forbes, Jack D. (2007), *The American Discovery of Europe.* Urbana, IL: University of Illinois Press.

Foreman, Carolyn Thomas (1943), *Indians Abroad: 1493-1938.* Norman, OK: University of Oklahoma Press.

Franklin, Adrian (2003), *Tourism: An Introduction.* London: Sage.

Fulford, Tim (2012), Transatlantic American Indians; in: Eve Tavor Bannet & Susan Manning (eds.), *Transatlantic Literary Studies, 1660-1830*: 106-123. Cambridge: Cambridge University Press.

Fulford, Tim & Kevin Hutchings. (2009), Introduction: The Indian Atlantic; in: *Native Americans and Anglo-American Culture, 1750-1850*: 1-38. Cambridge: Cambridge University Press.

Hall, C. Michael, Allan M. Williams, & Alan A. Lew (2004), Tourism: Conceptualizations, Institutions, and Issues; in: Michael Hall, Allan M. Williams, & Alan A. Lew (eds.), *A Companion to Tourism*: 3-22. Malden, MA: Blackwell.

Hamera, Judith & Alfred Bendixen (2009), Introduction: New Worlds and Old Lands – The Travel Book and the Construction of American Identity; in: Alfred Bendixen & Judith Hamera (eds.), *The Cambridge Companion to American Travel Writing*: 1-9. Cambridge: Cambridge University Press.

Jones, Peter (1860), *Life and Journals of Kah-Ke-Wa-Quo-Na-By (Rev. Peter Jones): Wesleyan Missionary.* (Anson Green, ed.). Toronto: Wesleyan Printing. Columbia University Online Archive; Web. June 4, 2013.

Knight, Sarah Kemble (1920), *The Journal of Madame Knight.* (Theodore Dwight, ed.). Boston: Small, Maynard and Co.

Knudsen, Daniel C., Anne K. Soper & Michelle M. Metro-Roland (2008), Landscape, Tourism, and Meaning: An Introduction; in: Daniel C. Knudsen *et al.* (eds.), *Landscape, Tourism, and Meaning*: 1-8. Burlington, VT: Ashgate Publishing.

Lickorish, Leonard L. & Carson L. Jenkins (1997), *An Introduction to Tourism.* Oxford: Reed Elsevier.

Mather, Cotton (1693/2012), The Wonders of the Invisible World; in: Nina Baym (ed.), *The Norton Anthology of American Literature* (vol. A, 8th ed.): 328-333. New York: Norton.

Michaelsen, Scott (1994), Narrative and Class in a Culture of Consumption: The Significance of Stories in Sarah Kemble Knight's Journal; in: *College Literature* 21 (2): 33-45.

Occom, Samson (2006), *The Collected Writings of Samson Occom, Mohegan.* (Joanna Brooks, ed.). New York: Oxford University Press.

Pratt, Mary Louise (1992), *Imperial Eyes: Travel Writing and Transculturation.* London: Routledge.

Pratt, Stephanie (2013), Iroquois Portrayed: Images of the Haudenosaunee from Three Centuries; in: Sylvia Kasprycki (ed.), *On the Trails of the Iroquois*: 43-49. Bonn: Bundeskunsthalle.

Peyer, Bernd C. (1997), *The Tutor'd Mind: Indian Missionary Writers in Antebellum America.* Amherst: University of Massachusetts Press.

Rosenberg, Ruth (1997), Samson Occom; in: Kenneth M. Roemer (ed.), *Native American Writers of the United States*: 203-207. Detroit, MI: Gale.

Ruoff, A. LaVonne Brown (2001), Reversing the Gaze: Early Native American Images of Europeans and Euro-Americans; in: Gretchen M. Bataille (ed.), *Native American Representations: First Encounters, Distorted Images, and Literary Appropriations*: 198-122. Lincoln, NE: University of Nebraska Press.

Smith, Donald B. (1987), *Sacred Feathers: The Reverend Peter Jones (Kahkewaquonaby) and the Mississauga Indians.* Toronto: University of Toronto Press.

Smith, Donald B. (2003), 'Jones, Peter', in: *Dictionary of Canadian Biography,* vol. 8. University of Toronto/Université Laval; Webpage, September 3, 2013.

Smith, Donald B. (2013), *Mississauga Portraits: Ojibwe Voices from Nineteenth-Century Canada.* Toronto: University of Toronto Press.

Stanford, Ann (1984), Sarah Kemble Knigh; in: Emory Elliott (ed.), *American Colonial Writers, 1606-1734*: 187-189. Detroit, MI: Gale.

Stephens, Robert O. (1964), The Odyssey of Sarah Kemble Knight; in: *College Language Association Journal* 7:247-55.

Stern, Julia (1997), To Relish and to Spew: Disgust as Cultural Critique in "The Journal of Madam Knight"; in: *Legacy* 14 (1):1-12.

Urry, John (1990), *The Tourist Gaze.* London: Sage.

Urry, John & Jonas Larsen (2011), *The Tourist Gaze 3.0.* London: Sage.

Vaughan, Alden T. (2006), *Transatlantic Encounters: American Indians in Britain, 1500-1776.* Cambridge: Cambridge University Press.

Vizenor, Gerald (2009), *Native Liberty: Natural Reason and Cultural Survivance.* Lincoln, NE: University of Nebraska Press.

Vizenor, Gerald (2003), Imagic Moments: Native Identities and Literary Modernity; in: Helmbrecht Breinig (ed.), *Imaginary (Re-)Locations: Tradition, Modernity, and the Market in Contemporary Native American Literature and Culture*: 167-183. Tübingen: Stauffenburg.

Vizenor, Gerald (2014), *Blue Ravens.* Middletown, CT: Wesleyan University Press.

Weaver, Jace (2011), The Red Atlantic: Transoceanic Cultural Exchange; in: *American Indian Quarterly* 35 (3):418-77.

Weaver, Jace (2014), *The Red Atlantic: American Indigenes and the Making of the Modern World, 1000-1927.* Chapel Hill, NC: University of North Carolina Press.

Native American Detours and the Quest for Authenticity

Dutch Tourism, Collecting and Research in the Southwest

Pieter Hovens

Introduction

In 1991 the National Museum of Ethnology in Leiden, The Netherlands, established a separate North American Department with a half-time curatorship, recognizing the importance of its collection from that part of the world (*cf.* Hovens 2011). An inventory of the then circa 2200 specimens was undertaken to identify opportunities for research, collecting, and exhibitions. The Southwest collection was by far the largest and varied, while from the Plains, Northeast and Northwest Coast the museum curated a basic collection. Notable was the presence of a substantial number of traditional Indian-made artifacts sold to western visitors, and items intentionally produced for that market. A survey of materials from Native North America in other Dutch museum collections led to the same conclusion (*cf.* Hovens 2015). The major customers for these goods were travelers and tourists that traversed and visited the North American West in ever increasing numbers since the 1880s when the transcontinental railroads were completed and cruises could be taken along the Pacific coast. The survey of Dutch museum collections eventually culminated in a research project on Indian tourism in Native North America, as it was also realized that tourism had become a major socio-economic and cultural factor in many tribal communities, and was promoted as a development strategy by American and Canadian federal, state and provincial governments (*cf.* Csargo 1988; Smith 1994; Ryan & Aicken 2005).[1] In the present article a selection of the preliminary results regarding the Southwest will be presented, the region where tourism had and still has the greatest impact on Indian communities.

When sociologists like Erik Cohen (1972) and Dean MacCannell (1973; 1976) pioneered the field of tourism research in the early to mid-seventies, anthropologists were quick to follow suit. In the mid-seventies Nelson Graburn

1 Funds for research in the U.S. and Canada for this project were provided by: the National Museum of Ethnology (Leiden), the Netherlands Science Foundation (NWO, The Hague), the Gratama Foundation, the Netherlands-America Foundation, United Airlines, and the American Embassy. The Roosevelt Study Center (Middelburg), The Harold S. Colton Research Center (Flagstaff, AZ) and the Laboratory of Anthropology (Santa Fe, NM) provided other assistance. Their support is gratefully acknowledged.

was instrumental in promoting anthropological interest in tourism as an agent of change in Fourth World communities. Although his primary focus was on material culture and the arts, he soon broadened his analysis to the phenomenon of tourism as a form of interethnic relations (Graburn 1976, 1983). A new specialization emerged, notably in the Anglo-Saxon world: the anthropology of tourism (e.g. Smith *et al.* 1977, 1980; Nash 1978; 1981; Van Den Berghe & Keyes 1984). The new specialization faced a struggle to be accepted as a field of academic study, both as a new discipline, but not in the least because of the less than serious image of leisure time as a human activity worth of scientific inquiry. However, with tourism becoming the largest industry in the global economy and its impact reaching into even the remotest corners of the world, the anthropology of tourism has also matured and is now addressing a myriad of issues in tourist encounters and exchanges from the perspectives of both hosts and guests (*cf.* Nash 1996, 2007; Chambers 1999; Stronza 2001).

Sociological and anthropological interest in tourism as worth of scientific inquiry lagged in The Netherlands. It also was a subject not easily embraced by the art historians and archaeologists that dominated the curatorial department at the National Museum of Ethnology in Leiden. Tourist art was regarded as inauthentic, hardly deserving serious scientific research. To bring the subject closer to home in more than one sense, the research of the North American Department focused on the involvement of the Dutch in Indian tourism since the 1880s. Ideally this also provides a stimulus for similar research in other European countries, insight into the historical development of this aspect of interethnic relations in Native North America, and a European perspective on ethnic imagery.

The experiences of the Dutch in the American Southwest are presented and paraphrased as they are, with a minimum of historical annotation, as the history of Indian-white relations and tourism has been extensively documented elsewhere. However, in separate articles on several individuals that are currently in preparation the historical context will be addressed more extensively.

Early imagery

The Netherlands is a small country, situated in a delta where several European rivers reach the North Sea that is connected to the Atlantic Ocean. Thus the Dutch have historically been a seafaring nation and became involved in world exploration, trade and colonization, competing with much larger nations such as Great Britain, France, Spain and Portugal. The New World and its Native inhabitants became familiar in Holland soon after its second discovery in 1492 through allegorical representations of the New World, travel narratives, and various treatises on the continent beyond the Atlantic. Between 1567 and 1652 the international scientific discussion on the origin of the aboriginal Americans was centered in the Netherlands because of the active participation of Dutch scholars and the residence or publication of works by European scholars in Holland. These included Johannes Lumnius, Antonio de Montesinos, Francois Caron, Menassah ben Israel, Isaac de la Peyrere, Hugo Grotius, Johannes de Laet, and Georg Hornius (Wauchope 1962; Huddleston 1976). The Dutch colony of New Netherland on the Hudson and Delaware Rivers (1609-1664) also generated publications and some rare imagery. However, the written accounts and visual representations of Native Americans generally remained accessible only to an educated upper class of nobility, clergy and major entrepreneurs, except on the rare occasion when a Native American was exhibited in a public place (Hamell 1987).

The Netherlands is a small country, situated on a multiple river delta connecting it to various parts of Europe, and on the North Sea, connecting it to the Atlantic Ocean and the world beyond. This explains the strong external orientation of the Hollanders and their prominent presence in global exploration and trade since the sixteenth century (*cf.* Coolhaas 1980). One expression of this interest is the plethora of 18th and 19th century Dutch translations of books on the exploration of the North American continent. Original accounts by Fernando De Soto, Louis Hennepin, Jacques Marquette, William Bartram, Jonathan Carver, Portlock and Dickson, Zebulon Pike, Lewis and Clark, Balduin Möllhausen, and others reached an educated Dutch audience and created an imagery about the northern parts of the New World and its Native peoples (Hovens i.p.b).

Firm foundations for the wider public imagery of North American Indians in The Netherlands were laid by the popular literature in the nineteenth century. From the 1820s the novels and short stories of James Fennimore Cooper in which the red men of the eastern woodlands figured prominently were translated into Dutch and found an appreciative audience. It was an early confrontation with the history of a continually moving frontier of westward trekking colonist and settlers, and forever retreating Indian tribes, struggling for their survival. In the 1860s a series of reprints of Cooper's works testified their popularity in Holland. When the novels and short stories of the German author Friedrich Gerstäcker came on the Dutch market in translation from the 1840s, they also became a popular success. They were often staged in the American West, from the Mississippi to California, and discussed the adventures of European settlers and gold seekers. Later Gerstäcker published narratives of his travels through North America that were translated in Dutch in the 1870s.

During the 1850s and 1860s three other European authors began to establish a reputation with adventure novels and stories set in North America and in which Native Americans figured more or less prominently: Mayne Reid, Gabriel Ferry, and Gustave Aimard. The books they published were reprinted repeatedly in Dutch translation into the early twentieth century (e.g. Eggermont-Molenaar 2010). From the 1870s several books of adventure stories set in North America and were published by Dutch authors Jan Goeverneur and Rinse Koopmans van Boekeren, and included Indians as main or secondary characters. In the 1880s J.H. Van Balen followed suit and produced fiction in which Chiefs Bear Tooth and Black Buffalo of the Sioux and warrior Panther Cat of the Seminoles were the main protagonists. Gradually Indians of North America also acquired their place in popular geographic journals and school books for teachers. At the occasion of the World's Fair in Amsterdam in 1883 the Dutch public was able to gaze at a group of Omahas staging a performance in full Indian regalia. From the 1890s the adventure novels set in the American West by German author Karl May gained a loyal following. From the 1930s American movies began to replace juvenile adventure novels as the major source of popular imagery about the American West and Native Americans.

In the course of the nineteenth century newspapers were becoming another important source of public imagery about American Indians. With the mushrooming of Dutch emigration to Michigan, Illinois, Indiana, Wisconsin, and Iowa in the 1840s, national newspapers began to report about American politics and society with increasing frequency. Keen on developing profitable business ventures, the Dutch financial and commercial sector required and received news about post-Civil War reconstruction and opportunities in agriculture and industry, trade and transportation. The westward moving frontier and the development of the trans-Mississippi West was followed with great interest, and soon the Dutch became the major foreign financiers of railroad development in the U.S. The earlier generation of Dutch emigrants spread out into Minnesota, the Dakotas, Nebraska, and Kansas, and a new generation left their homeland to settle in the Pacific Northwest, Texas, Colorado, New Mexico, and California. For decades these Dutch emigrants were a source of imagery about Native Americans through their letters to family and friends in The Netherlands, and through the emerging Dutch-American press whose productions found their way to The Netherlands. In the larger cities libraries and booksellers provided patrons with a number of current American newspapers (Hovens i.p.b).

This short outline of imagery about North American Indians in The Netherlands demonstrates that by the 1880s the Dutch public had been exposed to a variety of stories and images of the aboriginal inhabitants of the United States and Canada. Soon some would visit this region of the globe and experience interethnic encounters, and their number gradually increased as travel and tourism expanded rapidly since the transcontinental railroads were completed (*cf.* Schulte Nordholt 1982; Lammers 1989).

The transcontinental railroads

The "Aardrijkskundig Weekblad" (Geographic Weekly) was a popular publication established in 1880 by the National Museum of Ethnology in Leiden. Already in 1881 editor-in-chief Gualtherie J. Dozy, a geographer and historian, drew the attention of its readers to the rapid progress in the establishment of transcontinental railroads in North America. In an article he discussed their perceived need, early development, and imminent completion on both sides of the international border between the United States and Canada. The author predicted that this would immensely boost North America's trade and commerce and contribute to the rate of settlement by immigrants (Dozy 1881).

The readership of the weekly consisted in no small way of those people in The Netherlands with an interest in the Dutch East Indies (now: Indonesia), the sprawling insular Dutch colony in the Indian Ocean. Many Dutch families had members who lived there as owners and operators of plantations, processing plants, and trading companies. Others were involved in the colonial government and civil service, and soldiers did duty in the colonial army. Professional people worked in the fields of health and education, and missionaries of various denominations were proselytizing throughout the region. Transportation between the mother country and colony was mainly by steamship on a return ticket from Amsterdam or Rotterdam to Batavia (now: Jakarta), taking the shortest route through the Mediterranean to Port Said, through the Suez Canal (since 1869) and the Red Sea, and across the Indian Ocean to their final destination. The return journey followed the same route. However, with the completion of the transcontinental railroads in North America an alternative return route became possible: by steamer to China or Japan, and across the Pacific to a west coast port in North America where comfortable trains took the travelers across country to the east coast, from where a relatively short journey by steamer brought them back to Europe, and their home country. A reverse journey across the globe was also possible but much less used.

Not only Dozy's article made Dutch people aware of these new routes of train travel across North America. American railways had long been a prime object for Dutch investment and for a time the Dutch and British were the main investors in American railroads. For a time the Denver & Rio Grande Railroad was even completely Dutch-owned. These ventures received ample coverage in Dutch newspapers (Veenendaal 1995:passim; Hovens 2009:315-316). One of the earliest reports by a Dutch traveler on the western railroads was by T.G. Van der Meulen who held a public lecture in the Frisian town of Dokkum in 1881 about his experiences, holding his audience captive by stories about the comforts of steamship and railway travel, Indians of the Far West, and showing pair of beaded moccasins that awed the listeners (Leeuwarder Courant, Nov. 10, 1881:6). By the 1890s the newspaper-reading Dutch public was well aware of the United States as an up-and-coming country, as a country to cross efficiently and comfortably when visiting family and friends in the Dutch East Indies, and increasingly as an attractive destination to spend leisure time. By that time Thomas Cook of London and Lissone & Son of Amsterdam and The Hague were offering trans-Atlantic steamship tickets, trans-continental American railway tickets and hotel reservations in major cities and along the main railway lines across the American and Canadian West. Soon Indians became integrated into

North American cultural tourism that developed rapidly as a consequence of railroad construction, increasing amounts of leisure time, and target marketing.

Intermittent historical research over two decades has resulted in the identification of a number of Dutch who have played a role in Southwestern Indian tourism. Most published accounts of their journeys. Their backgrounds and interests were varied, as were their roles and relevance, as will be demonstrated in the following chronological review. Herman ten Kate's pioneering work in the 1880s has already been documented, analyzed and published. On Andrew Vanderwagen, the Postmas, Henry C. Balink, Lucy Schouten and Elisabeth Houtzager fuller studies will be published in the near future. In this presentation the role of the Arntzenius sisters is highlighted.

1880-1884: John Van de Moer and Thomas Tempelman Van der Hoeven

In the 1870s Dutch Navy officer John Van de Moer emigrated to the United States and worked for newspapers in Colorado reporting on mining activities. During a business trip to New Mexico in 1880 he visited Tesuque Indian Pueblo, and was enamored with traditional Indian life he observed. In his diary he noted that: "In some apartments I found women manufacturing pottery out of clay, which they shape into the funniest shapes, generally imitating some live object or other, either a man or an animal. They bake this pottery in a very primeval fashion, … to sell it to the traders, who again dispose of it to the collectors of curiosities, at very remunerative prices, as it can be got from the Indians very cheap" (Van de Moer 1956:194-195). This is the earliest Dutch report about the manufacture by Pueblo Indians of pottery curiosities for the outside market of Santa Fe traders who catered to a growing number of professional and leisure visitors to the territorial capital. The fact that these souvenirs were Indian-made and exotic in appearance was ample to satisfy the needs and tastes of this new clientele. Euro-American customers generally were not aware of the fact that these objects were only partly or even largely non-traditional (*cf.* Gaillard, this volume).

In 1885 Thomas Bastiaan Tempelman Van der Hoeven (1816-1901) donated a series of fourteen North American artefacts to the Leiden museum (series RMV 473), including seven pieces of Pueblo pottery from New Mexico. The benefactor was living in San Antonio at the time, practicing medicine, and trying his luck in mining and railway ventures. The Pueblo pottery was probably acquired during a business or pleasure trip to New Mexico, and included early Indian-made curiosities for the tourist trade as mentioned by Van de Moer.

1882-1883: Herman ten Kate, anthropologist

Herman Frederik Carel Ten Kate (1858-1931) was the first professionally trained anthropologist in The Netherlands and qualified in the four constituent fields of ethnology, archaeology, physical anthropology and ethnolinguistics at the universities of Leiden, Paris, Berlin, Göttingen and Heidelberg. As early

Picuris "Rain God," ca. 1880; Tempelman Van der Hoeven Collection (RMV 473-2).

as 1878 he published an article in a popular periodical about the resistance of Native American tribes against the encroachment onto their lands by white colonists, and tried to explain the actions of Nez Percé Chief Joseph and his people in the Pacific Northwest to a wide Dutch public. This was based on reports in American newspapers he read at Martinus Nijhoff Books and Publishers in The Hague. In the 1880s he spent two years of fieldwork in the United States, mostly in the Southwest, excavating prehistoric sites, carrying out physical measurements, recording Native languages, and making observations on traditional customs, cultural change and Indian-white relations. The 450 artifacts he collected are curated mainly at the National Museum of World Cultures (formerly: Ethnology) in Leiden, while most of the photographs he took and collected are at the Nederlands Fotomuseum (Netherlands Museum of Photography) in Rotterdam. Throughout his life Ten Kate would repeatedly publish articles in popular journals about Indian-white relations (Heyink 1983; Hovens and Groeneveld 1992; Hovens 1989; 1995; Hovens et.al. 2004, 2010).

An overriding motive to carry out fieldwork in North America was Ten Kate's realization that Indian cultures were changing rapidly as the result of the western colonization, and traditional culture traits were being lost at an increasing pace. The "salvage paradigm" is characteristic of much of his early work, although he was also keen on identifying those factors that were primarily responsible for the demise of Indians peoples and cultures. He discussed epidemics, interethnic warfare, forced settlement on reservations, missions, boarding schools, and federal Indian policy as major causes of cultural change and assimilation.

Ten Kate in Apache camp, Arizona Territory, 1883 (RMV 414Kd2).

The Dutch anthropologist also made a number of keen observations on the emergence of Indian tourism in the Southwest in his 1885 travel book, published in Dutch, and in an annotated English translation in 2004. He noted the proliferation of western materials in Native material culture, the impact of the transcontinental railroads on Indian-white relations, and the sale of arts and crafts to travelers, tourists and health-seekers as an important alternative source of income for an increasing number of Indian families. He commented on Indians adapting their arts and crafts to the tastes and needs of their white customers, and their staging of dances specifically for the entertainment of outsiders eager to pay for the privilege (Ten Kate 1885:passim; Hovens et.al. 2004:passim).

Despite these adverse conditions, Ten Kate noted a new economic niche available to at least some Indian tribes, although he had no clear idea about its future potential. While traveling through Upstate New York he observed that shops in Niagara Falls sold decorated birchbark containers and baskets made by Indians from that region for tourists visiting the natural wonder and keen on taking back a souvenir from their trip. He purchased several of these to be added to the collections of the National Museum of Ethnology in Leiden, the Netherlands. He continued his journey by train, taking the Atchison, Topeka & Santa Fe Railway to the American Southwest, just when the railroad company had completed its transcontinental link, and noted opportunities to purchase objects of Indian manufacture at railroad stations. During the stop in Wallace, New Mexico, he encountered Indians from nearby Santo Domingo Pueblo. They "offer turquoises and small painted pottery for sale. … The pottery, most of which has the color of putty and is painted with black ornamentation, is not unattractive. One would have to be very unfeeling not to buy a small item from the dark Pueblo girls, with a blush on their cheeks as fresh as a peach while they ask me, bashfully and comically at the same time, for a *real*." In Santa Fe the anthropologist witnessed Pueblo Indians performing traditional dances for white audiences, receiving payment for their presentations. He also noted that Las Vegas, New Mexico, was developing into a major spa because of its natural hot springs, attracting visitors from the whole country, a new market for Indian arts and crafts (ten Kate 1885; Hovens et.al. 2004:passim).

Ten Kate's collection contains tourist art from various tribes. Quechan pottery was produced and painted in traditional tribal style, but in shape imitated Victorian tableware Indian women saw in affluent white homes where they worked as domestics. Also popular were miniature clay dolls in traditional dress, miniature replicas in pottery and cloth of the Indian vendors the travelers acquired their souvenirs from. From New Mexico Pueblo Indians Ten Kate also collected clay curios produced specifically for the tourist market, buying these in their villages or at train stations (see also: Gaillard, this volume). By paying attention to the interaction between Indians and white travelers and visitors, by collecting innovative artifacts bridging Indian and western culture, almost

Quechan souvenirs: male and female clay figures (RMV 362-99 and 100).

tacitly acknowledging Indian agency in their dealings with Euro-Americans, Ten Kate's fieldwork and collecting in the 1880s is thoroughly modern (Heyink & Hodge 1931; Hovens et.al. 2010:16-17,39-44,135-136,143-146).

Although Ten Kate's fieldwork was partially driven by a sense of urgency that traditional tribal ways of life were rapidly changing under American rule and within the confines of Indian reservations, he also keenly observed that the tenacity to Indian customs was much stronger than expected. Among the New York State Iroquois he noticed that despite western dress, modern farming and elementary education adherence to traditional beliefs and ceremonies was still strong after several centuries of Anglo-American domination. In the Southwest the sedentary Hopis, Zunis and Pueblos proved that centuries of Spanish domination and repression had only had a limited impact on these societies, and that social, political and religious traditions remained strong. Under a thin outward veil of western material culture and daily practices tribal beliefs and customs still retained much of their authenticity. However, like his contemporaries Ten Kate was convinced that ultimately the Indians would vanish as a cultural group and biologically assimilate into the general American population (Hovens 1989:155-184).

Andrew Vanderwagen in Zuni home, ca. 1910 (Heritage Hall Archives, Calvin College, Grand Rapids, MI).

Between 1878 and 1925 Ten Kate published a series of articles on Native Americans in popular Dutch journals, addressing subjects like Indian resistance against Euro-American colonization, federal Indian policy, Christian missionary work, imagery of Native Americans in Euro-American art and literature. Some of this material was also published in English translations. In poetry, fiction, and painting Southwestern Indians played a major role, and Dutch educated readers of these periodicals were thus exposed to their culture, history and imagery (Ten Kate 1878, 1889, 1911, 1919, 1920, 1922; Hovens 1989:185-196,271-279).

1895-1905: Andrew Vanderwagen, missionary

The Vanderwagen family emigrated to Michigan where their son Andrew trained for the ministry and became a missionary of the Dutch Christian Reformed Church. In 1897 he was stationed at Zuni. Stuart Culin of the Brooklyn Museum visited the Indian pueblo and engaged the minister to collect for his institution. However, objects of religious significance were very difficult to obtain. Aware of the interest of white customers in authentic Indian artifacts, notably the more esoteric, the missionary engaged several Zuni men to make kachina dolls in 1904. This was done in secret in the basement of his mission house. Manufacture of these dolls for outsiders was deemed sacrilege and tribal members were threatened with capital punishment if caught in the sale of such objects. Because the carvers feared repercussions from their religious leaders, they discontinued their work after a while (Fane 1991:60-62,109). Although Vanderwagen used the extra income for the mission only, he was the first whiteman in Zuni to pioneer the production of kachina dolls for an outside clientele.[2] Vanderwagen's primary mission was to divest the Indians of their ancient beliefs and convert them to Christianity. The general belief was that conversion was almost impossible without changing traditional Indian lifestyles and adopting a civilized way of life, the Euro-American way. Thus churches and the federal government became allies in efforts directed at the cultural assimilation of the aboriginal population. Tribal cultural authenticity was not valued but instead became a target for the combined civilization offensive.

1903: Hendrik P. Muller

On his way for business and possibly as a diplomatic envoy Muller visited the United States in 1903 and travelled by train from Los Angeles to El Paso. In Needles, the entry point to Arizona, he saw about thirty Mojave Indians on the platform whom he found physically impressive because of their long stature, long black hair, facial tattoos and body paint. He bought some beadwork that they offered, but regarded it as insignificant (Muller 1905:161-2). From Williams he took the spur line north which brought him in two and a half hours to the South Rim of the Grand Canyon. The train was crowded with tourists who stayed overnight in a tent or a small hotel that included a restaurant. Prices were steep as all supplies had to be freighted in from a long distance and competition was absent. The next day most visitors descended the canyon on horseback, but Muller undertook the journey on foot, and was greatly impressed by the canyon and the river. He made his return journey to Williams on horseback and reboarded the AT&SF eastward. In Williams and Flagstaff he saw colorful Navajo blankets that were offered for sale.

Interested in seeing Indians in their original environment, Muller got off the train at dawn in Laguna Pueblo. The trading post was still closed and he slept a couple of hours on the porch of the house of a railroad foreman who supervised a crew of Indian laborers. The foreman referred Muller to an American land surveyor who had married a Laguna woman. Their son and his mixed blood friend served as his guides through the pueblo. In the trading post a Laguna woman bartered a number of sheep for a sewing machine. Most of the stock for trade consisted of farming equipment, colorful rolls of cotton and a variety of foodstuffs. In the small adobe church he admired the naturalistic Indian paintings of animals.

The women and children acted shy, but by offering small amounts of cash Muller was able to photograph an Indian youth and in gaining access to some of the houses. He also visited the government school and questioned the wisdom of settling Indians on the most infertile lands. With another surveyor, John

2 The Hopis produce kachina dolls in various styles for the collector and tourist market. Cheap Navaho-made replicas have recently been banned because of reproduction rights infringement. Zunis do prohibit production and sale of their *koko* to outsiders.

Mojave Indians, Needles, California (Muller 1905:161).

St. Stephen shrine, Acoma Pueblo, NM (Muller 1905:177).

Gunn, he made a trip by buckboard through the vicinity. A short visit was paid to Acoma Pueblo on Enchanted Mesa where Muller witnessed the veneration of Saint Stephen (San Esteban) in a tent where a shrine was erected, surrounded with Navajo and Hispanic blankets. The Indians offered weapons, fruits and pottery to their patron saint (1905:170-8). In Albuquerque Muller stayed at the luxury Alvarado Hotel, and subsequently he journeyed by train south to El Paso. Back in Holland he published a travel account in which he proved to be a non-judgmental observer.

1904: Aletta Jacobs, women's rights advocate

Aletta Jacobs (1954-1929) was raised in an educated and liberal Jewish family in the northeastern province of Groningen. Her father was a physician and she and her brother followed in his footsteps. She became the first woman in The Netherlands to attend high school and university, obtaining a Ph.D. in medicine in 1879 before settling in Amsterdam and opening a practice. During a trip to Great Britain she met compatriot Carel Victor Gerritsen, a grain trader and left-wing politician. The two kindred souls married in 1892, united in their ideas about and work on behalf of the poor and working class. Jacobs instructed underprivileged women in health and hygiene, including birth control, and published popular books and articles in these fields and on the rights of women at home, in the workplace, and in politics. She was a strong advocate for voting rights for women, a goal achieved in 1917.

In 1904 Jacobs terminated her medical practice in favor of her work for women's rights and the international peace movement in the public and political arena, both in The Netherlands and abroad. That year she and her husband visited the United States to acquaint themselves with social conditions in the land of promise and opportunity across the Atlantic. The couple funded their journey by selling their private book collection to the John Crerar Library in Chicago. The letters they wrote for several Dutch newspapers were subsequently published as a book (Gerritsen & Jacobs 1906).

Jacobs was disappointed about the upper class women in the eastern cities as they focused almost exclusively on conspicuously showing their affluence and expressing traditional ideas about the role of women in society. She was much more enthusiastic about the state of Colorado where women were allowed to vote. Jacobs and Gerritsen were impressed by the almost simultaneously development of railroads and the hospitality business, including hotels, restaurants and shops, catering to the travelling public. Most impressive were several hotels in an attractive architectural style with shops where Indian arts and crafts were sold in New Mexico and Arizona. The efficiency and cleanliness everywhere was impeccable. Gambling and drinking were major vices the couple witnessed in this region, corrupting all ethnic groups (Gerritsen & Jacobs 1906:105-6).

Near Holbrook the couple visited the Petrified Forest, and from Williams they travelled by spur line north to the Grand Canyon, a natural phenomenon that impressed her immensely. By horse and carriage she made a trip to the Navajo Indian Reservation where they were intrigued by the cliff dwellings of the prehistoric Anasazi Indians, precariously built on ridges and into recesses of canyon walls. It struck them that Indians with their own government and laws still lived on the plateaus of this region, and kept their traditions alive. However, they expected that they would disappear in the course of time, just as their prehistoric predecessors. The region and its Native peoples intrigued Jacobs greatly and she expressed the wish to be able to stay for weeks or several months to learn more about this fascinating corner of the world (Gerritsen & Jacobs 1906:111-114).

The couple travelled by Southern Pacific train from Utah to California and was pleasantly surprised about the speed and comfort of the trip. At many of the depots where the train stopped they encountered Indians. Jacobs wrote: "Because of the good care of the government many of them are partially civilized, although this sounds too strong, humanized is maybe the better term. Many speak some English and they all understand the language of money. … The women collected wild foods in the forests and prepared it, wove baskets and other trinkets they try to sell to travelers. That is sufficient to fulfill their needs. In several towns I saw the Indian women, recognizable from a distance because of their colorful dress, descending the mountains, carrying heavy baskets on their backs, sometimes topped with the baby. The men saunter slowly along them, smoking their pipes. If their humanization goes a step further, the men begin working, usually as loggers, and the women become lazy. In this stage of the humanization process whiskey poses the greatest threat. Although America has a law forbidding the sale of liquor to Indians, it seems that in this land of boundless opportunity … laws seem to exist to be ignored. Everywhere the Indians knew where to get their hands on alcohol, and use this knowledge liberally. If one meets a drunken Indian one can assume to meet the most civilized specimen of his race" (Utrechts Nieuwsblad, Nov. 11, 1904:1; Gerritsen & Jacobs 1906:156-158).

After their return home Jacobs and Gerritsen had time to reflect on their experiences before publishing their partially rewritten travel letters. Their book included a separate chapter on Native Americans, written principally by Jacobs. She emphasizes that despite what western novels might lead people to believe, Indians are still alive, though generally not well, in the American West. She paints the picture of Indians as tenaciously holding on to their traditional culture, despite a long-standing civilization offensive by the government and the churches. She wrote about the tattooed and painted faces she saw among the Mohaves and Apaches in Arizona, and the traditional whorl hairdos of the unmarried Hopi girls. Jacobs noted differences in the division of labor between men and women between villages and tribes. She also mentions the traditional rituals that were still practiced, most of them to promote rain and fertility, and that the public parts of these ceremonies could be attended by visitors and tourists. She advises the visitors to travel by train, stop at the four depots in Indian Pueblos, and spend a few hours or a day in the quaint villages where life seems frozen in time. Guides are always available, and here is an opportunity for observing people at work, making arts and crafts, and buying pottery, jewelry and weavings as souvenirs. She stressed that the Pueblos are a peaceful people, but that Indians have generally been ill treated by the government and the white Euro-American settlers. Alcohol had a devastating effect on many individuals and even whole communities, despite efforts by authorities and tribal leaders to curtail and even prohibit its trade and consumption. Jacobs believed that within a few generations the Indians would vanish before the onslaught of "western civilization" (Gerritsen & Jacobs 1906:170-178).

1910-1911: Reverend Walkotten and the Dutch Christian Reformed Indian missions

In the late nineteenth century the Dutch Christian Reformed Church (CRC) from the Dutch-American communities in the Upper Midwest (Michigan, Iowa, South Dakota) embarked on missionary work among Native Americans. The focus was on the Southwest and the CRC established a whole series of missions among the Navajos and the Zunis in Arizona and New Mexico. In addition to providing spiritual care, missionary workers became active in the fields of health and education, establishing a mission and boarding school at Rehoboth near Gallup (Dolfin 1921). In support of the transition from traditional ways of subsistence to achieving independence in the new cash economy the CRC missions supported vocational training for boys, but also sought ways to turn what was left of traditional arts and craft into marketable merchandise. Several plans were developed to teach Navajos to produce clean wool, carefully spun and well-dyed yarn, and sturdy and beautiful textiles that would provide decent financial returns for their makers. However, little was actually put in practice before 1940 and only after the war the economic potential of traditional Native arts and crafts received some appreciation. The work in these Indian missions was presented in various promotional publications, including two small books written by Reverend Henry Walkotten (1864-1925) and published in Dutch that reached an audience across the Atlantic (1909, 1910). From 1897 publications from the Dutch Christian Reformed Church reported on the development of missionary work among Navajos and Zunis. Such promotional literature attracted church members from the Upper Midwest and The Netherlands to the Southwest where they visited "their" missions, attended the annual Gallup Inter-Tribal Ceremonial, and purchased Indian arts and crafts.[3]

3 See also: 1946-1947: Rudolf van Reest, in this article. A book on the Indian missions of the Dutch Christian Reformed Church in the American Southwest is in progress.

1911: H.E. Dekker, hobo and gardener

In 1928 H.E. Dekker published a book about his adventures as a hobo travelling through the United States in 1911. Dekker failed in high school in 1909 and decided to try his hand at life. Unable to get a good job without a diploma in Holland, he decided to try his chances in America, the land of unlimited opportunities. For almost a year he worked at odd jobs as a farmhand, housepainter, and sales clerk in a grocery store in Michigan. Times were hard, and when the lost his last job Dekker decided to winter in the south where he expected the cost of living would be lower and the chances for work better. In December 1910 he purchased a train-ticket and traveled by way of Chicago to St. Louis where he worked in restaurants and for the Salvation Army, and learned about the life of the itinerant unemployed. As steady and decently paid employment could not be had in St. Louis, he decided to try his luck in the Promised Land, California that is. Soon he jumped on a westward bound train of the Union Pacific Railroad, and worked his way through Kansas City and Dodge City to La Junta in south-central Colorado. There he changed trains and jumped on a California Limited of the Santa Fe Railroad because it was headed south to warmer climes. Its regular occupants traveled quite luxuriously. They occupied comfortable chairs upholstered in red plush, and Black servants clad in white uniforms catered to their every need. The tables in the restaurant car were set with fine bone china, crystal glasses, and silver tableware. However, Dekker was not envious but convinced that one day he would also be able to travel in style. By way of Trinidad and Raton he reached Albuquerque where spring already made itself felt in the air. Covertly getting off the train he was suddenly faced with a railroad policeman waving his pistol in his face. He was arrested and incarcerated for five days in the jail at the depot, and then told to leave town immediately (Dekker 1928:1-126,131).

This adventure provided Dekker with an opportunity to become acquainted with the Albuquerque train depot. He found the city most interesting because of the many Indians flocking towards it from a wide region. They included Pueblos, Navajos and some Hopis and Apaches, and many were engaged in selling craftwork. He noted that the railway company encouraged their presence around the station as they provided an colorful spectacle for tourists and travelers who had an opportunity to pick up exotic souvenirs of their trip. Navajo men and women offered fine woolen blankets in a variety of colored patterns of mostly triangles for sale. Indian women sat quietly around the depot, those of the Hopis and Apaches surrounded by basketry woven of variously colored grasses, and Pueblo women amidst pottery, both undecorated and painted wares. The latter wore white deerskin leg covers. Contributing to the exoticism of the scene were babies swaddled on cradleboards and carried on their mothers' backs or positioned upright against the wall of the depot. Many Indians came to town with mule- or horse-drawn wagons, selling firewood, produce and arts and crafts to the city folk. They wore western dress, including wide-brimmed Stetsons, and the only peculiarity were their colored silk scarves (1928:127-128).

However, Dekker had to leave Albuquerque, and after experiencing the hospitality of an Indian family at Isleta Pueblo south of town, jumped on the next train heading for California. In Laguna Pueblo he spent a short while and to his surprise encountered several Indians who spoke English fluently and had been educated at Carlisle Indian Industrial School in Pennsylvania. He learned about nearby Acoma Pueblo but was unable to visit the intriguing Indian village perched atop of a steep mesa. He caught only a glimpse of Gallup and witnessed the loading of coal from the nearby mines, and the Navajo Indians buying provisions and goods at local stores and selling craftwork, mostly woolen blankets and silver jewelry. A kind waitress at the railroad depot provided Dekker with free sandwiches, and soon he was again on his way west, via Paquita and Adamana across the Arizona border (1928:129-148).

Dekker regarded Arizona as the ideal tourist destination. He was impressed by the Petrified Forest near Holbrook, and traversed the area partly on foot, studying the intriguing Indian rock art in the area. Major attractions were the remains of prehistoric Indian villages and towns, especially those of the Cliff Dwellers who had chosen abodes in hardly accessible rock crevices across northern Arizona. Their descendants, the Hopis, still lived in their adobe villages perched on the outcroppings of Black Mesa. The Painted Desert, aptly named because of the changing hues of the rocks at different times during the day and season, also created a lasting impression. While working for a while on a ranch in the Flagstaff area, Dekker became aware of the Grand Canyon and the number of tourists the great chasm attracted year. However, he was unable to visit the natural wonder at that time (1928:148-184). Soon he continued his journey, crossing the Colorado River at The Needles, and entering California. That state kept its promise and after studying landscape architecture at the University of California in Berkeley the Dutchman embarked on a successful career in the Los Angeles area. During this time he was able to work intermittently on the 1928 publication of his travel experiences of 1911.

1912: W.J. van Balen, publicist

Van Balen studied law but subsequently embarked on a career as journalist and writer of books on travel and historical subjects. He became increasingly interested in North America and in 1912 made his first major journey through Canada and the United States, publishing accounts in the newspaper *Het Vaderland*, and in 1913 a book that became a popular success. Because of the book's format it became the first Dutch travel guide to the American West. It was widely used by people with plans to visit the U.S. Van Balen stayed on the main routes of travel and elaborated on the Grand Canyon, Petrified Forest, Albuquerque and Santa Fe, noting services for tourists as well as opportunities to see and meet Indians and buy exotic souvenirs of Native manufacture. One of the best options was to buy arts and crafts from Indian vendors at the railway stations where they flocked to the trains during stops. Santa Fe offered a plethora of shops that carried Indian goods, and Van Balen noted that relations between Indians and entrepreneurs were cordial and friendly. During several excursions he was especially impressed by the enigmatic prehistoric cliff dwellings and petroglyphs of the ancestors of the Indians of the Four Corners region (Van Balen 1913:156-172). With his travel book Van Balen positioned Native Americans firmly within the realm of cultural tourism for a Dutch audience.

1913-1922: Theo F. Stomps and J.P. Lotsy, botanists

In 1913 Amsterdam professor Theo F. Stomps (1885-1973) visited the American Southwest. He was a protégé of the internationally known botanist, Amsterdam professor Hugo de Vries. His mentor was instrumental in arranging an associate professorship for him in 1910, and Stomps also became director of the Hortus Botanicus in the capital when De Vries retired. In Arizona the Dutch naturalist undertook botanical studies in Tucson area. Back in Holland he lectured widely in non-academic circles on flora, notably cacti, in the Sonora Desert, also paying specific attention to the role of these plants in the traditional lives of the Native inhabitants, as well as the fact that descendants of these tribes still lived in the region (Leeuwarder Courant, Oct. 6, 1922:5).

In March of 1922 the botanist J.P. (Johannes Paulus) Lotsy (1867-1931) boarded the S.S. Rijndam of the Holland America Line in Rotterdam harbor and crossed the Atlantic Ocean for a four-month visit to the United States. He planned to visit universities and scientific institutions and attend a number of conferences in his field of research. However, repeatedly he took the time to learn more about the country and its people, and in 1923 published a book about his experiences. At the American Museum of Natural History in New York Lotsy prepared himself for his journey west and was most impressed by the displays on the Grand Canyon and the Native peoples. By train he journeyed through the Delaware River Valley to Baltimore, and observed that unfortunately the Indians from the Dutch colonial days in this area had vanished, to be replaced by billboards loudly advertising a variety of products, notably chewing gum. In Chicago he enjoyed the Indian exhibits at the Field Museum and on the campus of the University of Wisconsin in Madison he was intrigued by the prehistoric effigy mounds (Lotsy 1923:27,47,95,132).

Lotsy repeatedly expressed his regret about the fate of the Indians. He pointed out that the Native tribes had lived with and from nature, without destroying it, only taking what they needed for their daily subsistence. This was in stark contrast with the exploitative nature of western civilization which had destroyed wildlife, notably the immense buffalo herds on the Plains, and had cultivated the wild land, subdued it, and turned into boring fields. Most Americans never gave a thought to the Indians they had displaced and whose land was forcibly taken. Now the tribes lived on infertile reservations in an impoverished state (Lotsy 1923:61,95,147).

Lotsy was pleasantly surprised by the establishments of the Fred Harvey Company along the railroad, who catered to the travelling public, providing them with clean hotel rooms and good food (1930:148,232). He enjoyed the train journey by the Golden Limited from El Paso to Tucson and Phoenix, and his trip through the blooming Sonora Desert. He was pleased by the playing children, ball kicking boys, fat women and men on horseback he saw at the little stations and in desert settlements. He noted the use of desert plants by the Papago, Pima and Maricopa Indians, not only their storage capacity for water, but also the harvest of saguaro fruits, the use of *Datura* as a narcotic, and rattlesnake weed from which they made an antidote for snakebites (1923:163-174,205,208-9,211,220-1).

From Phoenix Lotsy continued his train journey north and arrived in Ash Fork. Adjacent to the train station was a store which sold colorful Navajo blankets and other Indian curiosities to travelers and tourists. In Williams he saw many Indians and the white canvas tents and cabins in the cool mountain forests that attracted people from the hot and low Arizona desert during the summer months to cool off. He spent the night at the Harvey House Hotel and found his room pleasantly decorated with woolen Navajo blankets. From Williams he took the spur line to the Grand Canyon. At the terminus uniformed Chinese servants from the El Tovar welcomed the passengers and took their luggage to the hotel. The Dutch botanist was less impressed by the geological wonder of erosive rock than the living desert he had just transected (1923:231-234,237).

Lotsy witnessed the "war dance" that the Hopi Indians living at Grand Canyon Village performed every day near the hotel. However, he was unimpressed by the spectacle of wild dancing which he regarded as conspicuously directed at creating an impact upon the white public and thus little more than a carnival act. Instead he was favorably impressed by a number of dances performed by a group of Navajo Indians led by Hoshkay Yazzie who visited a local trader who had lived among them for several years. The group performed a war dance, victory dance and night chant, and the next day several medicine men made sand paintings. Lotsy noted an abundance of what he regarded as imitation Indian arts and crafts for in sale in New York and Salt Lake City (1930:239-242,360,478). Back in Holland he continued his scientific career and gained international recognition for his studies of botanical evolution.

1917-1963: Henry C. Balink, artist

The Dutch artist Henry C. Balink emigrated to North America after studying at the Royal Academy in Amsterdam. He settled in New Mexico in 1918 where he lived and worked until his death in 1963. Native Americans were his main

Henry C. Balink in his Santa Fe studio (photo by son Henry B. Balink, 1954).

subject, and he painted them in his studios in Taos and Santa Fe, in the pueblos of northern New Mexico, and on reservations during several journeys across the West (Hovens 2007).

Every day he sat sketching in the lobby of the La Fonda Hotel in Santa Fe when the guests arrived from the train. Those who showed an interest in his work were invited to his studio, and many left with at least one Indian portrait, either an etching or oil. Balink was part of the Taos and Santa Fe artistic communities that popularized the imagery of the American Indian between 1900 and 1945, especially when the railroad began using their work in advertizing, drawing scores of tourists to the Land of Enchantment. The Native American peoples and cultures of the Southwest were immortalized in the work of artists and writers and firmly incorporated in the popular imagery.[4]

1919: Hessel Postma and Lura May Love, senior honeymooners

In 1919 the Dutch psychiatrist Hessel Postma and his American wife, poet Lura May Love, traversed the Southwest on a belated honeymoon. Mrs. Postma's father, Methodist Episcopal Reverend Nathaniel Barrett Coulson Love (1830-1922),

4 A full biography of Balink will soon be published (Hovens i.p.a).

was a history buff and author of several treatises on Native Americans in the Old Northwest. This probably contributed to the Postmas interest in Indians during their leisure trip across the Southwest.

The couple visited the Museum of New Mexico/Laboratory of Anthropology where they marveled at the ethnographic collections. Director Edgar L. Hewett was instrumental in the donation of a collection of quality Pueblo pottery from the pottery improvement project supervised by Kenneth Chapman with the stipulation that it would be transferred to a major Dutch museum. Included were pieces by Maria and Julian Martinez from San Ildefonso. The Postmas also visited the Navajo and Hopi reservations and acquired Hopi-Tewa pottery, mostly Sykiatki Revival ware, some from Nampeyo and her family. On their return to the Netherlands they donated all 55 pieces Pueblo pottery as well as other Indian artifacts to the Leiden museum (Kaemlein 1967:142-143). Until 2002 this material was in storage, but the renovation of the permanent galleries enabled the exhibition of major ceramic pieces from this collection (Hovens 2015:35,164-181).[5]

Lura May Love, Mrs. Postma, published several volumes of poetry, written in a Romantic style. In 1926 she sent a poem entitled "Indian Prayer" to Hewett, inspired by her experiences in the Southwest. It was published in El Palacio (Postma 1926) and expresses her admiration for the reverent attitude shown by Indians toward nature and the gods and spirits that enable and sustain life.

1922: Herman Rutgers, students advocate

In 1922 the chairman Herman C. Rutgers of the Netherlands Christian Students Association attended the annual international conference of the world federation in Beijing of which he was an elected official, and the national conference of the American association in Estes Park, Colorado. He was a passenger on the luxury liner Aquitania which sailed from Southampton to New York. The Dutchman then found himself on the transcontinental train crossing the United States, a sign and symbol of the changes in the American West, a major factor in the destruction of the wilderness and the romanticism of Indian life. In an effort to recapture something of that not too distant past, he visited Buffalo Bills grave in Golden, west of Denver. Continuing his journey, he traveled south to Albuquerque, then west to Flagstaff, making a side trip to the Grand Canyon, before going to San Francisco. He was disappointed to see Indians dressed up in their traditional attire and performing dances as tourist attraction at the Albuquerque train station and the El Tovar hotel at the Grand Canyon rim. Equally disappointing were the other Indians he encountered, most of them employed as unskilled laborers by hotels and the railway companies. Rutgers was keenly aware of the fact that western education had had a great impact

5 A publication by Pieter Hovens and Bruce Bernstein on the Postmas and their collection is in progress.

on traditional ways of life of the America Indian. The Indians with whom he had personal contact were Red Owl and Grey Earth, Sioux representatives of Christian Indian schools in South Dakota who had visited their Dutch counterparts in the Dutch town of Nunspeet for a previous conference, and Mrs. Muskrat, a Cherokee teacher who was part of the American delegation to the Peking conference. Rutgers related his experiences in a book that was read among young academics (Rutgers 1922:1,40-45,185-193).

1923 Nathan de Vries: prohibition campaigner

In March 1923 a delegation of Dutch anti-alcohol protagonists crossed the Atlantic aboard the S.S. New Amsterdam on a fact finding mission to the United States. One of its members, entrepreneur and social-democrat politician Nathan Albert de Vries, kept a diary and published a popular book about this trip. The delegation not only visited major cities in the East, but also crossed the nation to California.

From Pittsburg De Vries and his companion P. Van der Meulen traveled by train to Santa Fe by way of Columbus, St. Louis, Kansas City, Las Vegas, New Mexico and Lamy where they take the spur line to "the city different". In Las Vegas they encountered two young Pueblo Indian boys on the platform, trying to sell souvenirs to the passengers on the train. De Vries was charmed by the quiet and colorful Santa Fe with its mixture of Indian, Spanish, Mexican and American culture traits. Culture dominated the city in architecture, dress, menu, language and art. The city had become a haven for intellectuals and artists to whom a number of exquisite hotels offered their hospitality services. Also the local museum catered to their tastes, showing work of white artists who had been living in the city and the surrounding area. On the plaza and in the surrounding streets De Vries talked to a number of Indians from whom he purchased crafts. De Vries was especially taken by the soft-hued Navajo blankets, made from the wool of their own sheep, dyed with mineral pigments and vegetal extracts. He also witnessed the Indian women selling firewood from their mule-drawn carts (De Vries 1924:76-86).

From Santa Fe De Vries made a journey by car to Tesuque, north of the city and a main port of call for organized tours. The women were grinding corn with their stone *manos* on slab *metates*, and offered pottery, necklaces and basketry for sale in an unobtrusive modest and friendly manner. He noticed the female ownership of the land and houses, the loss of their position as hunters and warriors by the men, and the co-existence of traditional and Christian beliefs. For a fee of 25 cents the women allowed a photograph, but charged 10 cents more if a baby was included, something the Dutchman regarded as hilarious. The children had learned their lesson well and fled into the houses as soon as a camera was pointed at them. Only the promise of a quarter could entice them to reappear. All inhabitants of Tesuque seemed accustomed to tourists and their requests and generally quietly submitted to their visits (1924:83,85-7).

De Vries deplored the fate of the Indians, overrun by whites, on the verge of extinction or total assimilation. They lived as strangers in their own land, their spirit almost broken. They were sometimes self-sufficient, but often depended on government support. Poor diet and tuberculosis took many lives. He regarded acceptance of education as their only real chance for survival, and noticed several young educated Pueblo Indian men that were employed by businesses in the city. He was also impressed by a young Hopi leader who had received a western-style education and regarded him as a promise for a better future (1924:77,81-2,84,87).

Like some educated contemporaries De Vries showed himself to be a Romantic realist, appreciating ancient Indian traditions, lamenting their passing, and regarding cultural adaptation as the only means of survival, the Indian peoples eventually becoming Indian Americans. This paradigm departed from the prevalent conviction of Indians as a vanishing race and gained increased acceptance in science and society as time progressed, also in The Netherlands.

Tesuque woman and child (De Vries 1924:82-83).

1922-1927: Peronne and Constance Arntzenius, twin adventurers

Twin-sisters Peronne and Constance Arntzenius from The Hague undertook four extensive camping trips through the United States between 1914 and 1927, some lasting a year or even longer. In total they stayed for about six years in the U.S. during this time. The girls longed for the pristine forests and mountains, wild fauna and flora, and what they called "primitive" peoples, preferring to travel rough trails through back country rather than smooth highways and tourist routes. In 1931 they shared their experiences with a wide Dutch public by publishing an illustrated travel narrative for which former Navy Secretary and scouting promoter J.J. Rambonnet wrote a preface (Arntzenius 1931:passim).

The Arntzenius sisters came from an upper middle-class family with modest means. Father Robert Arntzenius was secretary of the Lower Chamber at the Houses of Parliament in The Hague. Their mother Constance Boddaert was of Flemish nobility, She gave birth to triplets on May 20, 1883, Peronne, Constance and Paul, but passed away shortly afterwards. The children were raised in a household where the arts and sciences were valued highly. The family's wide social circle included many intellectuals and artists, and their socialization in this liberal environment allowed the girls to develop and pursue their interests

The Arntzenius twin sisters with their dog David (Arntzenius 1931:1).

and talents freely.[6] They became independent and free spirits, and when they were interviewed on one of their trips through the U.S. they stressed that they appreciated America because women had an equal chance with men (Feakins 1919). Their brother Paul became a well known landscape painter.

Between travels to the United States the Arntzenius family spent much of the Great War period in Zürich where they were part of the literary and artistic circle in of that city of refuge. The girls loathed that the German Kaiser had sought and received exile in Holland: for the repressive and arrogant nobility he represented; his pathetic efforts at being accepted as a man of the common people in the Netherlands; and trying to find recognition as a serious painter (Kokomo Daily Tribune, Oct. 17, 1919).

By 1910 the first Dutch translations of the works of Ernest Thompson Seton came on the market and inspired a new generation of people becoming alienated from an increasingly materialized and industrialized world with his stories of animals in the wilds and the traditional way of life and survival techniques of Native Americans (Seton 1911, 1920). The Englishman Seton had emigrated with his parents from England to Canada in 1866 when he was six years old. He trained as an artist in London and Paris, but became an author, illustrator, and naturalist. He began his career with publications about animals, natural history studies with illustrations by his own hand. Soon these were followed by animal stories for a wider public, factual stories about their natural lives, providing his readers with an intimate understanding of the habits and survival strategies of various species: the mustang, grizzly, wolf, coyote, bighorn sheep, silver fox, etc. In 1902 Seton founded the Woodcraft Indians youth organization that would develop into the American branch of the international scouting movement (1910), originally begun by Lord Baden Powell in 1907 in Great Britain. In 1903 he published a little book entitled "How To Play Indian" with directions for boys how to organize as an Indian tribe and live like Native Americans. More elaborate subsequent editions under different titles were published and in 1911 a Dutch translation appeared (Seton 1903; 1911).

The twin sisters came under the spell of Seton's books and their attention was increasingly drawn to the continent beyond their Atlantic horizon. Soon they were "playing Indian", camping out, learning to survive in nature with limited material possessions, first in their back garden, later during trips across the country. Seton's "Manual of the Woodcraft Indians" (1915) must have been inspiring, and they followed suit by spending much time in the outdoors, camping, boating, swimming, learning to make weapons and traps, tools and utensils, studying animal behavior, hunting and trapping wildlife, gathering edible plant food, cooking on a campfire, etc. They also learned how to handle still and movie cameras, to record events and experiences. Constance Arntzenius

6 A portrait of Peronne Arntzenius as a child, painted by artist Willem Tholen, a close friend of the family, was used for a Dutch postage stamp in 1957.

took it upon her to publish a translation of selected materials from Seton's writing as early as 1915 (Seton 1915a). While the sisters were in a privileged position and learnt about outdoor life on their own accord while using resources available to them, the scouting movement rooted and quickly blossomed in The Netherlands (Rambonnet 1932; Van der Steen 2010).

From 1914 the Arntzenius girls worked on the idea to realize their dream of an American journey. They had joined a scouting group in The Hague and went on trips to Eerbeek where national meetings were held. When they heard about an annual meeting of a relative new organization called The Campfire Girls in the U.S., an all-girl version of but independent from the Woodcraft League, they contacted the young organization and were promptly invited by its president Charlotte Vedder Gulick to join Camp WoHeLo on Lake Sebago, Cumberland County, in the forests of Maine as guests.[7]

The girls did not hesitate long and embarked on their first American journey on August 3, 1914 when they sailed on the SS Rotterdam to New York and stayed for a year, principally in the Northeast (1931:2-4). WoHeLo was short for Work, Health and Love, and the program of the campfire girls clearly focused on the domestic sphere. The camp accommodated 60 girls and staff in tents, and several cabins housed workshops and the kitchen with dining area. The staff consisted of physician Dr. Gulick and his wife Charlotte, as well as a number of paid female instructors who taught pottery, weaving, jewelry making, photography, dance, swimming, etc. The group spent two months at the lake, learning teamwork as a fundamental value. Life and activities had a strongly American Indian character, with accommodation in tents, engaging in arts and crafts, etc. Dr. Gulick was called *Timanous*, "leader" in Algonquian, and his wife *Hiitini*, "mother." A weekly campfire was organized with oratory, reporting activities of the week in verse. Treks through the countryside were undertaken with hilltop destinations, as were trips with "war canoes" on lakes and rivers, all the while observing the wildlife. The focus on Native American life and culture was the result of the Gulick's dissatisfaction with materialism that increasingly dominated society, while cultural values that made up civilization were constantly undermined. They regarded adolescence as a kind of rebirth, and wanted to promote high ideals of community and cooperation among youth. In 1914 physician Charles Eastman, of Sioux ancestry and named Ohiyesa, published "Indian Scout Talks," a guide for boy scouts and camp fire girls, containing information about Indian traditions. It proved to be a great source of inspiration for the organized youth movement (Eastman 1914; Arntzenius 1931:8-12; Buckler 1961:11-18,43-44; Cordery 2013:211-213).[8]

7 The Camp Fire Girls were officially incorporated as an organization in 1912, and in a few years listed 60.000 members.

8 The Camp Fire Girls have been the subject of numerous books by participants as well as outside observers; *e.g.* Buckler *et al.* 1961; Gulick 2000.

After their stint with the Campfire Girls the twins returned to New York City where they made the acquaintance of ornithologist Frank Chapman and Arctic explorer and Inuit-expert Vilhjalmur Stefansson at the Museum of Natural History. Chapman arranged for them to camp for a time on Gardiner's Island in Long Island Sound, enjoying the outdoors and the plentiful wildlife: hawks, owls, song birds, turtles, snakes, muskrats, beaver, and deer. The girls carried out several experiment with the hawk population for the museum curator, and filmed the birds, producing a documentary they hoped to sell. However, they were swindled out of the film and lost their investment. Back in New York City the girls played small roles in the film The Legend of Sleepy Hollow that starred W. Rogers, but the footage in which they figured ended up on the cutting floor (Arntzenius 1931:13-27).[9]

While camping and travelling in New York State in 1919 the sisters called upon Ernest Thompson Seton at his estate in Greenwich, north of New York City, and made the acquaintance of the celebrated author whose works they loved so much. Seton had established the Woodcraft League of North America in 1902 when he started summer camps at his estate, learning the participants a way of life inspired by Indian tribal ways of life and natural history studies. This outdoor educational program for boys combining of survival skills with playing Indian was popularized in his writings and lectures. Soon local groups organized and followed suit. When the sisters encountered again Ernest Thompson Seton in California again in 1922 he invited them to come to his estate again to perform folksongs during a "Woodcraft Indians" scouting course he taught (Arntzenius 1931:45-6; Witt 2010:95-106). In 1927 Seton and Clyde Fisher of the American Museum of Natural History travelled to the Southwest to shoot the documentary "Camping among the Indians" that was subsequently installed in a permanent gallery at the museum (Griffiths 2013). The twins were in the Southwest that same year but they did not meet Seton on this occasion.

The twins were able to finance their travels by cutting costs to a minimum. As experienced girl scouts they camped outdoors, in a tent, and when the wildlife necessitated this or the weather became colder, in their car. The generous American hospitality offered to them while on the road was also willingly accepted. In addition, they stayed with Dutch acquaintances or Dutch emigrants to whom they were referred by family and friends in Holland. They had also acquired sufficient technical knowledge to be able to maintain and repair their car when it broke down, with a few exceptions of course. They also did their own cooking on a campfire. During their first overland trip the twins bought a new Ford Model T Pickup for $ 600 in New York City. The girls kept their gear to a minimum. They slept in sleeping bags in their car on the front

9 Copies of the Arntzenius correspondence in the Stefansson Papers at Rauner Special Collections Library, Dartmouth College, Hanover, NH, were requested twice but never obtained.

On the road in Arizona (Arntzenius 1931:81).

and back seats. When staying longer in any one place, they attached a tent to the car in which they cooked on a little woodstove, ate and socialized with visitors.

Having their own car allowed the sisters to stay away from tourist traps and explore more isolated areas where nature and people were unspoilt by the onslaught of mass-tourism. They became convinced that the most difficult road was the best road, in a literal as well as figurative sense. Such choices also lowered the pace of travel, enabling people to take much more in of the environment, animals and people. This was especially satisfying as it meant a much stronger experience and impact. Music served the girls well during their travels. It paved the way for introduction to almost anyone, including Indians. Good maps were available everywhere, but on Indian reservations the lack of road signs could easily get people lost. Only in exceptional cases did one find signs along the road, as in the case of First Mesa on the Hopi reservation where Walpi was the destination of hundreds of visitors during the summer who came to attend the biennial Snake Dance (1931:28-32,199).

Much needed cash was earned by performing folksongs in various languages, including Dutch, Flemish, English, Scotch, Welsh, French, Italian, Greek, and Russian, to the accompaniment of a guitar and mandolin. In 1919 they specifically toured the northeastern U.S. to raise funds for their subsequent travels. To get bookings for shows they engaged William B. Feakins, the major American agent of lectures with offices in the Times Building at 500 Fifth Avenue in New York City. At one time or another he arranged lecture tours for Alexander Kerensky, Bertrand Russell, August Picard, Lincoln Steffens, and Hendrik Willem Van Loon (Herald Statesman, Yonkers, NY, March 26, 1946). He published a promotional brochure showing the sisters dressed in the traditional attire of the fishermen on the island of Urk, one wearing a lace cap and long apron, the other a striped shirt, and both wooden shoes (Feakins 1919). They used this pamphlet also during their later travels for promoting additional performances. In California they worked short time for wages, making lamp shades in the shape of tipis and doing secretarial work. On January 13, 1923 the Sausalito News announced a program at the Woman's Club bringing "the delightful little Arntzenius sisters from Holland, whose repertoire of European folk songs and dances, and the manner of getting them 'across' are said to be refreshingly buoyant and spontaneous." In early August 1923 they performed their folk songs before an audience of almost 1000 people in Wheeler Hall on the University of California Berkeley campus, raising a substantial amount (N.N. 1929). Small change was earned with occasional language and driving lessons. Back in The Netherlands they earned additional money by giving lectures, showing their slides, and singing folk songs of which they developed

The Arntzenius sisters in folk costume (Feakins 1919).

a considerable repertoire. During these performances they often dressed up in Navajo Indian costume, consisting of a velveteen shirt and a long calico skirt, and added with silver and turquoise jewelry. Their usual venues were schools and community centers (Arntzenius 1931:1-7,28-31; Het Vaderland, January 30, March 30 and April 3, 1928).

The Arntzenius sisters had first visited Santa Fe in 1920 and as so many others before and since were immediately taken by the mixture of Indian, Spanish, Mexican and American cultures in its people, architecture and way of life. A second visit took place two years later and they immediately noted a significant growth of the population and in 1927 they hardly recognized the town again after five years on their third visit. They attributed the rapid growth of Santa Fe to its healthy climate which drew health seekers from the East and California to northern New Mexico. Other attractions were the scenic beauty of the landscape which drew nature lovers from urban centers and artists, and the Indians of the Four Corners region whose tribal cultures fascinated intellectuals, artists and a large public. A positive aspect of Santa Fe's growth was that artists and intellectuals had organized to study and improve the life on reservations, principally by defending Indian land and water rights, and to protect and develop Native arts and crafts (1931:35-6).

They noted that traditional Indian arts were of high quality due to the time spent on their manufacture. They were impressed by blankets woven by Navajo women and the silver and turquoise jewelry crafted by their men, the painted pottery of the Rio Grande Pueblos, Zunis and Hopis, the basketry of the Apaches and the beadwork of the Plains tribes. However, they also noted that the quality of arts and crafts had deteriorated due to the influx of increasing numbers tourists. This market required mass production of cheap souvenirs and Indians, especially the younger generation, catered to the tastes of this new gullible clientele by mass-producing mediocre and inferior curios which they easily could dispose off. The "railway Indians" could be seen on every train station of the Atchison, Topeka and Santa Fe line, offering their merchandise to eager travelers and tourists. A number of artists, intellectuals and traders tried to stem this deterioration of traditional arts and crafts and encouraged the production of high quality pieces for a more discerning clientele (1931:35-7).

The traders played an important role in the upkeep and improvement of standards according to the sisters. Some of them employed the best craftspeople to produce the highest quality jewelry and textiles for a decent salary. One had hired the best Navajo weaver he was able to find and had her train younger girls in the intricacies of the weaving art. He was also trying to replace the strong commercial aniline dyes with vegetal dyes from Switzerland that were reminiscent of the natural pigments the Navajos had used traditionally but whose production was rather time-consuming and had therefore been abandoned. Finally he was acquiring capital to purchase Persian sheep as their wool was much better than that produced by the interbreeding of Indian and Merino sheep. However, the Indian trade was geared to making a profit, and many Indian traders had high quality arts and crafts as well as cheap souvenirs in stock for their varied customers (1931:37,86).

The sisters also yearned to acquire a few quality pieces of Indian crafts but their budget prohibited that because prices for quality products were comparatively high. Instead they visited Indian traders in isolated rural areas who accepted Indian articles in pawn and had sometimes high quality pieces for sale at a decent price. Thus they were able to purchase a pair of nice woven Navajo garters from a trader with whom they spent several days (1931:36-7).

When they heard about the Inter-Tribal Ceremonial, they decided to go to Gallup in 1922 or 1923. The road west was disastrous with long stretches of gravel and sand, lava fields, sagging bridges. In Gallup they made the acquaintance of Indian trader Mike Kirk, one of the originators of the Inter-Tribal Ceremonial. He was jovial, always cheerful, friendly and astute. He provided them with a "press" card in return for a copy of al photographs they took. They camped near the festival grounds, near the Indian camp with between 2000 and 2500 representatives of ten tribes. Parades, games and horse races took place all day. In the early evening cars were placed in a circle around the dance ground. Their lamps provided the light for the Indian dancers, as did several campfires in the circle, creating a fantastic atmosphere. The Fire Dance was the most spectacular event as burning torches were beaten on the back of the dancers until they extinguished. The dances of the Pueblo Indians were less dramatic but restrained and graceful, as was the appearance of the Zuni *olla* maidens, carrying their large intricately decorated water pots on their heads, clad in white shirts, dark mantas, decked out in silver and turquoise necklaces and bracelets (1931:38-40,86-87). The girls also visited nearby Zuni Pueblo and c amped near the Christian Reformed Mission of the Dutch Reverend Herman Fryling who had been working among the Indians for 28 years as Vanderwagen's successor.

They noted that all Indian children were obliged to attend several years of school where white teachers and missionaries taught them that their traditional beliefs and way of life should be abandoned as they were of no value, even evil. In such conditions it was not surprising that no young Navajos were willing to be trained many years as singers anymore, and that some medicine men had exploited their position by spreading rumors of witchcraft and demanding substantial payment for their services combating this evil. Many Indian parents opposed the forced removal of their children to often faraway schools they were unable to visit because of the costs involved as the sisters were told by a distressed Hopi mother in Walpi. The girls were aware that the condition in the boarding schools often left much to be desired and were relieved to hear that a government inquiry into the treatment of Indian pupils was planned. Many children who returned after three years were hardly able to fit into their local communities again as social and cultural traditions often conflicted with new values and norms they learned in white institutions. However, they were also not accepted in white communities who still regarded them as Indians, thus creating a culturally homeless generation (1931:40-41,82-3).

In 1923 and 1927 they visited the Hopi villages on Black Mesa. Only with difficulty they reached their destination, once being stuck in the wash until the mail truck bailed them out. They were impressed with the mesa-top location of the villages, especially Walpi on First Mesa which they visited. They admired the adobe architecture, their neat appearance inside, the affective treatment of children, especially by the men. Also their hospitality they found remarkable, offering them peaches to cool off after their steep ascent on foot. They were also invited for meals of white beans, sheep fat, cooked corn mush and *piki*, traditional flatbread. To express their appreciation the girls sang several songs and showed photographs of their American travels. This gesture was much appreciated by their hosts who returned the musical favor (1931:80-82,84-5,195-7).

In Mishongnovi they attended one of the many dances aimed at bringing rain, being invited by a 15-year old Hopi girl from Walpi who also acted as guide and interpreter. It was a women's dance for which the participants had been preparing and fasting for sixteen days. During that time they were prohibited from eating sugar and salt, and were only allowed to drink the absolute minimum. If rain appeared within four days after the dance, the women had performed their duties well; if not, one or more of them were suspected of breaking the rules on fasting, and continued drought was regarded as punishment of such infraction. This was the case when the sisters visited as there was no rain for four weeks. The sanctity of the performance was expressed in the solemnity of the dance and the reverence of the spectators, aligned along the plaza and sitting on the rooftops where the sisters had also been assigned a place (1931:83-4).

In 1927 they had an opportunity to see the snake dance at Walpi. It was held on August 23 and on that day the twins among several hundred white visitors climbed First Mesa in a 90 F heat. They positioned themselves on the plaza around 11 a.m. to see the dance that was to be performed in the late afternoon. They knew about the sacred significance of the dance, aimed at the bringing of rain to bring fertility to the fields. They also knew about the gathering of the snakes, their ritual washing and dusting with sacred corn meal, the drinking of an antidote against snakebite by the dancers. The snake dance was performed on the ninth day of secret ceremonies in the kiva, protected from the gaze of uninitiated women men. Finally the dance commenced. The Antelope priests emerged from the underground kiva with their torsos painted, clad in kilts, moccasins and colorful woven belts, carrying rattles. They danced and sang, positioned in a single file, not moving from their spot.

Then the snake dancers emerged, also painted and dressed in ceremonial attire. First they danced, but then, one by one stooped in front of the *kisi*, a brush hut, from which they took a rattlesnake and put it in their mouth. Each dancer was immediately joined by a companion who diverted the attention of the snake by stroking its head and back with a feather, thus protecting the carrier from a possibly fatal bite. All snakes are thus treated before a group of elaborately dressed women appears, dusting the dancers with sacred cornmeal from their baskets. Then they draw a circle on the plaza floor with the meal into which the snakes are thrown. Finally the dancers dash forward, grasp as many snakes as they can carry, and run down the trails to the plain where the reptiles are released. The dance was successful as a downpour drenched dancers and spectators alike. The next day the twins witnessed the dance at Mishongnovi. They liked this performance better because it was much less crowded and there were only few whites present. At Keams Canyon they camped, washed, rested and developed their films at the office of the Indian Agent (1931:85).

In 1923 they also visited Acoma and Isleta. It was a tiresome trip by car along a sandy road to Enchanted Mesa. On an adjacent mesa Acoma Pueblo set as an eagle's nest, only accessible by a few narrow and steep trails. Having seen their visitors from afar, they were welcomed on the top of the mesa by several women who offered tacky souvenirs, including pottery, for sale. They were also charged a two-dollar entry-fee and a five-dollar camera-fee unless the photographs were used for educational purposes. The explanation of the sisters that they showed their photographs during lectures was not accepted and because they refused to pay the camera-fee, they were accompanied on their tour of the pueblo by an

Indian "guard" in Acoma (Arntzenius 1931:92).

Acoma woman who watched that they would not surreptitiously take pictures. However, they managed to photograph their "guard" with her consent and in return for the promise to send her a copy, and the church. After developing their film in Santa Fe, they mailed her the photograph. The sisters were appalled at the commercialism of the Acomas which they attributed to the steady stream of white visitors (1931:91-2,198). They did not realize that they had encountered the first vestiges of self-determination in tourism management by a Native community.

When they heard that the Green Dance was being performed in Isleta, they visited the pueblo from Santa Fe. They enjoyed the colorful dance, the dancers decorated with spruce boughs, kilts and wearing large masks. *Koshares*, sacred clowns wearing beaded clothing, a sack mask and an elaborate headdress, enlivened the performance with their antics and, when necessary, kept order among spectators. They did not hesitate to attack white visitors who tried to take pictures in secret, and destroyed their cameras on the spot. Later, in Jemez Pueblo, they would experience how cameras were taken from visitors and kept until after the dance when they were returned (1931:93,198).

The Pueblo Indians performed a number of sacred dances that white people were not allowed to observe. When these dances took place, the village was closed off and sentries posted along the roads leading into the pueblo, turning back all unwanted visitors. The sentries were known to slice the tires of cars of persistent whites, and one time the sisters saw sentries jumping on the footboard of a car and smash the window with a club, forcing the driver to return (1931:93).

In 1923 they made a trip from Gallup to Canyon de Chelly on the Navajo Indian Reservation. Trader Mike Kirk had provided them with a letter of recommendation for his colleague Cozy McSparron in Chinlee who provided

Eagle Dance at Tesuque Pueblo (Arntzenius 1931:190).

the sisters with horses. They trekked through the majestic canyon for a whole day and were awed by its reddish-brown perpendicular walls, the rock alcoves at the bottom and the prehistoric Indian ruins built in the crevices, notably White House Ruin. This was also an occasion to get to know the Navajo way of life and they witnessed women weaving outside their *hogans* and men tending their flocks of sheep. An offer to buy a silver belt buckle from an Indian cowboy for $ 5 did not initially result in a purchase as its owner wanted three dollars more, an amount the sisters unfortunately could not spare. Later they regretted to let this opportunity pass and they asked McSparron to buy the buckle for them, paying him in advance. Months later, back in the Netherlands, they received a small parcel by post, containing the coveted artifact (1931:87-91).

In 1927 the twins visited the trading post of Ramon Hubble at Ganado, the son who trod in his prominent father's footsteps. Among the whites and Navajos the Hubbles had a reputation of being honest traders, and they were well liked on and outside the reservation. As far as the twins were concerned this reputation was deserved, because they were warmly welcomed by Hubbell Jr., his wife and their two sons, given a comfortable bedroom and their car was parked in a garage. They admired the museum-like interior of the house, decorated with Navajo rugs, western paintings, Indian basketry and Hispanic weavings and woodcarvings.

When hearing about their interest in the Navajos, Hubbell invited them to a *yeibichai*, a healing ceremony. After a ride of an hour through a darkening desert, they arrived at a *hogan* into which they were invited. The "singer", the medicine man who performed the nine-day ceremony, allowed them to attend that night's ritual, meant to banish all evil, witchcraft and sickness, and cure and heal the spirit as well as the body by injecting them with harmony and beauty. Prayers, chants and sand painting were performed by the singer, all to be carried

Navajo medicine men working on the sand painting for the curing ritual (Arntzenius 1931:206).

out precisely as tradition prescribed, otherwise the goal of the ritual would not be achieved. Three patients were present, two women and one man, sitting on a blanket against the wall, their faces painted with red and white designs. From time to time they were served an emetic, part of the curing procedure. At daybreak the singer and his seven helpers began designing a picture on the *hogan* floor, using a variety of colored sands. Gradually stylized images of a variety of deities appeared, enclosed by a rainbow. A curing ceremony was an expensive affair because it attracted family and friends who socialized and danced, and had to be fed. There was also the food and fee for the singer and his assistants (1931:202-5).

Hubbell told them that Navajos used both the hospital and the medicine men. Many Navajos used their singers as a last recourse when the hospital physician had judged their illness as incurable. In a number of cases patients had completely recovered, testimony to the power of the singers. On the other hand, there were also cases known in which patients had become worse because of the treatment with native medicines from medicine men, and had to be cured in the hospital.

The night before they left they attended a "girls dance", honoring the girls who had reached puberty. The girls were dressed on colorful cotton dresses and shawl, and chose their dancing partners among the artificially reluctant young men, draped in blankets of various colors and designs. Some were drawn from their horses, the girl often being aided by her friends. They let go of their partners when they paid a coin of sufficient value, otherwise they faced another round. Several hundred young people participated in the pleasant spectacle (1931:205-7).

Their four-day stay was thoroughly enjoyed by all. Mrs. Ramon Hubble confided in the twins that it was becoming increasingly difficult to uphold traditional hospitality because of the increasing number of visitors and the fact that some abused it (1931:205).

Before leaving the reservation they witnessed a sheep dip. There were only few dipping stations on the reservations and Navajos came from a large surrounding region with their flocks. The women had dressed in their finest calico and velvet clothes and wore concha belts and silver and turquoise jewelry. Some had painted their faces with ochre to prevent sunburn. That morning 7000 sheep went through the dip (1931:208-10).[10]

The Arntzenius sisters are an example of individuals in Europe and North America feeling a degree of estrangement from civilization. In response they embarked on a search for a more authentic lifestyle. This they found in the semi-arid deserts of the American Southwest where Native peoples tenaciously tried

10 The twins also spent time in Nevada with the Washoes (1922-24), and in Montana with the Crows (1926-27). Constance Arntzenius passed away in January 1941 in Monterrey, Mexico. Peronne Arntzenius died on November 27, 1953, and is buried at Forest Lawn Memorial Park in Glendale, Los Angeles County.

to hold on to their ancient and cherished ways of life, despite centuries of Euro-American domination. In the end the sisters chose to settle in the United States where nearer to the wilderness and Native peoples they could more easily escape the alienating forces of their own culture.

1926: an anonymous travel party

In 1926 an anonymous Dutchman published his experiences about a trip undertaken with several compatriots across the American West in the Leeuwarder Courant, a provincial newspaper. They travelled by car and camped along the way. A few nights were spent in Santa Fe, but the author had difficulty in getting used to the town with its unfamiliar Indian-style adobe architecture and historic Hispanic character. They encountered Indians during a shopping trip on and around the plaza and were surprised that they could hardly speak English. The next day a nearby Indian pueblo was visited and the experience left the Dutch travel party a bit shaken. They found little of interest in the village, except for the little church they secretly photographed, because a sign stated that this was forbidden. However, when the Native residents noticed what they were up to they emerged from their mud huts and approached the intrusive visitors in what the Dutch felt was a threatening manner, after which they quickly jumped in their car and sped away. Along the highway they stopped at a roadside stand where Indians sold painted pottery. The visitors purchased several pieces and tried to photograph the sellers, but refrained from doing so after being faced with strongly voiced objections. The amount of money the Indians demanded for having their picture taken was prohibitive, ten dollars in silver coins, as they distrusted paper money (Leeuwarder Courant, Nov. 2, 1926:9).

1928: the Gratamas, a grand tour

Successful investor Ludolf Gratama and his wife Wilhelmina Schultz-Van Haegen, member of a wealthy family, embarked on a grand tour around the world in 1927. In the United States they spent a number of months with family and friends in the American West in 1928. Their unpublished manuscript about this part of their journey and a series of photographs was recently discovered and most of it published in Dutch (Hovens and Van der Hooft 2010). Their experiences in the Southwest are detailed in the contribution by Mette van der Hooft to this volume of tourism studies. It is surprising that both this manuscript and the book they published on the Pacific leg of their journey lack clear references to their motives for travelling to distant lands and meeting Native peoples and are fairly factual descriptions of their encounters with peoples from other cultures (*cf.* Gratama 1931).

1930-1932: Chief White Horse Eagle in the Netherlands

The public lectures, travel books and translations of the works of Ernest Thompson Seton by the Arntzenius sisters did much to promote scouting in the Netherlands. The movement drew much inspiration from Seton's ideology, rooted in the life of natural man, Native Americans particularly. In 1930 and 1932 Osage Chief White Horse Eagle from Oklahoma, by that time a centenarian, was hosted at the annual scouting jamborees in Holland and held a number of public lectures on Indian customs. He gained notoriety because of the 1930 Dutch translation of his autobiography (1930, 1930a). Divided into three parts, the book contained sections on the history of Indian-white relations and on the Native peoples of the Southwest, in addition to the autobiography. It

Chief White Horse Eagle, ca. 1930 (private collection).

was popularized through the chief's visits to the Netherlands and the exposure he received in the Polygoon News that was shown in all movie theatres across the country. The author devoted chapters to the Rio Grande Pueblos, Taos, Hopis, Navajos, Apaches, Pimas and Havasupais, and discussed subjects like Santa Clara and Hopi-Tewa pottery, Navaho weaving, jewelry, and sandpainting, Hopi kiva ceremonies and the Snake Dance, and Pima, Havasupai, and Apache basketry. Such presentations played a role in focusing the attention of a wide Dutch public on the American Southwest and promoted visits to the region and its Native American inhabitants.[11]

1930s Rudolf Steinmetz, historian and poet

In the 1930s Rudolf Steinmetz made several journeys to and through the United States. He travelled by Greyhound bus and by backpacking and hitchhiking, an early example of a tourist type that would become much more numerous after the war. He was the son of Sebald Rudolf Steinmetz who occupied the chair in social geography at the University of Amsterdam. Steinmetz Jr. was a historian and poet, and was known to have national-socialist sympathies. Shortly before the outbreak of the Second World War he published an informative and reflective book about the most eye-catching aspects of America and its way of life for a European. One-third of his book focuses on the American West, the region that he regarded as the quintessential America, in sharp contrast to the Europeanized East (Steinmetz 1939).

Steinmetz saw the white settlers in the Southwest as strangers in a land which they had conquered but had not been able to accommodate to. They remained strangers, exploiters and enemies of the living natural environment, tribeless and on unfamiliar hunting grounds, perennially searching for water and profit. Only the Indians were authentically rooted in this environment and were really organically part of it in a way the whites would never be. The Dutchman regarded the Southwest with its long Spanish heritage and relatively short American history as a reflection of a Eurocentric colonial society. The Euro-American East had gained political and economic dominance, and most of the population in the Southwest adhered to lifestyles rooted in Mediterranean tradition. This Hispanic population had mingled to a certain extent with Native Indians, and the original inhabitants, conquered and destitute, were pushed to the geographic and social margins of society. It is with these aboriginal inhabitants that his sympathies lay. However, Southwest society had kept a strong commitment to land and community, and, to a certain extent, rooted organically into its natural surroundings. This could not be said of the Euro-Americans who had

11 The Native American identity of Chief White Horse Eagle has been questioned by American and European historians and anthropologists. Sioux Indians with Buffalo Bill's entourage regarded him as an Afro-American, and it is quite probably that the man was of mixed descent.

not blended in with the land and had kept themselves separate from the Native and Hispanic population (1939:331-2,337-8).

Santa Fe had become a Mecca for tourists travelling by car. According to Steinmetz its attraction consisted of an artificial exoticism, created out of its Indian and Hispanic heritage, with the most visual expression the adobe architecture carried to extremes. At the Grand Canyon he abhorred the facilities developed for tourist, spoiling the natural experience. The Dutchman visited a number of Indian pueblos in New Mexico that he described with much realism, shunning romanticizing: gray, multi-storied blocks of small adobe houses, situated around a central plaza, the whole complex surrounded by small one-story mud abodes along narrow, wooden sheds, and small fields with vegetables and fruits, the whole creating a quiet and frugal impression, lying in a relentless baking sun. Steinmetz observed many Indians along the roads travelling with mule-drawn carts, and selling crafts from roadside tables. They were also to be seen in the larger towns, plying their wares from door to door. Indians also were employed in the tourist industry, especially restaurants and hotels, albeit in the most menial of jobs (1939:333-334).

After a visit to the mighty Grand Canyon, Steinmetz travelled across the Navajo and Mescalero Indian Reservations in Arizona and New Mexico. Cameron was a desert oasis providing decent lodging in a small hotel and a cabin camp, public showers, good food in a restaurant and café, served by Indian and Hispanic waitresses, and an abundance of Indian arts and crafts for sale. Steinmetz was grateful for the free meal he received from the trader's wife. A *hogan*, a traditional Navajo home, is situated next to the trading post and occupied by a disheveled Indian family that offers itself and its humble abode to be photographed for a small fee. Many tourists accept and let the shutters of their cameras do the clicking. Throughout the day many Indians, both Navajos and Hopis, visit the post to trade. They bring sheep, fleeces, sometimes horses or mules, often woolen blankets, silver jewelry, and pottery in return for

Navajo Indians selling arts and crafts along the highway (Steinmetz 1939:352-353).

foodstuffs, tools and equipment, kitchen utensils, and cash. Pride rather than modesty characterized the attitude of the Hopis whom Steinmetz regarded as the nobility among the Indian tribes, although he was also impressed by the Navajos (1939:340-348).

At the Fort Defiance Agency Steinmetz received assistance from government employees in making several trips across the Navajo reservation. He made the acquaintance of a *natani*, a headman who lived nearby and showed him his treasure of woven blankets and silver and turquoise jewelry. Another trip was made to Canyon de Chelly in trading post automotive vehicle especially outfitted for desert travel with broad tires and an extra powerful engine. Steinmetz was pleasantly impressed with the verdant canyon and its more manageable size than the gigantic chasm to the northwest. He admired the remains of prehistoric Anasazi settlements, notable White House Ruin, and their strategic location as to defensibility and access to water and fields. Unfortunately the archaeological site was cordoned off by the Park Service with barbed wire, so he was unable to explore the buildings (1939:308-316).

On the Navajo Indian reservation Steinmetz found the administration of the Indians by the government benevolent and wise, although based on racial superiority and partially also on guilt. The government provided healthcare, education, low-skilled employment and income-support. However, he also noted that the Navajos resented the interference of the government into affairs they considered tribal and private. Christianization was left to the private enterprises of the different religious denominations, although in many cases Indians retained their traditional beliefs and rituals even after Christian conversion (1939:305-12,316).

From director Hewett of the Laboratory of Anthropology Steinmetz received a letter of recommendation for the Indian Agent at Mescalero and was thus well received and assisted when he arrived on the Apache reservation. He had a similar letter for a Mescalero Apache Indian from an ethnologist who had been working among Indians for 25 years; the Apache man was collecting data, had a wooden leg, and was known as somewhat of an obstructionist by the Indian Agent. During his stay at Mescalero Steinmetz also made the acquaintance of a government inspector who spent his holiday there (1939: 317-323).

Having witnessed the nomadic Navajos with their sheep herds and the Apaches with their cattle herds Steinmetz was left with the impression that these tribes lived a relatively unencumbered life without concern for abode or property, satisfied with life and liberty. However, he deemed the nomads cursed, expressed as much in their radiance, passion and anger as in their resignation. The native peoples of the Southwest conveyed an impression of gloom which Steinmetz attributed to the dismal prospects of their destiny. This was expressed by their conduct, characterized by reticence and distrust that went beyond cultural modes of prescribed behavior. Only on horseback did they relive something of their independent and proud past, and they appeared one with their animals. However, the Dutchman was quick to point out that even the horse was an introduction by whites and he considered Indians riding on horseback as engaged in a last meal before their final dance of death on the edge of their grave (1939:297-304,327).

1932: Tollien Schuurman, Olympic athlete

Schuurman was the first woman to run the 100 meters in under 12 seconds. In 1932 the Dutch athlete made a cross-country railroad journey from New York to Los Angeles, headed for the Olympic Games. She published her itinerary in the Leeuwarder Courant (Sept. 17, 1932:10), a major regional newspaper. Stops were made in St. Louis, Kansas City, and Albuquerque. On their approach to the latter city she saw cowboys on horseback and the adobe homes of Indians, congregated in dusty pueblos around a central plaza. The train stopped for half an hour at the Albuquerque depot and Schuurman's diary relates: "There is a large Indian house where one can buy all kinds of souvenirs. Many travelers avail themselves of this service. Indian women squat in front of the house under parasols, surrounded by their merchandise, mostly pottery vessels with painted designs. They are eager to sell something and look at you almost pleading with their dark and sad eyes. When the train departs the stocky women wrap their merchandise together, some maybe satisfied, others disappointed." This is just one example of reports by Dutch travelers about fleeting encounters with Indians while traversing the Southwest as travelers rather than tourists.

1932: J.G. Sleeswijk, scientist

In the early 1930s, professor of technical hygiene J.G. Sleeswijk (1879-1969) of the Technical Academy in Delft traveled through the United States, and published a general book on the country, inspired by his own observations (Sleeswijk 1932). This included remarks on tourism, national parks and American Indians. He regarded the variation in natural scenery as one of the main attractions for tourists, American and foreign alike. He noted that because of the size of the country and the wide differences in regional attractions, the advertising for tourists was organized regionally or locally through the Chambers of Commerce and their publicity departments. Promotion of the West was also actively engaged in by the railroads and on a smaller scale by hotel chains. He regarded the automobile as the ultimate means to disentangle the American from the metropolis and give him the time and opportunity to relax in nature, peace and quiet. This was not limited to an annual holiday, but also had grown into a mass phenomenon during weekends. An increasing number of people had gained more leisure time when Saturdays became days off, and people left by car for their destinations on Friday nights. Auto courts abounded and catered to their needs. Major cities, adjacent Canada without prohibition laws and the Niagara Falls were main attractions to differing clienteles (1932:185-195).

Anasazi cliff dwellings in Arizona (Sleeswijk 1932:144-145).

The romance and adventure of the American West attracted many, and the Indians played a major role in this attraction. The Apaches had an image of epic proportions in the European mind, the result of the impact of popular juvenile literature. Sleeswijk became ecstatic when he traveled through former Apache territory by train across Arizona. However, soon he realized that the tribe had been forced to settle on reservations, that Apaches wore citizen's dress and that Indian children attended school, thus losing much of their authenticity (1932:129-131).

In southwestern Colorado Sleeswijk visited the Anasazi cliff dwellings at Mesa Verde. He noted the numerous archaeological excavations taking place in the Southwest and praised the policy of the federal government of protecting these sites and turning them into national monuments, providing interpretation services for visitors. He also appreciated the national park system as it was a public facility, open to visitors of every means as parks provided simple campgrounds as well as luxury hotels. He regarded the U.S. national parks and monuments as a prime example of environmental, scientific, educational and recreational policy to be worthy of emulation by other nations (1932:127-133).

Sleeswijk deplored the cruel history of Indian-white relations that had resulted in the reduction of once proud and independent Indian nations to powerless wards of the government through disease, war and alcohol. Now they were penned in on reservations and under constant harassment from whites because of their remaining land and natural resources. The author was able to discuss his impressions with civil servants from the Bureau of Indian Affairs in Washington D.C. and was surprised that his critical views were shared. Commissioner

Charles J. Roads had just received approval from Interior Secretary Ray Lyman Wilbur for a plan to improve the educational opportunities for Indian children, an approach appreciated by Sleeswijk, who did not fail to add that this would eventually result in the complete assimilation of the Indian in the American melting pot (1932:249-254).

1933-39: Mrs. Sophie Armstrong-Welters, on holiday

In early 1933 a Dutch woman (1888-1985) and her American husband, living in San Francisco, undertook a Southwestern trip by private car, camping and lodging, depending on facilities. Mrs. Armstrong-Welters published her experiences in two regional newspapers in The Netherlands (Leeuwarder Courant [LC] and Alkmaarsche Courant [AC]). Their first destination was Mount Zion National Park. From there they reached the North Rim of the Grand Canyon. In this region she noted prehistoric Indian cliff dwellings, and told her readers that Mormons and the aboriginal inhabitants had a long history of violent conflict about the land and its resources. The travelers enjoyed the spectacular scenery of the canyon, the Colorado River flowing as a silver ribbon in the deep, the forested plateaus, and the numerous deer. The author of the itinerary informed the readers about the history of Grand Canyon, its "discovery" by Spanish explorer Don Lopez de Gardenas, and subsequent "rediscovery" by American trappers, and Major John Wesley Powell's expedition through the canyon by way of the Colorado River in 1869. She elaborated on the construction of the railway and the construction of roads, and the facilities for visitors, including inner canyon tours, nature walks, and public lectures by Park Rangers. About the Indians of the region she related that Indians, led by the whiteman John D. Lee, had massacred immigrants on the California Trail at Mountain Meadows in 1857. In the early 1920s hundreds of Navajo Indians had been involved in an effort by the National Park Service to catch wild horses and relocate them partially to the South Rim (AC: June 17, 1933:9; June 24, 1933:6; LC: July 21, 1933:9; July 28, 1933:13-14; AC July 1, 1933:8).

Indian culture was also featured in her published letters, especially from the moment when she entered the Painted Desert that owed its name to the colored rocks with various oxidizing minerals contained in them. Armstrong-Welters visited the Navajo Indians on their sprawling reservation that incorporated much of the Painted Desert. She presented them as the Bedouins of the desert, a nomadic tribe with large flocks of sheep, goats, and horses, living in temporary camps until the grazing was depleted, necessitating continual changes of residence across a large territory. They lived in *hogans*, traditional huts constructed from logs and poles, stone and mud, and ceremonially blessed when they were ready for occupation. Near their abodes women sat at upright looms, weaving colorful blankets, a craft learned from Pueblo Indians. These were sold to white traders and customers for decent prices. A number of men had learned silversmithing and made various kinds of jewelry, necklaces, bracelets, rings, belts, buttons, etc., using silver coins as raw material. According to the writer it was the originality of their design and their "barbaric" origin that made them so attractive in the eyes of white collectors. The Navajos had mastered the desert, satisfied with few material goods, free of fear, industrious and independent. Mrs. Armstrong-Welters was clearly impressed by them although she held an ethnocentric bias (AC: July 1, 1933:8; LC: Aug. 2, 1933:10).

From the trader at Cedar Ridge the couple learned that the Navajo women usually made small blankets and that it was difficult to persuade them to produce larger ones, for which there was a demand that thus could not easily be satisfied. This had much to do with their immediate needs. The women sold their blankets every week to four weeks, usually to the local trader who gave them credit of foodstuffs and merchandise at his store. While camping at the trading post the travelers prepared lunch and when two Navajo men let it be known that they were hungry, they shared their food with them. With gusto the Indians ate a tin of sardines, despite the taboo on eating fish. When asked about this they denied that this was fish, because it was "canned stuff" (LC: Aug. 2, 1933:10; also: Alkmaarsche Courant, July 1, 1933:8). Mrs. Armstrong-Welters informed her readers that the Navahos collected the colored rocks in the Painted Desert. These were ground down to fine powders for use by medicine men in the sand paintings of deities, required for curing rituals. She saw a dozen men working on a large painting, artfully funneling the colored sands through their fingers, creating patterns representing gods, spirits, cornstalks, and celestial bodies (July 28, 1933:14).

The Hopi mesas were next on their itinerary. These Indians caught rattlesnakes in the Painted Desert for the biennial Snake Dance in their elevated villages, perched on the rim of Black Mesa. They were a peaceful people, the Quakers among the Indian tribes. Horticulture supplied them with much of what they needed, and they tended villages in niche areas where sufficient moisture was available during the growing season (AC: July 1, 1933:8; LC: July 28, 1933:14; Aug. 2, 1933:10).

Mrs. Armstrong-Welters appreciated the nicely situated campgrounds which the forest service provided for travelers. She stressed that camping there was preferable to lodging at cheap hotels when it came to hygiene and comfort, and that the outdoors had a healthy effect (Aug. 2, 1933:10). Before returning to California a visit to the Havasupai Indians was undertaken. From Hotel El Tovar on the South Rim the party descended into the Grand Canyon. The only settlement in the gorge was a small hamlet called Supai, the focal point of the reservation of the Havasupai Indians. They grew squash, melons, beans, onions, chilies, peaches and figs, facilitated by the excellent climate and soil. Armstrong-Welters was impressed by the people as well as their natural environment, and tantalized her readers by stressing that she saw more natural wonders on this 12-mile trip that other people during a lifetime. The group returned to California, using the Fred Harvey restaurants established on the AT&SF Railway for lunch and dinner, enjoying the "electrically cooled" facilities (AC: July 7, 1933:10; LC: Aug. 12, 1933:9).

1935 Skyscraper: European tourists in North America

Under the pseudonym of "Wolkenkrabber" (Skyscraper), a Dutchman living in New York published a series of "Amerikaansche Notities" (American Notes) in the provincial newspaper Leeuwarder Courant. On August 31, 1935, he addressed the growing European tourism in North America. This was especially attributed to the devaluation of the American currency by a third against most European currencies, and especially the Dutch guilder and Swiss francs were strong. The pre-eminence of the dollar was challenged. Whereas previously Americans went to Europe in droves and enjoyed their holidays and travels in relative luxury there, the tables were now turned. In 1933 the American government reported 34.000 foreign tourists as having visited the U.S.; in 1934 their number had risen to 50.000, and for 1935 even more were expected. Also the composition of European tourists was changing. No longer only people from the upper class crossed the Atlantic, but also for members of the well-to-do middle class a trip to and across North America became a financially viable option if one chose to work hard and save up for such a venture, such an adventure.

The author also mentioned differences between American tourism in Europe and European tourism in America. Americans mostly travelled individually, while many Europeans came in organized group: as members of professional associations, as company managers, etc. They frequently combined business and pleasure. According to the author a major difference was that Americans came to Europe to experience culture and history, while such things were virtually absent in America (sic!). Europeans came to see phenomena such as the New York skyline, Broadway, Black Harlem and the Niagara Falls. In the eastern states popular attractions were office towers with air conditioning and elevators, the Empire State Building, the George Washington Brown, the Holland Tunnel, technical marvels and proof of American ingenuity and enterprise. The Europeans bypassed museums, libraries, churches, zoos and parks because such institutions were too familiar to them. They knew too little about American history to visit places associated with past presidents or other major historical figures. However, America did offer attractions, but these were located in the West: Yellowstone National Park and the Pueblo Indians of New Mexico, requiring a journey almost the same distance as they had already travelled from Europe. Some American politicians, including Senator Royal S. Copeland, realized the importance of this development in these times of economic hardship and stressed the need for their embassies in Europe to assume responsibility for the promotion of tourism to the United States (Leeuwarder Courant, Aug. 31, 1935:18).

1946-1947: Rudolf van Reest, publicist

Rudolf van Reest was a pseudonym of author Karel Cornelis van Spronsen (1897-1979), a prolific author of novels and non-fiction books. As a journalist he worked for several Dutch newspapers. During the Second World War he was active in the Dutch resistance movement, and after 1945 was put in charge of cleansing the Dutch media from newspapers and people that had been collaborating with the German occupiers of The Netherlands. After the war he worked for the newspaper Trouw that originated in 1943 as an underground publication.

Van Reest made a first journey to the U.S. in 1939 with a passenger ship from the Holland America Line. In 1946 he was less lucky as the Netherlands government had commandeered the ship on which he was set to sail, as it was required to transport seamen to pick up new ships in North America. However, he managed to get on a freighter that had a few passenger cabins and it took him and his wife in two weeks to Montreal. From there he travelled on to the U.S. and after his return home published a popular book about his experiences (Van Reest 1948).

Van Reest had great appreciation for the policy regarding the establishment of national parks as a conservation measure, but feared the ruin of the parks because of their development as tourist attractions by the enterprising Americans. The parks had been made accessible for automobiles which brought people in increasing droves to the park. Campgrounds, hotels, and stores catered to the needs of visitors, and artificial attractions such as golf courses, swimming pools and cinemas were being developed (1948:132-3).

Indian members of the Rehoboth (NM) congregation (Van Reest 1948:160-161).

En route from Los Angeles to Chicago, Van Reest crossed Arizona and New Mexico and visited the Grand Canyon and the Dutch Christian Reformed establishment for Indians at Rehoboth, a few miles east of the town of Gallup. It consisted of a mission and a boarding school (Dolfin 1921:97-121). From Rehoboth he made a trip by car through the surrounding area. He saw Navajo women working on vertical looms outside their *hogans*, and appreciated the soft tones, interesting designs and harmonious composition of their woolen blankets (1948:162,165).

Van Reest was aware of the "Indian problem", the result of the violent conquest of America by Euro-Americans, the dispossession of the Indians and their forced settlement on reservations, reduced to dependency. However, he also noted that their numbers were increasing again and that they were not a vanishing race anymore. Another positive prospect for the future was Christianity, as it ended their destructive fatalism and turned them into enterprising citizens. However, the land provided very limited opportunities for agriculture or ranching and economic development was a major concern for the tribe and the missionaries (1948:161-5,171).

1950-51: Wicher Van der Sleen, publicist and bead collector

The foremost publicist propagating the natural and cultural attractions of North America in the Netherlands during the 1950s was Wicher Gosen Nicolaas van der Sleen (1886-1867). He was a productive travel writer and also became known for his extensive collection of beads from around the world. Although he studied chemistry in Amsterdam, his interest went far beyond that academic discipline. Before World War II he repeatedly undertook extensive journeys, notably through the Himalayas and the Indonesian archipelago. The natural history collections he accumulated during these trips were donated to the University of Amsterdam and the Museum of Nature in Enschede. His travel books were well received by an increasingly educated and affluent middle class. To recoup the expenses of his travels, he held lectures for associations and schools. During the war he also gave educational and recreational lectures for his compatriots during the years they were interned in Japanese prison camps in Indonesia (Jurriaanse-Helle 1994).

After the war Van der Sleen married Marianne van Wessem, a woman whose affluence allowed him a life of travel and collecting and researching beads, becoming an expert in this field and authoring an English-language reference work on the subject (Van der Sleen 1967). In the late thirties and early fifties he travelled through the U.S. and Canada and in his travel book commented upon tourism and the Native peoples. He advertised the practicalities of travel in the American West, including easy access to the country, the frequent gas stations and well equipped trailer parks, free tourist information services of local chambers of commerce, good facilities in national parks.

Pueblo designs (Van der Sleen 1953:262).

Van der Sleen's travel books are dotted with data on Native American culture and history. He discusses origins and migrations, prehistoric architecture and even the methodology of tree-ring dating, cultural diversity, specific customs, Spanish colonization in the Greater Southwest, Indian wars and missions, government policies, living conditions on reservations and arts and crafts (1953:passim). He also documents his visits to archaeological and historical sites such as Casa Grande Ruins, the Papago Indian mission church of San Xavier del Bac, and Tonto National Monument (1953:190-193,202-5). He used designs on Pueblo pottery as an emblematic finish of each chapter.

In Palm Springs, California, Van der Sleen was amazed that the American tourists knew nothing about the springs as they stayed on the main street with its luxury hotels, fine restaurants and expensive shops. The springs could be found one block further and were exploited by the Indians. The bathhouses were neatly kept. To enjoy a hike in beautiful Palm Canyon one had to pay two quarters to the Indian at the entrance to the reservation to get access. At the Date Festival in Indio they saw local Indians participating in the festivities. In Yuma on the California-Arizona border he encountered Quechan Indian women selling silver and turquoise jewelry at the railway depot and under the arcades in the main street (1953:179-189). By that time the production of their own traditional pottery and beadwork had ceased virtually completely, and they had taken recourse to peddling Navajo Indian jewelry to passing travelers and tourists.

In south-central Arizona Van der Sleen noted the increasing popularity of this region for Americans from the northeastern United States to pass the cold winter months in a much more pleasant clime. Vacationers also flocked to the region in growing numbers, attracted by the colorful desert dotted with saguaros, and bright flowering succulents and bushes, the warm and healthy climate, the Indian and Hispanic heritage of the region, the art and history museums, the national parks and monuments, and the attraction of a western lifestyle, including ranching, rodeos and a mix of tasty cuisines. Two specific developments he noted were the mushrooming of dude-ranches and retirement communities in the guise of trailer parks (1953:195-201). At San Xavier del Bac near the city of Tucson he was surprised to find Papago Indians living in traditional huts with *ramadas* in front, grinding corn by hand with a rolling stone *mano* on a flat and rectangular stone *metate*, baking tortillas, riding horses and mules bareback, and transporting their harvest and firewood on heavy creaking wagons reminiscent of frontier times (1953:202).

At the Grand Canyon Van der Sleen was overwhelmed by the chasm and its magnificent natural setting on the periphery of the Colorado Plateau and the Painted Desert. He presents his readers with a natural history of the phenomenon, a history of its discovery and exploration, a guide to its educational attractions, and some practical information for prospective visitors. Van der Sleen camped near the Watchtower and described its construction and interior murals by Hopi artist Fred

Van der Sleen among saguaros in Arizona (Van der Sleen 1953:145).

Kabotie. At the Cameron Trading Post he saw the Navajo *hogan* (which he mistook for a Hopi dwelling) where Indians stayed who came to sell their weavings, jewelry and pottery to the local trader and to passing tourists (1953:222-217).

In 1976 Van der Sleen's widow donated her husband's large and worldwide collection of beads to the Allard Pierson Museum of Archaeology of the University of Amsterdam. Surprisingly it contains relatively few beads from North America and none from the Southwest (*cf.* Hovens 2015:65).

1951-1955: Lucy Schouten, psychologist

In the early 1950s Lucy Schouten studied psychology and anthropology at the University of Arizona. She took courses on Minority Peoples with Edward Spicer and introductory anthropology and Indian art and material culture with Clara Lee Tanner. The then current culture-and-personality paradigm led to fieldwork on reservations. At the intertribal Santa Fe Indian School and at Indian day and boarding schools across the Southwest she collected drawings from Indian children for ethno-psychological analysis. At Hopi she met Italian psychology professor Dalla Volta who did similar research at the University of Genoa. About 90 drawings from Schouten have survived and are curated here in Leiden (Hovens 2015:58-59; Hovens and Bernstein 2015:188-191), while 40 of Amedeo Dalla Volta's drawings are in Italy in a Genovese museum. A number of the Leiden drawings contain references to tourism: women weaving on their looms, men fashioning silver jewelry, white people visiting, etc.

Silversmith by N.N., ca. 1953 (RMV 6003-76).

To extend her stay Lucy Schouten worked on several reservations in the Southwest, notably at trading posts and lodges. She befriended a number of Indian families and stayed with some of them for a while, observing their way of dealing with tradition and tourism. She not only attended the Gallup Intertribal Ceremonial and Flagstaff Pow-Wow, but was also present at numerous traditional dances on reservations. At Hopi she saw virtually the whole calendrical cycle of kachina dances and the Snake Dance, and at the various Pueblos she was present during the festivities in celebration of their patron saints. She became acquainted with Hopi artist Fred Kabotie, San Ildefonso potters Maria Martinez and Popovi Da, author Oliver LaFarge, artist Henry Balink, traders Harry Goulding and Cozy McSparron, Franciscan missionary and Navajo ethnographer Father Berard Haile, and many others. Kabotie assisted Schouten with acquiring Indian children's drawings at the high school in Oraibi where he taught art.

Among the Apaches in Arizona Schouten noticed that tourism was becoming an important source of income. The Indians advertised campgrounds that were built along creeks, and hunting and fishing opportunities on the reservations for which permits could be purchased. Tourist resorts were encroaching on the reservation borders. At San Carlos and on the Jicarilla Indian Reservation, Schouten observed Apache women engaged in making beadwork. The *kinaldaa* or girl's puberty ceremony on the Mescalero Indian Reservation in New Mexico still had traditional meaning but seemed to have partially developed into a tourist attraction, complete with printed programs and widespread advertising in the region.

Lucy Schouten on horseback at Grand Canyon (ca. 1953).

Among the Navajos Schouten used several occasions to do fieldwork. With Navajo mothers she talked about child rearing, and she took notes on the practices and mythology surrounding birth practices and the construction of cradleboards, and with men she discussed cosmology, horses, silversmithing and healing rituals. In 1951 most adult Navajos refused to be photographed and even rejected payments that were offered.

Tourists preferring to visit the larger cities of the Southwest also had ample opportunity to get to know and see something of the American Indian. Tucson had been attracting wealthy tourists for a long time, and expensive resorts and dude ranches had sprung up in the area, notably the foothills of the Catalina Mountains. Some shops and stores in the city presented themselves as "Indian Village" or "Trading Post" and offered western dress and Indian arts and crafts to appreciative customers from North America and Europe. Several entrepreneurs hired Indian artisans to work in their establishments so customers could watch them while working on jewelry and beadwork. Some Navajos demonstrated sand painting, drawing mythological figures with colored sand as was done in healing ceremonies. In the latter case, photography was strictly forbidden. Some performed dances, clad in Plains-style garb, replete with colored feathers and fringed buckskin dress, conforming to white stereotypes of Red Indians. Thus tourists were able to experience some staged authenticity in an urban environment.

Schouten returned to the Netherlands in the spring of 1955 and became active as a publicist and public lecturer in Holland and Belgium, using her American experiences as source material. She held several seasonal appointments at community colleges in major cities. In her classes, public lectures, and articles for popular magazines Schouten showed a strong realism, based on her own experiences over many years, and tried to correct the overly positive imagery of her readers and audience when it came to contemporary Indian life.

Through experience with Indians on reservations over a number of years Schouten was keenly aware of their conditions. Ancient traditions and the lures and demands of western culture competed with each other, affecting every Native American community and individual. The impact of civilization was reaching into even the remotest Indian communities. However, she also witnessed the benefits that western education could provide to American Indians to face present and future challenges, as well as the opportunities of tourism to make a living in their traditional homelands and beyond.[12]

1950s: Star gazers

A number of Dutch astronomers became involved in developing the academic discipline at the University of Arizona from the 1950s, and the concurrent construction of and research with telescopes in the Southwest desert (e.g. on Kitt Peak). They included Bart Jan Bok and Gerard Kuiper from Leiden University. Some did research at the Sunspot telescope near Alamogordo in New Mexico, like Cornelis Zwaan who went on to become professor of astronomy at Utrecht University. Most came under the spell of the Southwest and were fascinated by the Indians and traditions that had survived. Some collected a variety of Indian arts and crafts. They all showed visiting Dutch family and friends around who, back in The Netherlands, shared their stories about Indians, tribal dances, pow wows and traditional crafts with family and acquaintances in Holland (*cf.* Rutten 1999).[13]

1960-61: Karel van 't Veer, publicist

Karel Van 't Veer is the penname of Dr. K.L. de Bouvère S.C.J., a scientist of the University of Amsterdam, working for Euratom, the European atomic research agency. He was also a popular writer and journalist. In 1960-61 the Dutchman made a trip through the United States. During that time he wrote a series of articles for "De Volkskrant", one of the largest daily newspapers in the Netherlands, relating his experiences and sharing with readers his insight into America, the nation and the people. In 1961 the Netherlands Automobile Association (ANWB) awarded the writer a prize in recognition for this series, after which the columns were edited and published in book form (Van 't Veer 1962).

---

12 A publication on Schouten's life and work, focusing on the American Southwest, is nearing completion.

13 After the death of her husband the author visited Prisca Zwaan and surveyed the small private collection of Southwestern Indian arts and crafts, including a Sun kachina especially made for Cornelis Zwaan when the Hopi carver learned about his profession.

In the American West Van 't Veer encountered a primordial landscape, a confrontation with creation in the making. He noted that in contrast to Europe, tourism in North America had emerged when regions were still wild and pristine, hardly touched by the hand of man. Landscapes, animals and Indians were saved by protective measures, notably the creation of national parks and Indian reservations, and had thus been protected against the unchecked exploitation of profitable resources by American capitalist entrepreneurs (1962:34-36). Van 't Veer found travel in the United States cheap, whether one chose to go by car, train or airplane. However, lodging was more expensive than in Europe, as were meals, which were generally not very good in taste (1962:213-215).

The Dutch traveler wrote, "I lost my heart in Santa Fe," charmed by the un-American architecture, whether Pueblo adobe or Spanish colonial, and the road network that was shaped by the landscape rather than the rulers and measuring instruments of government surveyors. The capitol building and the governor's mansion were no imitations of their counterparts in Washington D.C. The predominant language of the locals was a melodious Spanish, and the Hispanic males looked like real men in their jeans and colored shirts, and the Hispanic women like ladies, without make-up and stuck-up hairdos. It was like Spain transplanted, with its culture and cuisine, and rodeo replacing bullfighting.

Van 't Veer was also impressed by the prehistoric cliff dwellings and the living Pueblo descendants of their inhabitants, regarded as more industries and of higher moral stature than those in other regions of the American West. He was fascinated by the history of Spanish conquest, the Mexican interregnum, and the establishment of American rule at the terminus of the Santa Fe Trail. On his visits to Indian pueblos he found Indian life significantly transformed as the result of Spanish colonization, especially as exemplified in language and dress. Also American ways had made inroads, and almost everyone owned cars. Most families were dependent on government welfare. They were a poor but smiling people. With some reservation he noted that the Indians frequently catered to the tastes of tourist, donning traditional costume for performing dances or taking photographs for an appropriate monetary reward. They also engaged in the production of arts and crafts for the tourist market, but he regarded the souvenirs as superfluous knickknacks/trash, but sufficiently profitable to contribute to the income of Indian families. He reported a conversation with a Navajo silversmith who became talkative when he discovered that he was not a tourist and potential client but a European traveling through. The craftsman cynically remarked that he took a silver dollar, turned it into a piece of jewelry in fifteen minutes, and then wrapped himself in an Indian blanket, and sat in front of a house or shop where tourists came to gaze at him and purchased the item for five dollars. However, Van 't Veer fell for what he considered to be the romance of Santa Fe and its tri-ethnic populace, although he expected that this charm would not last but crumble under the onslaught of Americanization.

Examples were the employment of Pueblo Indians at the laboratories in nearby Los Alamos, the birthplace of the atom bomb (1962:215-221).

Arizona surpassed all other American states Van 't Veer visited in natural beauty. The Painted Desert and Petrified Forest were only preliminaries to the most grandiose of natural spectacles: the chasm of the Grand Canyon. This natural wonder could not be grasped with any faculty or skill man possessed, but instigated an unforgettable experience. Only the photography in Arizona Highways, the promotional magazine of the state's automobile association, succeeded in modestly approaching the magnificence of the canyon and other Arizona landscapes. In contrast to Yosemite, the Grand Canyon was not overcrowded, offered a range of well-developed educational opportunities and decent facilities for overnight stays. Indians of the surrounding region, frequently staged dances on the rim for an awed and paying public. On his visit to Hoover Dam which controlled the Colorado River, the journalist had to admit that in the end he was more impressed by God's creation of man in his image than as a creator of so much natural beauty (1962:225-229).

1951-1986: Peter Voute, physician

Voute was a Dutch physician who settled in New Mexico where he pursued his professional career. He worked in Lea County, taking care of people employed in the oil fields. After working for a time in the Pecos Valley among Hispanics, he moved to Santa Fe. Voute had to admit to himself that he felt more in tune with what he called the mellow Hispanic ambiance than the raw Anglo-American pioneering spirit. His first encounters with Indians were limited to the Native people selling their arts and crafts under the portal of the Palace of the Governors in Santa Fe. However, he never considered them as typical of the general Indian population, although he initially had no idea about the latter. That would change during several trips he undertook through the Southwest. The first was to the town of Aztec, New Mexico, where he was impressed with the ancient Indian ruins. Voute assumed that their civilization must have been quite sophisticated as they were able to live together with thousands of people in a large population center consisting of one main building complex. He continued his journey across the New Mexican part of the Navajo Indian Reservation. In the 1950s wagon trails connected most communities that dotted the sprawling reservation, and few roads were paved. Most Indians lived in traditional *hogans*, and the Dutchman felt that a great material barrier existed between these Indian homes without utilities, and the state-of-the-art whitemen's modern hospital and boarding school that were being constructed at the time in Shiprock. He wondered how the Navajos would be able to adapt to the transition. The Indians were master craftspeople and their woven rugs and silver jewelry was sold through the local trading posts. They used the cash to buy the western goods that were required for survival, including kerosene for cooking and heating (Voute:1987:24-26).

Having caught his interest, from then on Voute made other trips to learn more about the Indians of New Mexico. The Dutch physician was particularly attracted to San Ildefonso Pueblo where he became acquainted with the famous potter Maria Martinez and her family. He always took family and friends from the Netherlands there for a visit. He explored the Pajarito Plateau and became well acquainted with the ruins of Tuonyi. He also studied Adolph Bandelier's writings and was impressed by his scientific drive as well as empathy with the Indians he expressed. An important feat of the archaeologist was the establishment of Bandelier National Monument to protect the ruins in Frijoles Canyon of the Pajarito Plateau, and becoming a major tourist attraction in the region. However, the culture of the Indians and the work of Adolph Bandelier were overshadowed in 1942 with the establishment of the Los Alamos nuclear research laboratory where the first atomic bomb was developed. Voute had mixed feeling about the new nuclear era and its unforeseen and awesome impact on humanity and civilization (Voute 1987:200-203).

1973-1979: Koos Heyink, book trader, publisher and collector

Jacobus (Koos) Heyink (1906-1997) became interested in foreign lands and peoples because of visits from Protestant missionaries to his father who was a part-time deacon. North American Indians caught his imagination through the juvenile literature of his day, notably the immensely popular books of the German author Karl May. He corresponded with anthropologist Herman ten Kate whose scientific work he valued (Heyink & Hodge 1931). He opened a bookshop and began editing a newsletter for aficionados of the German author, at the same time it attracted people interested in Native Americans. The Karl May newsletter evolved into the bi-monthly, now quarterly, periodical "De Kiva" highlighting Native American cultures and history. It carried the accounts of his trips to the American West, undertaken in 1973 and 1979, the latter partly funded by the American government (Heyink 1973a,b; 1979a,b).

Heyink repeatedly commented on the various classes of artifacts on offer. However, he warned prospective buyers to beware, as some of the basketry was imported from Mexico, some weavings were of poor quality or made only from commercially produced yarns. His advice was to learn more about the arts and crafts market first before buying, and suggested visits to museums as a good way to prepare oneself and acquire basic knowledge about quality aspects. He regarded the government-funded Institute of Indian Art in Santa Fe as a good way to support the artistic development of Native peoples of talent. In San Juan Pueblo they witnessed a Buffalo Dance in 1979 and got into trouble when he began taking pictures. They were approached by several angry Indians who asked to see their permit. Heyink showed the photography permit he had obtained at the Governor's office after paying the required fee, but was told that this was not valid, and thus he had to put his camera away. He afterwards learned that the angry Indians represented the faction of the War Chief who was involved in a power struggle with the governor and tried to obtain control of camera fees. In Taos Pueblo he saw how the Indians tried to control tourism by allowing restricted access and photography, and asking fees for both, thus developing tourism as a source of income. Local artisans sold their work from small shops on the plaza, the accessible central area of the village. The corn dance he saw in Taos was somewhat disappointing to him because the costumes of the participants were rather fragmentary as many western items of dress dominated, only offset by some traditional items, such as belts. Coiffures were very generally short and tidy, and the singing and dancing more muted and reserved than what he had witnessed elsewhere.

Because Heyink would publish his travel experiences the U.S. Council on International Relations had arranged a number of meetings with Indian leaders in New Mexico: Dave Warren, director of research at the Institute of American Indian Art in Santa Fe, Joe Herrera, executive director of the New Mexico Commission on Indian Affairs, Allan Martinez, educational counselor of the Eight Northern Pueblos Council, and J. Ramos Roybal, governor of San Ildefonso Pueblo. Heyink was pleasantly surprised to discover that many Pueblo Indian communities had retained much of their traditions and were governing their own communities according to a mixture of traditional and western standards. However, he also noted that straddling the divide between tradition and modernity was becoming increasingly difficult, and that divisions between traditional and modern factions seemed to increase in severity. Especially programs for economic development, mostly promoted by outsiders, caused much friction, such as the development of Cochiti Lake and the mining near Black Mesa. The traditionalists were often faced with accusations of opposing "development" and "progress", a powerful psychological strategy in a country based on and driven by these principles. Heyink feared that white economic interests in land, water, and other natural resources would prevail, aided by the federal Bureau of Indian Affairs, and in the end the Indians would lose out. However, he signaled one positive trend: the way Indians were using education as a primary tool to survive in the modern world. They talked about education as providing the means for self-government, autonomy, and sovereignty. Heyink was sympathetic to Indian traditions and traditional leadership, critical of the more radical political activism of some Indian organizations, but hopeful that the increasing number of educated of Indian youth would be able to bridge the divide between cultures and pave the way for a better future.

Heyink's travel accounts motivated many readers to follow suit and visit the Southwest to learn more about Native American life in this region. Some related their own experiences to the readers of De Kiva journal. Annual meetings were organized for the members with a program of speakers on Indian subjects,

Navajo pictorial weaving, ca. 1975, Heyink collection (MGL.MG920).

Houtzager at Navajo hogan in Tuba City, ca. 1970 (RMV).

showings of slides and films, and the sale of books, records and arts and crafts. The small private object collection Heyink aggregated is now at Groningen University Museum (Hovens 2015:73-75), and he donated his imagery collection to the Leiden museum.

1957-1978: Elisabeth Houtzager, museum director and folk art collector

Elisabeth Houtzager (1907-2001) was an only child of a successful businessman. She studied art history and modern European languages, and was appointed as director of the Central Museum in Utrecht, specializing in religious art. Throughout her life she travelled the globe, on her own as well as the ICOM-representative of The Netherlands attending the annual museum conferences around the world. She began collecting nativity groups, soon to be expanded to folk art in general, seeking out handmade objects amidst industrially produced goods. In the end she had 800 nativity groups, including some Native North American, which she donated to a Dutch museum dedicated to the Near East (Berkelbach van Sprenkel 1988). Mrs. Houtzager had fallen in love with the American Southwest and was delighted when she encountered a new curator in Leiden with whom she could share her interest. This eventually resulted in the donation of her 4000-piece worldwide folk art collection to the Leiden museum in 1994. Included are several hundred pieces of pottery and basketry, and tourist curios from all across North America (Hovens 2015:56-57; Hovens & Bernstein 2015:192-197). She occasionally lectured about her collecting activities for academically trained audiences.

Houtzager kept diaries of her travels. In the Southwest she was frequently accompanied by Navajo trader Sally Lippincott Wagner, long-time resident, deeply involved with the Indians and a critic of Indian affairs. This provided great access to Indian communities. She wrote about her encounters with potters Helen Cordero (Cochiti), Monica Silva (Santo Domingo), Maria Martinez, Popovi Da and Blue Corn (San Ildefonso), and many others, and how she acquired artworks from them.

She also elaborated on the great variety of venues where Indian and crafts were for sale, and where she acquired part of her collection throughout the years: museum shops, souvenir shops in Santa Fe and at the Grand Canyon, trading posts on reservations, roadside stands of Indian families, and homes of Indian craftspeople. On several occasions she attended Indian dances, facing opposition when she wanted to take photographs. In Santa Fe she saw the Alexander Girard Collection exhibited at the Museum of International Folk Art, her greatest inspirations for collecting and presentation, and the format for her own collection, her display at home and the Houtzager exhibition at our museum (Glassie 1989; Larsen 1995; Hovens & Blijlevens 1994). She occasionally lectured about her collecting for highly educated audiences.[14]

14 A publication on Houtzager and her North American collection of Indian "folk art" is in progress.

Jar by Elva Nampeyo, Hopi-Tewa, late 1960s; Houtzager collection (RMV 5715-2555).

Margot Spiegel- Kraemer.

1975-2000 Margot Spiegel, artist

In 1975 ceramic artist Margot Spiegel-Kraemer sought inspiration for her work outside Europe. Crossing the globe she encountered Pueblo potters in the Southwest and immediately fell in love with the country and its Native inhabitants. Over the years she established long-lasting friendships with potters and others craftspeople, including Joseph Lonewolf of Santa Clara Pueblo, Bill and Mary Martin and Dorothy and Onofré Trujillo at Cochiti, Paul Pino's family at Laguna, and Felipe Ortega at Lamadera, NM (Jicarilla Apache). Margot gradually mastered the ancient techniques of Pueblo ceramics from her friends and taught other Dutch craftspeople what she had learned. Since 1995 she has hosted some of her Pueblo friends in The Netherlands and conducted collaborative workshops for interested ceramicists. Her impact was underpinned by the publication of several books on the cultural background and technical aspects of Pueblo Indian pottery, including the various ways of firing, a partial autobiography and biography, a 2013 exhibition of the collection at the Leiden museum (Hovens 2015:58-59; Hovens & Bernstein 2015:204-205). She also lectured widely, and has just finished a book with photographs of Southwestern rock art (Spiegel-Kraemer 1990, 1993, 1997, 2014; Canté 1993).

Spiegel's attitude toward the Pueblo peoples was notably shaped by her appreciation of traditional painted pottery. She recognized its authenticity originating in prehistoric times as many finely shaped and decorated vessels had been excavated in archeological sites. Moreover, rock paintings contained motifs that were still in use when embellishing pottery with abstract and naturalistic designs. However, Spiegel noticed a disinterest among the younger generation to continue making pottery, and the few who did tended to introduce new elements that she regarded as a departure from communal traditions. She felt that authenticity was being compromised, and that Pueblo pottery was on its way to lose its distinctiveness as a traditional Native American art form.

Post-war tourism and exhibitions

The post-war reconstruction of Western Europe resulted in a society in which leisure was increasingly valued and disposable income rose with the expanding global economy. This enabled the middle class to travel abroad to spend their vacation. Major travel companies began to advertize trips to North America, promoting the national parks in the West. Organized tours were popular, but soon individual tours were on offer for the more independently minded. Movies and television boosted the romance of Route 66, and promoted it as a way to get to know the real America. News reports about the emerging Red Power movement in the 1970s resulted in the realization among the wider Dutch public that Native peoples were still part of contemporary North American society, and Indians were added to the attractions of the West as advertized by the Dutch tourist industry. Indian advocacy groups in Holland like the Lakota Foundation and NANAI (Netherlands Action-group North American Indians) began to offer occasional organized tours focused on Native communities, notably in South Dakota and the Southwest. A plethora of books on Native American culture, history and literature became available in Dutch (Hovens 2015:82-83).

From the Columbus Quincentennial in 1992 Dutch museums also began to focus on Native North America (Hovens 2015:54,59-62,68-69,76,79,81). The international event was commemorated by exhibitions on Southwestern Indian weavings at the Textile Museum in Tilburg (Gelijns 1992), and on Herman ten Kate's research and collecting, mainly in the Southwest, at the National Museum of Ethnology in Leiden (Govaert 1993) and the Wereldmuseum in Rotterdam (Groeneveld & Hovens 1992). In the 1990s the Leiden museum's curator obtained two modest grants from the National Ethnological Acquisitions Funds to acquire contemporary Pueblo pottery and Southwestern silver jewelry, including specimens relevant to the subject of tourism. In addition, historic postcards and Indian souvenirs were collected on an occasional basis. In 1998 the America Museum in Cuyk organized a presentation on the cultures and arts of the Southwestern Indians (Gilsing 1998), and the Leiden Museum showed some Southwestern materials in addition to their large exhibition on the Plains Indians (Hovens 1998; Maas-Frankort & Van Santen 1999). In 2012-13 an exhibition on the First Nations of the Northwest Coast was staged (Provezi 2012). Playing Indian has remained popular in The Netherlands since the Arntzenius twins translated Ernest Thompson Seton's works, and the youth movement took it up in an organized way. Even the National Museum of Ethnology in Leiden played its part with programs for children, including dressing up, making arts and crafts, and storytelling, as exhibition-related activities or as part of its general educational and recreational program (Hovens 2015:45-46,55,57,62).

Travel programs on Dutch television frequently included Route 66 and the American West and always selected Native American attractions as special features. A number of shops began to offer Indian arts and crafts to a growing clientele, and more recently some began to offer their merchandise through websites. The annual Western Lifestyle Experience in The Netherlands became the largest show of its kind in Europe, and always had a substantial Indian section with a program of dances, craft demonstrations and sales of beadwork and jewelry. Almost every year pow wow groups from North America visit Holland to perform before captivated audiences, and enactments of fur trade rendezvous and making replicas of Indian dress is something in which quite a few Dutch engage (*cf.* Kalshoven 2012). Cause and consequence is that since the 1990s the Dutch crossed the Atlantic in ever increasing numbers to spend their leisure time and learn about the fascinating multicultural history of the United States.

Conclusions

There is a plethora of Dutch historical sources on travel through the United States, and especially the Southwest figures prominently. As Doerry (1990) has pointed out: "No other literary region in America ... has proven as durable and as universal as the Southwest. ... The Southwest is an extraordinarily adaptable and fertile literary region." In the Dutch sources much attention is paid to railway connections, the quality of railroad cars, restaurants and hotels at the depots along the line, and opportunities to purchase Indian-made arts and crafts as souvenirs, and see visit Indians in the own communities. It is as if travelers want to convey the message that the Wild West and its natural and cultural attractions can be visited safely, easily, and in comfort. A few make just that point explicitly.

The Dutch were among the pioneering tourists in the Southwest, and some of them have left a specific legacy. Several Dutchmen were among the first visitors to the Southwest in the early 1880s to purchase a new type of Indian handmade object, curios, specifically produced by Pueblo Indians for the non-Indian market of travelers, tourists and collectors: John Van de Moer, Thomas Tempelman Van der Hoeven, and Herman ten Kate, and there were others that left no written or material record. At Zuni missionary Andrew Vanderwagen pioneered the production of kachina dolls for this emerging market. His home has been renovated and added to by his heirs and is now part of Halona Plaza, an attractive bed-and-breakfast in the center of Zuni Pueblo. Many members of the Vanderwagen family have become involved in the Indians arts and crafts trade, in Zuni, in Gallup, and on the Navajo reservation.

Dutch painter Henry C. Balink contributed to the popular imagery of the American Indian among visitors to the Southwest like his fellow artists in Taos and Santa Fe. Indian portraits and scenes of daily life painted by him are on permanent exhibit at Woolaroc in Bartlesville, Oklahoma, and several museums in the Southwest curate works by him. In the 1990s his large "Indian Pottery" canvas took pride of place in the exhibition galleries at the New Mexico Museum of Art in Santa Fe. Hessel Postma and Lura May Love, Lucy Schouten, Elisabeth Houtzager and Margot Spiegel donated their private collections of Indian arts and crafts to Dutch museums where some pieces are on permanent display. The role of these fairly independent women needs further exploration (*cf.* Jacobs 1999; Auerbach 2006:145-167). Koos Heyink laid the foundations for organized cultural tours of Dutch to the American West, with Native American culture and history as a primary focus. Voluntary associations engaged in Indian culture and history like the Lakota Stichting and NANAI became involved in such undertakings, and commercial travel companies followed suit. Museums in The Netherlands have contributed to the interest of the Dutch audience in Native Americans and have played a role in promoting the American West as a destination for tourists, as feedback from returning visitors testify.

Since the early years and decades since the emergence of the tourist market the importance of the leisure economy in the Southwest grew incessantly. Increased leisure time and disposable income brought increasing numbers of Americans, Canadians, Europeans, and more recently Asians, to the Four Corners region. As tourism developed into an industry, the market for arts and crafts expanded substantially, employment opportunities in the hospitality business mushroomed, opportunities for Native entrepreneurs arose, and tribes began to manage the tourist hordes by employing professionals, preferably educated specialists from their own cultural background. Emulating State Tourism Departments, sometimes in cooperation with them, some tribes and Indian entrepreneurs have realized the potential of European tourists and are actively engaged in promoting attractions across the Atlantic. Tribal casinos and resorts, the professional management of the pueblos of Taos and Acoma as tourist destinations, the proliferation of galleries and shops selling Indian art and crafts, Santa Fe's Indian Market, all testify to this growth. Increasing Native control over these developments is an indication of sovereignty also being realized in this arena.

Reviewing the historic cavalcade of Dutch characters that visited the Southwest we have seen occasional and passive consumers of exotic landscapes and Native cultures; socially engaged professionals concerned with the destiny of underprivileged groups in society and moved by the Indians' historic and contemporary fate; scientifically inquiring minds trying to come to grasps with different cultures, consequences of colonization, and government policies regarding Native peoples; missionaries trying to salvage heathen souls and bring Christian civilization; and various propagandists of the American Southwest, touting the attractions of its climate, landscape and Native peoples. Some, notably intellectuals, came explicitly in search of human authenticity, experiencing at least some degree of alienation in their own culture. Others simply came and consumed cultural otherness as exotically authentic, ignorant of its often at least partially contrived character. Many of these Southwest visitors published travel letters in Dutch newspapers, articles in popular magazines, and books, and some lectured occasionally or over a long period about their experiences in the American West. They thus influenced a wide Dutch audience, especially those planning an American holiday trip in the choice of attractions to visit. The Dutch presence in the tourist throngs traversing the Southwest these days cannot be overlooked. They have become an integral part of the phenomenon of Indian tourism.

Epilogue: colonialism, tourism and authenticity

The production and consumption of ethnic imagery and tourist art and the political, economic and cultural arena in which this transfer of ideas and objects takes place has a major impact on Native American and Canadian First Nation societies and peoples. It therefore merits serious scientific research. This is being undertaken in the United States and Canada, while Europe still has to catch up.

Tourism has been considered to be one of the manifold manifestations of colonialism (e.g. Nash 1978). It is part of what Patricia Nelson Limerick (1987) calls the "legacy of conquest" in North America. This is exemplified in the recurrent efforts at claiming Indian lands and challenges of treaty rights when it comes to the development of national parks and tourist sites, the appropriation of Indians as exotic tourist attractions, and the transformation of traditional Native arts and crafts into cheap tourist curios. Edmund Carpenter has stated: "Fakes imitate. Souvenirs substitute. Conquered people sell images of their gods, their art, whatever, to their conquerors. It's the most available trade item they have. But, no matter how well concealed, souvenirs always bear the unmistakable mark of conquest," and "… separate the spurious from the authentic, that is, made by Indians for Indians. … about half of all museum collections and nearly all private holdings are souvenirs" (2005:53-54).[15]

Tourism is a form of interethnic relations involving intercultural contact and confrontation, and has significant impacts on ethnic stratification and the formation of ethnic identities (Van den Berghe 1994). Modern tourism is characterized by externally imposed social stratification based on class and race, and on the symbolic transformation of this situation into marketable commodities such as art, literature, crafts and performances. These lend themselves to mystification of (neo)colonial relations of structural inequality between ethnic groups by creating exoticized, stereotyped imagery, neglecting the stark realities of daily life (Rodriguez 1994). Native arts and crafts are exchanged for cash during direct or indirect cultural encounters between host populations and visiting guests. This places souvenirs as the material culture of tourism at the heart of intercultural relations (*cf.* Hitchcock and Teague 2000).

Authenticity is a frequently encountered term in tourism studies and has engaged the attention of scientists from different disciplines (e.g. MacCannell 1973; Handler 1986; Cohen 1988; Bendix 1994; Nash 1996:141-142; Meethan 2001). However, among a wide public and among collectors as well it is a little understood concept. My initial proposition for curatorial research purposes is that ethnic souvenirs and staged performances are to be considered as intrinsically authentic in the sense that they are created by real people, for real people, in real circumstances.[16] One cannot get more authentic than that! As such, their origin, development, production, marketing, consumption and meaning merit serious study from the perspective of both the hosts and the guests.[17]

---

15 A contrasting image is provided by the increasing of Native control of tourism in its various manifestations, including access to communities, sites, and events, the adoption of tourism as a strategy for economic development, the development of the casino industry, and investment of tourism earnings in social services and cultural affairs. Indian sovereignty in tourism is rapidly gaining ground (*cf.* Blundell 1993; Markovitz 2001/2002; Fixico 2013:170-191).

16 Inspired by sociologist William Thomas (1928:572).

17 The author is engaged in research for an ethnohistory of Gallup as "Indian Capital of the World," as well the description and analysis of a number of tourist collections from Native North America in Dutch museums.

References

Arntzenius, Peronne and Arntzenius, Constance (1931), *Op Bezoek bij Mensch en Dier: Kampeerreizen door de Vereenigde Staten*. Haarlem: Tjeenk Willink.

Auerbach, Jerold S. (2006), *Explorers in Eden: Pueblo Indians and the Promised Land*. Albuquerque, NM: University of New Mexico Press.

Bendix, Regina (1993-1994), The Quest for Authenticity in Tourism and Folklife Studies; in: *Pennsylvania Folklife* 43 (2):67-70.

Berkelbach van Sprenkel, C. (1988), *En Legden Hem in een Kribbe: Kerstkribben uit de Collectie Elisabeth Houtzager*. Berg en Dal: Bijbels Openlucht Museum.

Blundell, Valda (1993), Aboriginal Empowerment and the Souvenir Trade in Canada; in: *Journal of Tourism Research* 20 (1): 64-87.

Buckler, Helen *et al.* (1961), *Wo-He-Lo: the Story of the Camp Fire Girls, 1910-1960*. New York: Holt, Rinehart and Winston.

Canté, Fred (1990), *Mijn Indianen: Stimulerende Souvenirs van Margot Spiegel-Kraemer*. The Hague: De Nieuwe Haagsche.

Carpenter, Edmund (2005), *Chief and Greed*. North Andover, MS: Persimmon Press.

Chambers, Erve (1999), *Native Tours: the Anthropology of Travel and Tourism*. Prospect Heights, IL: Waveland Press.

Cohen, Erik (1972), Toward a Sociology of International Tourism; in: *Social Research* 39:164-182.

Cohen, Erik (1988), Authenticity and Commoditization in Tourism; in: *Annals of Tourism Research* 15:371-386.

Coolhaas, W.Ph. (1980), *A Critical Survey of Studies on Dutch Colonial History*. The Hague: Martinus Nijhoff.

Cordery, Stacy A. (2013), *Juliette Gordon Law: the Remarkable Founder of the Girl Scouts*. New York, NY: Penguin Books.

Csargo, Lilla D. (1988), *Indian Tourism Overview*. Ottawa: Indian and Northern Affairs.

Dekker, H.E. (1928), *Als Zwerver door Amerika*. Haarlem: Tjeenk Willink & Zoon.

De Vries, Nathan Albert (1924), *De Nieuwe Wereld: Amerika 1923*. Groningen: Wolters.

Doerry, Karl W. (1990), Literary Conquista: the Southwest as Literary Emblem; in: *Journal of the Southwest* 32:438-450.

Dolfin, John (1921), *Bringing the Gospel in Hogan and Pueblo*. Grand Rapids, MI: Van Noord.

Dozy, G.J. (1881), De Nieuwe Inter-Oceanische Spoorlijnen in de Vereenigde Staten; in: *Aardrijkskundig Weekblad* 2 (37):161-166.

Eastman, Charles Alexander (1914), *Indian Scout Talks: a Guide for Boy Scouts and Camp Fire Girls*. Boston, MS: Little, Brown, and Company.

Eggermont-Molenaar, Mary (2010), *Gustave Aimard: Feiten, Fictie, Frictie*. N.p.: Privately printed.

Fane, Diana (1991), *Objects of Myth and Memory: American Indian Art at the Brooklyn Museum*. New York and Seattle: The Brooklyn Museum and the University of Washington Press.

Feakins, William B. (1919), *The Arntzenius Sisters: Folk-Songs and Dances*. New York: William B. Feakins Management.

Fixico, Donald L. (2013), *Indian Resilience and Rebuilding: Indigenous Nations in the Modern American West*. Tucson, AZ: University of Arizona Press.

Gelijns, Helena (1992), *Eeuwen van Weven bij de Hopi en Navajo Indianen*. Tilburg: Textielmuseum.

Gerritsen, C.V. and Jacobs, Aletta H. (1906), *Brieven uit en over Amerika*. Amsterdam: Stoomboekdrukkerij F. Van Van Rossen.

Gilsing, Lise (1998), *In het Spoor van Navajo, Hopi en Pueblo Indianen*. Cuyk: Amerika Museum.

Glassie, Henry (1989), *The Spirit of Folk Art: the Girard Collection at the Museum of International Folk Art*. New York: Harry N. Abrams.

Govaert, Wouter (1993), The Case against Designers: Exhibition Review of Onder Indianen; in: *European Review of Native American Studies* 7 (1):52-53.

Gratama, L.R. (1931), *Onder de Bewoners der Betooverende Zuidzee Eilanden*. Amsterdam: Allert de Lange.

Graburn, Nelson H.H., ed. (1976), *Ethnic and Tourist Arts: Cultural Expressions of the Fourth World*. Berkeley, CA: University of California Press.

Graburn, Nelson H.H. (1983), The Anthropology of Tourism; in: *Annals of Tourism Research* 10 (1):9-33.

Griffiths, Alison (2013), Camping Among the Indians: Visual Education and the Sponsored Expedition Film at the American Museum of Natural History; in: J.A. Bell, et.al., eds., *Recreating First Contact: Expeditions, Anthropology, and Popular Culture*: 90-108. Washington, DC.: Smithsonian Institution Press.

Anneke Groeneveld and Pieter Hovens (1992), *Odagot: Indianen gefotografeerd, 1860-1920/Odagot: Photographs of American Indians, 1860-1920.* Amsterdam: Fragment Uitgeverij.

Gulick, Charlotte Hewson (2000), *Wohelo: Down Through the Years; Memories of Camping at the Luther Gulick Camps, 1907-1930.* South Caso, ME: Wohelo Press.

Hammell, George R. (1987), Mohawks Abroad: the 1764 Amsterdam Etching of Sychnecta; in: C.F. Feest, ed. *Indians and Europe: an Interdisciplinary Collection of Essays*:175-194. Aachen: Rader-Herodot.

Handler, Richard W. (1986), Authenticity; in: *Anthropology Today* 2:2-4.

Heyink, J. (1973a), Amerika reis 1973; in: *De Kiva* 10 (3):50-52; 10 (4):63-66; (repr. *De Kiva* 34/4:128-133; 1997).

Heyink, J. (1973b), Verleden en Heden in Nieuw Mexico: Reisbrief aan de Kiva-Abonnees; in: *De Kiva* 10 (4):75-77 (repr. *De Kiva* 34/4:126-127; 1997).

Heyink (1979a), Amerika reis 1979: van Oklahoma naar Santa Fe, Pueblo San Juan en Taos; in: *De Kiva* 16 (6):90-92.

Heyink, J. (1979b), Amerika reis 1979: een Bezoek aan Taos Pueblo; in: *De Kiva* 16 (6):99-101.

Heyink, J. (1983), *Dr. Herman F.C. ten Kate en de Apache Indianen.* Bennebroek: Kiva Reeks nr. 5.

Heyink, J. and Hodge, F.W. (1931), Herman Frederik Carel ten Kate; in: *American Anthropologist* 33:415-418.

Hitchcock, Michael and Teague, Ken (2000), *The Material Culture of Tourism.* Aldershot and Burlington, UK: Ashgate.

Hovens, Pieter (1989), *Herman F.C. ten Kate (1858-1931) en de Antropologie der Noord Amerikaanse Indianen.* Ph.D.-thesis; Nijmegen/Meppel: Radboud University/Krips.

- ed. (1995), Ten Kate's Hemenway Expedition Diary, 1887-1888; in: *Journal of the Southwest* 37/4:635-700.

- (1998) *Indianen.* Leiden: Rijksmuseum voor Volkenkunde.

- (2007) Portraying Native North America: the Life and Work of Henry C. Balink, 1882-1963; in: *European Review of Native American Studies* 21 (2):35-42.

- (2009), 'Dutch Pioneers and Native Americans; in: H. Krabbendam et.al., eds., *Four Centuries of Dutch-American Relations, 1609-2009*: 307-317. Amsterdam: Boom.

- et.al. (2010), *North American Indian Material Culture: the Ten Kate Collection, 1882-1888.* Leiden and Altenstadt: Rijksmuseum voor Volkenkunde and ZKF Publishers.

- (2011) Moccasins and Wooden Shoes: the North American Collection at the Rijksmuseum voor Volkenkunde, The Netherlands; in: *American Indian Art Magazine* 36/3:64-74.

- (2014) *Southwestern Native American Detours and the Quest for Authenticity: Tourism, Collecting and Research in The Netherlands*; Paper presented at the American Indian Workshop, National Museum of Ethnology, Leiden, May 23, 2014.

- (2015) Collectors, Collections and Museums: Native North Americana in The Netherlands; in: Pieter Hovens and Bruce Bernstein, eds., North American Indian Art: Masterpieces and Museum Collections in The Netherlands: 5-95. Leiden and Altenstadt: National Museum of Ethnology and ZKF Publishers.

- (i.p.a), *A Portrait of Native North America: Henry C. Balink and the Art of Taos and Santa Fe.* (in preparation).

- (i.p.b) *Imagining Native North America: Sources and Developments in The Netherlands.* Zoetermeer (in preparation).

Hovens, Pieter; and Bernstein, Bruce, eds. (2015), *North American Indian Art: Masterpieces and Museum Collections from The Netherlands.* Leiden and Altenstadt: National Museum of Ethnology and ZKF Publishers.

Hovens, Pieter; and Blijlevens, Saskia, eds. (1994), *Volkskunst van Verre: de Collectie Elisabeth Houtzager.* Leiden: Rijksmuseum voor Volkenkunde.

Hovens, Pieter; and Groeneveld, Anneke (1992), *Odagot: Photographs of Indians, 1880-1920.* Amsterdam: Fragment Uitgeverij.

Hovens, P.; Orr, W.J.; and Hieb, L.A., eds. (2004), *Herman Ten Kate: Travels and Researches in Native North America, 1882-1883.* Albuquerque, NM: University of New Mexico Press (annotated translation of Ten Kate 1885).

Hovens, Pieter; and Van der Hooft, Mette (2010) Van Drenthe naar het Wilde Westen: de Grand Tour van Ludolf Gratama en Johanna Schultz van Haegen door Indiaans Amerika (1928); in: *Drenthse Volksalmanak* 2010:1-27.

Hovens, Pieter; and Van der Hooft, Mette (i.p.) Studying and Promoting Southwestern Native America: the Career and Collection of Lucy Schouten, 1950-1970 (manuscript in progress).

Huddleston, Lee Eldridge (1967), *Origins of the American Indians: European concepts, 1492-1729.* Austin, TX: University of Texas Press.

Jacobs, Margaret D. (1999), *Engendered Encounters: Feminism and Pueblo Cultures, 1879-1935.* Lincoln, NE: University of Nebraska Press.

Jurriaans-Helle, Geralda (1994), *Kralen Verhalen.* Amsterdam: Allard Pierson Museum.

Kaemlein, Wilma R. (1967), *An Inventory of Southwestern American Indian Specimens in European Museums.* Tucson, AZ: Arizona State Museum.

Kalshoven, Petra Tjitske (2012), *Creating the Indian: Knowledge, Desire and Play in Indianist Reenactment.* New York and Oxford: Berghahn Books.

Lammers, A. (1989), *Uncle Sam en Jan Salie: Hoe Nederland Amerika Ontdekte.* Amsterdam: Balans.

Larsen, Jack Lenor (1995), *Folk Art from the Global Village: the Girard Collection at the Museum of International Folk Art.* Santa Fe, NM: Museum of New Mexico Press.

Limerick, Patricia Nelson (1987), *The Legacy of Conquest: the Unbroken Past of the American West.* New York: Norton.

Lotsy, J.P. (1923), *Van den Atlantischen Oceaan naar de Stille Zuidzee in 1922: Dagboek van een Botanicus die niet alleen naar Planten keek.* The Hague: Naeff.

Maas-Frankort, Diantha, and Van Santen, Caroline (1999), Exhibition Review: Indian Stories; in: *European Review of Native American Studies* 13 (1):53-54.

MacCannell, Dean (1973), Staged Authenticity: a Look at Touristing; in: *American Journal of Sociology* 79:589-603.

MacCannell, Dean (1976), *The Tourist: a New Theory of the Leisure Class.* New York: Schocken Books.

Markowitz, Kristal (2001-2002), Cultural Tourism: Exploration or Exploitation of American Indians? in: *American Indian Law Review* 26 (2):233-260.

Meethan, K. (2001), *Tourism in Global Society: Place, Consumption, Culture.* Basingstoke, UK: Palgrave.

Muller, Hendrik P.N. (1905), *Door het Land van Columbus: Een Reisverhaal.* Haarlem: De Erven Bohn.

Nash, Denison (1978), Tourism as a Form of Imperialism; in: V. Smith, ed., *Hosts and Guests: the Anthropology of Tourism*: 37-54. Philadelphia: University of Pennsylvania Press.

Nash, Dennison (1978), An Anthropological Approach to Tourism; in: V. Smith ed., *Tourism and Economic Change*:133-152. Williamsburg, VA: William and Mary Press.

Nash, Dennison (1981), Tourism as an Anthropological Subject; in: *Current Anthropology* 22:461-481; 1981.

Nash, Dennison (1996), *Anthropology of Tourism.* Oxford: Pergamon Press.

Nash, Dennison, ed. (2007), *The Study of Tourism: Anthropology and Sociological Beginnings.* Amsterdam: Elsevier.

N.N. (1929), *The Misses Arntzenius: Twin-Adventurists.* Cape Town, n.p.

Postma, Lura May Love (1926), Indian Prayer; in: *El Palacio* 10 (4):83-85.

Provezi, Mariangela (2012), *Consultations of the Muses.* M.A.-thesis; Leiden: University of Leiden.

Rambonnet, J.J. *Padvinders: de Padvindersbeweging.* G.W. de Boer; Middelburg, 1932.

Rodriguez, Sylvia (1994), *Tourist Gaze, Gentrification, and the Commodification of Subjectivity in Taos*; in: R.V. Francaviglia and D.E. Narrett, eds., *Essays on the Changing Images of the Southwest*: 105-123. Arlington: Texas A & M University Press.

Rutgers, Herman C. (1922) *Door Amerika, Japan en Korea naar China.* Zeist: Ploegsma.

Rutten, Rob (1999) Cornelis Zwaan, 1928-1999; in: *Bulletin of the American Astronomical Society* 31/5:1612-1613.

Ryan, C. and Aicken, M., eds. (2005), *Indigenous Tourism: the Commodification and Management of Culture.* Amsterdam: Elsevier.

Schulte Nordholt, J.W. (1982), Dutch Travelers in the U.S.: a Tale of Energy and Ambivalence; in: J.W. Schulte Nordholt and R.P. Swierenga eds., *A Bilateral Centennial*: 251-266. Amsterdam and New York: Meulenhoff and Octagon.

Seton, Ernest Thompson (1903), *How to Play Indian*. Philadelphia, PA: Curtis.

Seton, Ernest Thompson (1911), *Twee Padvinders: de Avonturen van Twee Jongens die als Indianen Leefden*. Amsterdam: Scheltens & Giltay.

Seton, Ernest Thompson (1915), *Manual of the Woodcraft Indians*. Garden City, NY: Doubleday, Page and Company.

Seton, Ernest Thomson (1915a; C. Arntzenius transl.), *Bloemlezing uit de Werken van Ernest Thomson Seton*. Amsterdam: Versluys.

Smith, D.A. (1994), The Issue of Compatibility between Cultural Integrity and Economic Development among Native American Tribes; in: *American Indian Culture and Research Journal* 18 (2):177-205.

Smith, Valene L. ed. (1977), *Hosts and Guests: the Anthropology of Tourism*. Philadelphia, PA: University of Pennsylvania Press.

Smith, Valene L. ed. (1980), *Tourism and Development: Anthropological Perspectives*; Annals of Tourism Research 7 (1); 1980.

Spiegel-Kraemer, Margot (1990), *De Aarde Spreekt: Oude Keramiektechnieken en Hun Hedendaagse Toepassingen*. The Hague: Privately printed.

- (1993), *Sprekend Vuur*. The Hague: De Nieuwe Haagsche.

- (1997), *De Aarde Spreekt en Sprekend Vuur*. The Hague: Uitgeverij De Nieuwe Haagsche.

- (2014), *Tekens aan de Wand: Mijn Indianen in Beeld*. N.p.: Blurb.

Steinmetz, Rudolf (1939), *Menschenleven in Amerika*. Amsterdam: Nederlandsche Keurboekerij.

Stronza, Amanda (2001), Anthropology of Tourism: Forging New Ground for Ecotourism and Other Alternatives; in: *Annual Review of Anthropology* 30:261-283.

Ten Kate, Herman F.C. (1878) Amerikaansche Toestanden; in: *Omnibus* 10:366-369.

- (1885), *Reizen en Onderzoekingen in Noord Amerika*. Leiden: E.J. Brill (see: Hovens et.al. 2004 for English translation).

- (1889) Iets over het Indiaansch Vraagstuk in de Vereenigde Staten; in: *Tijdschrift van het Aardrijkskundig Genootschap* 6:582-588.

- (1911), On Paintings of North American Indians and their Ethnographical Value; in: *Anthropos* 6:521-545.

- (1919) De Indiaan in de Letterkunde; in: *De Gids* 83 (3): 63-128.

- (1920) De Noord-Amerikaansche Indiaan als Bondgenoot in de Oorlogen der Blanken; in: *Tijdschrift van het Aardrijkkundig Genootschap* 37:681-687.

- (1922) The Indian in Literature; in: *Annual Report of the Smithsonian Institution for 1921*:507-528.

Thomas, William (1928), *The Child in America: Behavior Problems and Programs.* New York: A.A. Knopf.

Van Balen, W.J. (1913), *Door Amerika: Van Reizen en Trekken.* Amsterdam: Maatschappij voor Goede en Goedkope Literatuur.

Vandemoer, J.J. (1956), *Diaries, Newspaper Articles and Letters.* Denver, CO: Colorado Historical Society.

VandenBerghe, Pierre L., Keyes, C., eds. (1984), *Tourism and Re-created Ethnicity.* Annals of Tourism Research 11 (3).

Van den Berghe, Pierre L. (1994), *The Quest for the Other: Ethnic Tourism in San Cristobal, Mexico.* Seattle and London: University of Washington Press.

Van der Sleen, Wicher G.N. (1953), *Tussen Texas en Pacific.* Tilburg: Nederland's Boekhuis.

Van der Sleen, Wicher G.N. (1967), *A Handbook on Beads.* Liège: Musée du Verre.

Van der Steen, Jan – *Padvinders: 100 Jaar Scouting in Nederland.*Walburg Pres; Zutphen, 2010.

Van Reest, Rudolf (1948), *Van Kust tot Kust: Verslag van een Reis door Amerika.* Goes: Oosterbaan & Le Cointre.

Van 't Veer, Karel (1962), *Op Houten Schoenen: Kris Kras door Amerika.* Utrecht: De Fontein.

Veenendaal, Augustus J. (1995), *Slow Train to Paradise: How Dutch Investment Helped Build American Railroads.* Stanford: Stanford University Press.

Voute, J. Peter (1987), *Stranger in New Mexico: a Doctor's Journey, 1951-1986.* Albuquerque: University of New Mexico Press.

Walkotten, Henry (1909), *De Navaho Indianen: een Deel van het Zendingsveld der Christelijk Gereformeerde Kerk.* Grand Rapids, MI: Grand Rapids Printing Company.

Walkotten, Henry (1910), *De Zuni Indianen: een Deel van het Zendingsveld der Christelijk Gereformeerde Kerk*; Grand Rapids, MI: Sevensma.

Wauchope, Robert (1962), *Lost Tribes and Sunken Continents: Myth and Method in the Study of the American Indians*. Chicago, IL: University of Chicago Press.

White Horse Eagle, Big Chief (1930), *We Indians: The Passing of a Great Race; Being the Recollections of the Last of the Great Indian Chiefs, White Horse Eagle*. London: Butterworth.

White Horse Eagle, Big Chief (1930a), *Wij Indianen: Herinneringen van het Laatste Grote Opperhoofd*. Leiden: A.W. Sijthoff.

Witt, David L. (2010), *Ernest Thompson Seton: the Life and Legacy of an Artist and Conservationist*. Layton, UT: Gibbs Smith.

Collecting Souvenirs

Alphonse Pinart's Collection of Pueblo Curios

Eloïse J. Galliard

While studying the history of the collections of Native artifacts from the Southwest and California housed in French museums (Galliard 2014), it emerged that at the end of the 19th century two French scientists brought two interesting and important collections of objects from this part of the United States over to France. One of these men was Léon de Cessac (1841-1891). He gathered the most important collection of Native archaeological artifacts from the Santa Barbara Channel Islands (Galliard 2014; Reichlen and Heizer 1964). The other, Alphonse Pinart (1852-1911), was a young scientist from the North of France. He took part in an expedition to the North Pacific coast in 1871 and1872 (Parmenter 1966) and brought from this expedition the most important

Alphonse Pinart (left) and Léon de Cessac in California (photograph 1956.137.070, courtesy of the History Center of San Luis Obispo).

collection of Kodiak masks to France, currently housed in the Château-Musée in Boulogne-sur-Mer. He joined de Cessac in California in 1878 for linguistic studies among the several tribes. A few years later Pinart made several studies in Mexico before a stay in New Mexico where he gathered Pueblo curios, small clay objects made for the tourist market, with Aaron Gold of Santa Fe being one of the most prominent dealers. Because of the number of items it contains, more than a hundred, and also because all these objects are of an early date, created in the late 1870's and in the early 1880's, this collection of curios now housed at the Musée du quai Branly in Paris is culturally, historically and scientifically important. This collection illustrates a historical and cultural phenomenon, "curios," souvenirs created by Anglos, with exotic Indian connotations, made by the Native Indians, and sold to the tourists, a curious mixture of ideas expressed in collectable artifacts. This paper documents this phenomenon, the creation of and the interest in Pueblo curios, through the presentation of Pinart's collection, and tries to demonstrate why this specific collection is still important today.

A Creation Story: the Development of the Curio Trade in the American Southwest[1]

Aaron Gold (1845-1884) who sold his Pueblo Indian curios to Alphonse Pinart was the son of Louis Gold, a Jewish immigrant from Poland, who opened a shop in Santa Fe in the late 1850s. In 1867 Aaron and his brother Abe started to work with their father at the Louis Gold and Sons Trading Post. After several years of partnership with his father and brother, Aaron operated his own business, a saloon and shop named Gold's Provision House in 1875 (Anderson 2002:51-66)[2]. A few years later he began to sell Indian artifacts and curios. According to Jonathan Batkin it is not known who the first dealer of Indian curios was in Santa Fe. But it seems that Aaron Gold was the first to display Native artifacts (Batkin 1999b:286), and he became quickly the most important trader of the town. Photographs taken in 1880 by Ben Wittick and now preserved at the Museum of New Mexico in Santa Fe show Aaron Gold in his trading post[3]. Aaron's brother Jake (Isaac Jacob Gold 1851-1905) was also involved in Santa Fe's trading posts, especially with his "Gold's Free Museum", open in 1883 on San Francisco Street, the town's main street, where even today it is the place where one can find curio

1 A similar development occurred on the North West Coast, where the Haidas of the Queen Charlotte Islands created model totem poles and pipes, carved in soft stone argillite, for seamen, traders, and tourists. Many of these small objects are now in museums collections in North America and Europe.

2 Aaron Gold seems to be one of the most important dealers of Santa Fe at this time, and he remains a famous trader. There seems to be no surviving archival material about his shop. According to Jonathan Batkin (personal communication, August 18, 2012), and after some additional research in Santa Fe repositories, no records about his activities have come to light. However, ledger books of Jake Gold are curated at the Fray Angélico Chavez History Library in Santa Fe.

3 Other pictures depict Jake's or J.S. Candelario's shops. Jesus Sito Candelario (1864-1938) was another dealer of Santa Fe. His shop was next to Aaron Gold's on San Francisco Street.

shops offering "Indian" goods to crowds of visitors and tourists. Like Jake Gold several other traders presented their shops as museums, which gave their Indian merchandise an "older" and more "authentic" appearance.

Both Aaron and Jake Gold sold Indian curios. These pottery objects were made for the traders by the Natives inhabitants of the pueblos surrounding Santa Fe. The Indian craftspeople quickly understood that this work could become a new and important source of income in the American cash economy. It is probable that Aaron Gold created a special kind of Pueblo curios: the Rain Gods. But invented imagery by Anglos or not, curios were always Indian-made. Some postcards or advertisements present Pueblo women making curios and Rain Gods. These photographs became iconic images of the Wild West, just like the postcards showing Indian women selling painted pottery at train stations along the Atcheson, Topeka & Santa Fe Railway. Santo Domingo, Santa Fe (from the Lamy station), Albuquerque and Laguna were the major stops for such interethnic tourist trade. Curios were also offered through mail order catalogs to customers farther afield. Ceramic curios thus quickly became a part of the popular representation of New Mexico.

In Santa Fe Alphonse Pinart bought dozens of pieces from Aaron Gold in 1881. Other European and American scientists attracted to the Southwest to study and collect the "Vanishing Race" purchased artifacts at Jake Gold's Free Museum or at Candelario's trading post, as can be deduced from the surviving ledger books of these businesses (Candelario 1881). However, tourists were the main customers of these trading establishments. Between the late 1870s and the early 1880s the Southwest of the United States, and more specifically Santa Fe, became one of the most popular places of the country for a leisurely visit. This was mainly because it was the Wild West, now subdued and safe, and on the way to the promise California represented. The transcontinental railway opened up the Southwest in 1880-1882. This new and fast way of travel brought tourists to the region in ever increasing numbers. They came to discover this "Land of Enchantment"[4] and see "real" and "authentic" Natives.

Batkin (1999b:282) notes that "By 1880 Pueblo potters had been adapting their wares to meet the needs and tastes of the Europeans for nearly three hundred years." Because of their experience of contact with Europeans, and with the intervention of traders such as Aaron Gold, Native artisans knew exactly how to respond to the new market of visitors and tourists. Anglos had a specific idea of what they wanted, what they wanted to buy, and what they wanted to bring back home: a small part of the Southwest, an artifact as a memento, preferably a unique one. They did not reflect about its authenticity, but needed only to believe in its authenticity. In the end they purchased a fantasy of the Southwest.

4 Official motto of the State of New Mexico.

At that time the Southwest was synonymous with wilderness: expansive places, with empty lands, where Native tribes, seen as the last authentic survivors of their ancestors were still living in their traditional ways. Anglos wanted to take home a souvenir of this exoticism. But Native artifacts were not only "exotic" like objects from Africa or the Pacific could be: these artifacts, and thus the curios, needed to be old and natural, exemplifying the primitive and linking Anglos and the first people who lived on their lands. Thus the curios for the tourist market needed to be Indian-made, look old, and contain references to Native spiritual life. Some entrepreneurs were quick to understand the mind-set of Southwestern visitors. The best example is Fred Harvey who developed hotels and souvenir shops at major railway stations, attracting Anglo-American and European tourists into a wild Southwest partially of his own design (Dilworth 1996).

Indian-made Curios

Pueblo Indian artifacts sold by Aaron Gold and purchased by Alphonse Pinart are of three kinds: ceramics for daily use and two types of curios: Rain Gods and Clay People. The utilitarian series consists of bowls and jars with black or brown designs, and black ceramics typical of Santa Clara and San Ildefonso, notably ollas and plates. From the early 17th century until the late 19th century shapes of and designs on the ceramics changed because of the changing interethnic environment. Initially Pueblos only made ceramics for their own use, but they soon adapted their production when the Spanish colonized the Rio Grande Valley. In the 18th century a lot of clay vessels were made and sold to the Spaniards for use in settlers' households. By 1880 Pueblos adapted ceramic production again, this time to the emerging tourist market.

Alphonse Pinart collected pots, plates and jars. Not as kitchenware, but as souvenirs. He also purchased miniatures of utilitarian wares, and small non-utilitarian pottery items, of complicated shape, with simple designs and surface finish. As Edwin L. Wade (1988:169) reminds us, full-sized ceramics, "too bulky to transport easily by train, were replaced by smaller, decorative forms."

Rain Gods are clay figures, roughly made, hand-modeled, and shaped like seated nude males, often with prominent genitalia. Some figures have horns on their head, some hold pots, pipes, or bows and arrows. A Rain God purports to depict a Native deity, not specifically Tewa, Hopi or Zuni, but generically "Indian." One encounters gods of rain, gods of corn or gods of joy, but "Rain God" remains the common name for them.[5]

It is said that Aaron Gold created them in the late 1870s to give Anglos an opportunity to take home something embodying Native spirituality, something they had encountered in one form or the other during their stay and was regarded as quintessential Southwestern Indian. However, in the late 19th

5 H.H.Tammen distinguished these Rain Gods he was selling by mail-order in 1882. A page of his catalog, *Western Echoes*, was published by Batkin (1999b:296).

Century scholars regarded Rain Gods as having religious connotations and such images reaching back into prehistory. Some of them were purchased by scientists and ended up in American museums, classed as antiquities, idols, deities, effigies or archaeological artifacts (Anderson 2002:26; Batkin 1999b:286). In Europe a similar development took place. The first Rain God was collected in July 1879 by the Geological and Geographical Survey of Ferdinand V. Hayden (Anderson 2002:56). This clay figure is today housed in the National Museum of Natural History, registered as a "Rude Pottery Image". Rain Gods could be solemn in appearance, but many looked comical, reminiscent of the clowns that appear during dances among the Pueblos or the Hopis. This idea endured in the 20th century and in the catalogue of the Musée de l'Homme in Paris Claude Lévi-Strauss labelled Alphonse Pinart's Rain Gods as "Clowns" (Inventaire: no date).

The artifacts seemingly to embody Native spirituality needed to be Indian-made to be regarded as authentic. Thus the traders asked the Indians to make them. Rain Gods, mythological figures, were made mostly at Tesuque Pueblo, and some production took place at Zia and Nambé. Clay People looked more realistic. These large hollow and painted figures were made predominantly at Cochiti Pueblo. The pueblos of Tesuque and Cochiti are really close to Santa Fe. It was easy for the traders to visit there periodically and bring back curios in order to sell them in their trading posts in Santa Fe.

The making of anthropomorphic or zoomorphic figures is a very old tradition in the Southwest. Such figured can be found in prehistoric cultures, such as the Mimbres. When the Spanish arrived, priests tried to erase Pueblo religion and its "idols." However, Pueblo religious and art traditions survived despite repression (Babcock 1986:11). When the region became a part of the United States in 1848, the pressure on the Native peoples decreased, and initially they were allowed to practice their traditional religion. When Colonel James Stevenson arrived in Cochiti at the end of the 1879 he gathered the earliest clay figures from Cochiti for the Bureau of American Ethnology in Washington, DC. The emergence of tourism in New Mexico opened up a new market for such ceramic images, and Stevenson specifically noticed that Cochiti potters produced large numbers of figurative ceramics for the tourist trade (Stevenson 1883:330).

The clay figurines changed with the arrival of the tourists. Cochiti produced less and less animal or birds effigies after 1880, which means that the effigies of Pinart's collection might be some of the last made at this time. These figurines became much smaller, and thus more suited to the tourist souvenir market (Babcock 1986:17). Most of clay figures from Cochiti depict human beings, and Anglos more particularly, as priests or cowboys. Cochiti potters also began to depict figures inspired by performers from travelling carnivals and circuses, such as acrobats or entertainers. Two human figures are in the Pinart collection. One of them is wearing a vest (MqB 71.1881.80.8) and could be a cowboy. The other one (MqB 71.1881.80.6) wears a large cross around his neck and may represent a priest. Different pueblos specialized in different ceramic creations when it came to figurative curios. The potters at Tesuque, a Tewa-speaking pueblo, made non-traditional figures invented by an Anglo, purportedly depicting Indian gods. At Cochiti, a Keresan-speaking pueblo, Native craftspeople produced anthropomorphic figures representing Anglos.

Collecting Curios: Scientific Interest

The Pinart collection contains many utilitarian ceramics of daily use, and some Rain Gods and Clay People. At the end of the 19th century private collectors bought same kind of curios, and there seems to have been no marked degree of preference for either of the two figurative types of ceramics. However, in intent one can distinguish two different approaches in the purchase of Pueblo curios by travelers and tourists as mementos of their journey. Acquisition of Rain Gods may be regarded as stemming from a need to collect the "primitive," a vestige of traditional tribal culture, of Indian metaphysics. Jonathan King (2000:340) noted that these "crude figures" were also "associated with evolutionary schemes of social development" that were popularly shared. However, collecting Clay People, realistic or comical renditions of Anglo-American outsiders, satisfied a generally shared need to bring back a memento, a real souvenir, irrespective of its cultural meaning, except that it was handmade by a Native craftsperson.

One wonders whether Anglos were aware of what they were collecting when they purchased Cochiti figures. For their makers the Clay People were humorous and critical depictions of "the other," notably Anglo-Americans. As Barbara Babcock (1986:17) noted: "Cochiti potters produced a profusion of Anglo professionals – cowboys, priests, businessmen, and carnival and circus entertainers ... Whether the whiteman realized it or not, what he purchased and described as "primitive idols" or "eccentric grotesque" were in fact, portraits of himself".

Although these figurative clay curios were initially made for tourists, one encounters them also in museum collections, in North America and in Europe. Museum records often record their purchase in the field by scientists. In 1881 Alphonse Pinart spent three months in New Mexico. This was not his first trip in the Southwest: he was there in 1876, then spent time in California with Léon de Cessac in 1878. While in the Southwest in 1881 Pinart stayed in Santa Fe and purchased a number of curios from the Gold Brothers. Photographs taken in 1880 in Aaron and Jake Gold's Trading Post show curios like those now curated at the Musée du quai Branly[6], notably the bird figurine MqB 71.1881.80.86[7], the pot MqB 71.1881.80.25, and the "cowboy" MqB 71.1881.80.8. According to Duane Anderson (2002:57) the five Rain Gods in Pinart's collection were also

6 The most interesting picture in which several pieces from the Musée du quai Branly are shown was taken by W.P. Bliss (from the collection of Val R. Berryman, Williamston, Michigan).

7 A similar one can be seen in front of Jake Gold's in a picture taken by Ben Wittick in 1880 (Museum of New Mexico Photo Archives, negative number 1692).

purchased from Aaron Gold[8]. Since there no records of Aaron Gold's trading post survive, we can only assume that Alphonse Pinart bought his entire collection from Gold. This was not uncommon at this time when to amass substantial museum collections scientists would purchase large numbers of pieces from traders. Ceramic Pueblo curios bought from Aaron Gold are now represented in a number of American collections, such as at the University of Kansas Museum of Anthropology. Pinart was also known to buy artifacts from other collectors. After he married Zelia Nuttal who also became an anthropologist and descended from an affluent family, he spent private means on collection tribal arts.

A year earlier, in August 1880, Swiss-American anthropologist Adolph Bandelier (1840-1914) was in Santa Fe. Like Pinart he purchased artifacts from Aaron Gold and other traders like J.S. Candelario and Charles Marsh for the Berlin Museum of Anthropology (Lange 1966:360). For almost five years Pinart and Bandelier competed when it came to collecting in the Southwest and in Mexico[9]. Also during those years Colonel James Stevenson and his wife Matilda Coxe Stevenson from the Smithsonian Institution bought "non-traditional" objects directly from Indians as well as from traders in Santa Fe like Jake Gold (Batkin, 1999b:285; Wade, 1988:171). James Stevenson never mentioned that he purchased part of his collections from entrepreneurs. But the ceramics he gathered are identical to ones sold by the traders. Thus, Pinart was no exception when it came to collecting for scientific purposes: many scholars did business with Anglo-American and Hispanic entrepreneurs in the Southwest. All means were acceptable save the last vestiges of the Vanishing Indian. Traders understood that really quickly and "guaranteed the ultimate rarity of objects" (Batkin 1999b:294).

By the year 2000 about five hundred Rain Gods were identified in museum collections (King 2000:341).[10]Shortly after they appeared on the market for the first time around 1880, some curators or museum staff began to denounce the production of curios: "These figures are crudely made of clay, not after aboriginal models, but from suggestions of whites, and in many cases as attested to by the semi-obscene character of the work, by a very vulgar element of the white population" (Holmes 1889). William Henry Holmes of the Bureau of American Ethnology stated that New Mexico "is flooded with cheap and, scientifically speaking, worthless earthenware made by the Pueblo Indians to supply the tourist trade" (Holmes 1889, in Batkin 1999b:286). Thus, in the course of the 1880's scientists became aware that tourism was having an impact on Native lives, and "the interest of traders [...] in promoting these ceramic 'curiosities' became an excuse of disinterest on the part of serious students and

8 Artifacts housed at the Musée du quai Branly, numbers 71.1881.80.39 through 43.

9 Some details of this competitiveness can be gleaned from Bandelier's Journals (Lange and Riley 1970:232).

10 In Wilma Kaemlein's 1967 survey about 40 Rain Gods and 20 Clay people were documented in European collections. However, her inventory was incomplete.

collectors of Pueblo pottery who were inclined to dismiss historic figurines as commercial origin, as 'touristic art' at best" (Babcock 1986:11).

Considering Victorian morality the prominent genitalia of the figurines might have shocked potential customers. One wonders why so many were sold. Possibly collectors and tourists rationalized that they were in the Wild West, beyond the borders of Christian civilization, where other rules applied. Moreover, the artifacts were Native-made, produced by primitive heathen peoples, and thus outside the realm of western standards. Because Rain Gods did not depict humans bur represented tribal deities, their characteristics might be considered as "acceptable" to a certain degree.

Holmes' point of view was shared by others scholars such as Kenneth Chapman and Edgar Lee Hewett. Jonathan Batkin (1999: note 4) reminds us that "Kenneth Chapman, responsible for building the major pottery collections of Santa Fe, rejected some pottery collected in 1886 as 'grotesque for museums'", and in the 1940's the anthropologist Bertha P. Dutton (1963:236) noted: "At Tesuque [...] most of the present output consists of cheap, gaudily painted (with show card colors) novelty items that are made expressly for the tourist trade. They cannot even be classed as true Indian ceramics."[11]After the Second World War a number of American anthropology museums deaccessioned much of their tourist art.

Re-Appraisal

The question to be addressed next is: what happened once collections of Pueblo Indian curios entered museums? In Paris the Pueblo curios from Alphonse Pinart were seemingly forgotten, never displayed. Thus a most interesting collection of Pueblo ceramics lies now dormant in storage facilities. Scholars like Duane Anderson and Jonathan Batkin must be credited for giving those culturally hybrid productions central stage in for scientific researchers: Batkin organized a stunning exhibition about Clay People at the Wheelwright Museum in 1999[12], and Duane Anderson published a richly illustrated book on Rain Gods in 2002. When writing his book Anderson contacted 147 museums around the world in order to discover which institution housed Tesuque figures. About 70 museums replied and he collected pictures of clay figures from Tesuque. The Musée de l'Homme in Paris sent a picture of the five Rain Gods from the Pinart collection it curated and this ended up as an illustrated in the monograph (Anderson 2002:57).

---

11 Ten years earlier Marius Barbeau studied the curio phenomenon among the Haida and published a collection of myths illustrated with Haida carvings in 1953.

12 *Clay People: Pueblo Indian Figurative Traditions*, Wheelwright Museum of the American Indian, Santa Fe, New Mexico, May 14 – October 27, 1999.

Already in the 1960s Wilma Kaemlein of the Arizona State Museum inventoried Native American artifacts in European museum collections. According to her study 35 Rain Gods are today housed in 15 European museums, of which eight are in France: five at the Musée du quai Branly, two at the Musées Historiques in Le Havre, and one is a part of the André Breton's collection, displayed in the museum of modern art, the Centre Georges Pompidou. About 100 curios from Tesuque and 150 curios from Cochiti are preserved in European museums such as the British Museum in London, the Rijksmuseum voor Volkenkunde in Leiden, the Netherlands, and the Pitt Rivers Museum in Oxford (Kaemlein 1967:passim).

Interest in Pueblo ceramic figurines in general and clay curios specifically has piqued recently as new publications demonstrate. This renewal of academic interest in figurines and curios is equaled by the recent work by Native artists. Virgil Ortiz, a prominent contemporary artist from Cochiti, is known for his modern clay figures, inspired by earlier historic figures and curios from the northern Pueblos.

The storytellers, created by Helen Cordero of Cochiti Pueblo in the 1960s, can be regarded as a new type of Clay People. The seated posture reminds one of Rain Gods. When they were created, Storytellers were Indian productions, made by and for internal consumption. However, soon they were produced for the outside market, in ever increasing numbers. Today, even Rain Gods are produced again at Tesuque Pueblo and are offered during markets and fairs.

In the booths at the Santa Fe Indian Market one encounters real curios. Each clay figure is an ironic rendering of American symbols: the Statue of Liberty (dressed as a Pueblo woman) and the major holidays (Halloween, Thanksgiving, Easter, Christmas). As Clay People those Indian-made figures represent Anglos and are made to be sold to them.

Among the Pueblos of the Southwest curios are an old but persisting phenomenon. What can be said about the curios that are offered for sale at Santa Fe's Indian Market today? They represent a modern revival of an older tradition, reaching back to the late 19th century. They are produced at a similar intercultural meeting ground of contemporary Native American artists and craftspeople, predominantly Anglo-American tourists and collectors, and contemporary scientists who study these arifacts and put them in the spotlight in exhibitions and publications.

Santa Fe Indian Market, 2012 (photo by Eloïse J. Galliard).

Clay figures by Max Early, Laguna Pueblo, displayed at the Santa Fe Indian Market in 2013 (photo by Eloïse Galliard).

References

Anderson, D. (2002), *When Rain Gods Reigned: From Curios to Art at Tesuque Pueblo.* Santa Fe, NM: Museum of New Mexico Press.

Babcock, B.A., G. Monthan & D. Monthan (1986), *The Pueblo Storyteller: Development of a Figurative Ceramic Tradition.* Tucson, AZ: University of Arizona Press.

Barbeau, M. (1953), *Haida Myths Illustrated in Argillite Carving.* Ottawa: Department of Resources and Development, National Museums of Canada Press.

Batkin, J. (ed.) (1999a), *Clay People: Pueblo Figurative Traditions.* Santa Fe, NM: Wheelwright Museum of the American Indian.

Batkin, J. (1999b), Tourism is Overrated, Pueblo Pottery and the Early Curio Trade, 1880-1910; in: R. Phillips & C.B. Steiner, eds., *Unpacking Culture Art and Commodity in Colonial and Postcolonial Worlds*, 282-297. Berkeley, CA: University of California Press.

Candelario, J.S. (1881), Ledger Book, Box 35-5. Santa Fe Archive, Chavez Library.

Dilworth, L. (1996), *Imagining Indians in the Southwest, Persistent Visions of a Primitive Past.* Washington, DC: Smithsonian Institution.

Dutton, B.P. (1963), *Indians of the Southwest.* Santa Fe, NM: Southwestern Association on Indian Affairs.

Galliard, E.J. (2014), *Le Far West sans ses bagages. Voyageurs scientifiques français dans le Grand Sud-Ouest des États-Unis: une histoire des collections.* Thesis of Troisième Cycle, presented at the École du Louvre, under the direction of Federica Tamarozzi, Muséed'Ethnographie de Genève, on January 2014.

Holmes, W.H. (1889), The Debasement of Pueblo Art: in: *American Anthropologist*, 2: 320.

Inventaire (no date), Inventaire des collections du Musée d'Ethnographie du Trocadéro, Catalogue n°8 (n°11491-11523). Paris: Archives du Musée du quai Branly, D000559 / 28740.

Kaemlein, W.R. (1967), *An Inventory of Southwestern American Indian Specimens in European Museums.* Tucson, AZ: Arizona State Museum.

King, J.C.H. (2000), 'Clay People', in: *American Anthropologist*, 102 (2): 337-344.

Lange, C. & C.L. Riley (1960), *The Southwestern Journals of Adolph F. Bandelier, 1880 – 1882.* Albuquerque, NM: University of New Mexico Press.

Lange, C. & C.L. Riley (1970), *The Southwestern Journals of Adolph F. Bandelier, 1883 – 1884*. Albuquerque, NM: University of New Mexico Press.

Parmenter, R. (1966), *Explorer, linguist and Ethnologist; a Descriptive Bibliography of the Published Works of Alphonse Louis Pinart, with Notes on his Life*. Los Angeles, CA: Southwest Museum.

Reichlen, H. & R. Heizer (1964), The Scientific Expedition of Léon de Cessac to California, 1977-1879; in: *Report of the University of California – Archaeological Survey*, 61: 5-25. Berkeley, CA: University of California.

Stevenson, J. (1883), Illustrated Catalog of the Collections Obtained from the Indians of New Mexico and Arizona in 1879; in: *Second Annual Report of the Bureau of Ethnology to the Secretary of the Smithsonian Institution, 1880-81*, 311-428. Washington: Smithsonian Institution.

Wade, E.L. (1988), The Ethnic Art Market in the American Southwest 1880-1980; in: G.W. Stocking Jr., ed., *Objects and Others, Essays on Museums and Material Culture,* 167-191.Madison, WI: University of Wisconsin Press.

Going West

The Grand Tour of Ludolf Gratama and Johanna Schultz van Haegen (1928)

Mette van der Hooft

The Grand Tour in Europe and North America

In the Western tradition (touristic) travel and sightseeing are usually regarded as rooting in Christian medieval pilgrimages, Renaissance trading and exploration expeditions. Although some sightseeing was possibly always part of an itinerary, it was certainly not the main reason for undertaking hazardous journeys. Travel gradually became more leisurely and recreational in the eighteenth century when enlightened ideals of personal improvement begin to manifest themselves in phenomena such as the European Grand Tour (Chambers 2010:9-10). The travellers were commonly wealthy young men for whom it was thought essential for their cultural upbringing to visit European capitals with their art collections, churches and palaces. Other increasingly important motivations for travel in this period were experiencing wild nature and viewing scenic places that combined landscape with historic monuments and exotically dressed people (Phillips 1998:26). In the nineteenth century tourism or travel in general seems to have gained a solid foothold as a tool for social distinction. There was a competitive as well as a romantic edge to it; the distance travelled and the level of uniqueness of the sights visited contributed to one's social standing (Chambers 2010:13). To other wealthy members of society, travel agencies such as Thomas Cook offered all-inclusive packages through Europe. These "less unique" experiences derived from the Grand Tour traditions but reduced the amount of effort individuals had to spend on organizing their own vacations. In the nineteenth century the rapid development of new forms of transportation such as trains and steamships accelerated the growth of the tourist travel industry. An increasing number of people were able to undertake a journey, close to home or even to other continents (Chambers 2010:16).

While the European Grand Tour had a more or less fixed format, this phenomenon was exported to colonial settings where itineraries were developed that combined natural wonders, ancient history and exotic and picturesque peoples. In the American Northeast visits to Indian villages were combined with the sightseeing of waterfalls or other scenic places. Ruth Phillips (1998:25, note 47) found that this development took place rather early in this particular region. In the late eighteenth century for example British officers and their spouses already made excursions to Indian villages to watch dances performed specifically for their entertainment. Indian villages and a visit to Niagara Falls, one of the most popular destinations in the Northeast, were often combined. By 1830 the falls were part of at least two fixed itineraries; the Northern Tour and the American Grand Tour (Phillips 1998:26, after Sears 1989:4; Jasen 1995:35). Like in Europe, novel methods of transportation that formerly carried raw materials from remote areas were adapted to bring travellers comfortably to these very same remote areas in North America. Motivations for travel were similar. City dwellers were trying to escape the strains of modern urban and industrial society in order to enjoy unspoilt nature and exotic peoples (Chambers 2010:16-17). Previously hard to reach regions were more easily accessible by railroads, steamships and eventually by car and tourist areas could be developed. This was not only an advantage for tourists. Indians made use ofrailroads to travel to tourist destinations in order to sell their handmade arts and crafts. Souvenirs sold at vacation resorts and train stations provided much needed cash income for Indian families (Phillips 1998:34-36). Many parts of North America witnessed such a similar development.

In the Pacific Northwest shippers who transported lumber and fish began carrying a new kind of cargo in the 1880's: tourists. Many holiday makers travelled to the Northwest by way of the transcontinental railroad that was completed in 1882. The railroad connected this remote part of North America with the large cities in the East. The region's breathtaking coastline, icy glaciers, fascinating wildlife, and exotic Indian villages with their spectacular totem poles attracted many visitors who wanted to experience the Northwest. Steamships offered great travel opportunities in this region. The Inside Passage, a steamship route, brought tourists from San Francisco or Seattle to Alaska while making stops at several destinations in between (Glass & Jonaitis 2010:61-62). On the docks travellers were greeted by Indian women who offered handmade souvenirs for sale. Northwest coast cruises remain an extremely popular tourist activity today.

In Florida the construction of the Tamiami Trail in the 1920's was key to the development of Seminole tourism. The highway initially disrupted traditional Indian life as it cut straight through canoe trails. However, the Seminoles used the raised roadbed to put up camps above the water line while they travelled to and from Miami. En route, tour buses stopped nearby for tourists to visit the camps and have their photographs taken with the Indians. Soon, the Seminoles charged admission fees to their villages where tourists could visit and experience traditional life and buy souvenirs. Visiting Indian villages along the Tamiami Trail became increasingly popular and was even discussed in northern newspapers. Visitors could see authentic Indian life for themselves or possibly visit the little zoo with local wildlife attached to it. The villages operated independently from the white-run commercial Seminole show villages and became an important source of income to Seminole families (West 1998:14,32-34).

The Gratamas' main destination in North America, the Southwest, was opened to travellers by the Atchison, Topeka and Santa Fe Railroad, in conjunction with entrepreneur Fred Harvey in the 1880's. Harvey made the rather rough Southwest more attractive to travellers by providing clean and affordable restaurants and accommodations along the railroad. His hotels at main destinations such as the Grand Canyon and Santa Fe made wild nature and Indian cultures accessible to tourists. He made clever use of Indian imagery in advertisements and staged demonstrations of Indian craftsmanship in some of his hotels. After World War One the importance of railroads decreased in the Southwest while the use of cars was on the rise. Keeping up with the changes Harvey developed the Indian Detours. Tourists could now visit even remoter natural wonders and Indian villages by car with a private driver and guide (Chambers 2010:26-27).

In 1925 the Gratama's embarked on their journey around the world that lasted nearly three and a half years, one of the prime examples of a Grand Tour. They were people of means, travelled to remote areas and were curious about nature, history and new cultures. They did not depend on travel agencies or packaged tours, but were masters of their own itineraries.

Ludolf Reinier Gratama and Johanna Hendrike Schultz van Haegen

Ludolf Reinier Gratama was born on March 4, 1875, and attended high school partly in Germany. On October 3, 1901, he married Johanna Hendrika Schultz van Haegen, who saw the light on June 23, 1878 in the city of Breda, in the province of North-Brabant. Like her husband she originated from a wealthy family. During her youth she showed a keen interest in the arts and was quite talented at watercolors and sketching. Ludolf Gratama accumulated his wealth through a series of fortunate business investments that enabled the couple to undertake their Grand Tour as was customary for wealthy European couples.[1] Visits to European capital cities were fairly common and journeys to the Holy Land and the Egyptian pyramids were not unheard of. The Gratamas however were much more ambitious and prepared to walk new paths. They were driven by their interest in non-western peoples and cultures and their search for lucrative investment opportunities abroad (Hovens & Van der Hooft 2010).

They were not the first in their family who were culturally and historically interested or wanted to travel. In 1819 one of their forebears, mr. S. Gratama founded a historical society for the purpose of studying the Drents language and history. Some family members participated in excavations and started private collections of antiquities. In 1854 the basis for the *Drents Museum* was established by concentrating several archaeological collections in the Assen town hall.[2] One of the prominent committee members of the *Provinciaal Museum*

1 Family archive Gratama; Drents Archief: no 291-295.

2 Drenthe is a province in the northeast of the Netherlands. Assen is its capital city.

Mr. and Mrs. Gratama ca. 1935 (Drents Archief; photo nr. DA 75300138).

van Oudheden (Provincial Museum of Antiquities) was Lucas Oldenhuis Gratama who convinced the provincial government to buy the *hunebedden*, the megalithic structures, in order to preserve them for future generations (Peters 2000:270-273). Painter Arie van der Boon (1886-1961) travelled multiple times through Europe with his spouse Henriëtte Elise Gratama, made possible by her fortune.[3]

Itinerary

The first part of their travels took the Gratama couple through Europe, followed by several Asian countries. They continued their journey through Australia and New Zealand where they stayed with friends for several months. In New Zealand they became acquainted with the culture of the Maori, the indigenous population. In the Pacific the Gratamas travelled to other Polynesian archipelagos: the Society Islands, Samoa, Tonga, Fiji and Hawaii. Ludolf Gratama kept a travel journal and their Pacific itinerary was eventually published in 1931, illustrated with Mrs. Gratama's artwork. A recurring theme in the book is their critique of Christian mission work and its impact on Polynesian daily life, such as the imposition of western dress. The cover is a painted portrait of an unknown

3 Encyclopedie Drenthe Online.

Cover of Gratama's Pacific publication.

woman by Mrs. Gratama. Her hobby enabled interaction with Polynesians more easily. People were curious about these westerners and often couldn't resist the offer of a trip in their car as a thank you for posing in return (Gratama 1931).

Arriving from Hawaii, the Gratamas landed in California (1928) and boarded the train to Phoenix, Arizona where acquaintances of Mrs. Gratama lived. The romance and the adventure of the Southwest attracted them to the Four Corners area where the state borders of Arizona, New Mexico, Colorado and Utah meet. Photographs and articles on the natural surroundings and prehistoric Indian settlements in National Geographic Magazine had caught their interest. As travellers with a larger budget they could afford a rental car with driver, a former cowboy named Jack Young, to go off the beaten track to areas where Indians lived who had more or less managed to maintain much of their traditional cultures. The Gratama's personal view on Indians seems to have been somewhat mixed. On the one hand Indians were admired because of their sense of humour, hospitality, friendliness and artistry. On the other hand they were referred to as 'red skins' and their way of living called primitive while the American government was criticized for its treatment of Indians.

As he did before in Polynesia, Mr. Gratama wrote a journal on the Southwestern part of their itinerary. The handwritten manuscript entitled *Roodhuiden: Reizen door Arizona, New Mexico, Indian Territory, Utah (1928)*[4] ('Redskins: Travels through Arizona, New Mexico, Indian Territory, Utah (1928)') together with the photographs were found in the *Drents Archief* in Assen, the Netherlands. Considering the editorial notes it contained, the manuscript was very likely intended for publication, but unfortunately and for unknown reasons, it was never printed. Although the manuscript provides (sometimes very) detailed information on historic events, natural surroundings and peoples it remains somewhat unclear on their itinerary as a whole. The author, Mr. Gratama himself, continuously jumps back and forth between occurrences. It seems likely that they travelled for at least a few months in the Southwest, while the photo albums document their journey onwards to British Columbia. Their manuscript speaks of the Southwest only.

The Gratama account focuses on three classic Grand Tour themes: ancient history of the region, contemporary Indian cultures and the wonders of nature. This article presents some of the most interesting episodes from the manuscript to a larger audience, as was the original intention of the couple. The emphasis is on the encounters with Indians, wild nature, ancient ruins and the remarkably rough travel conditions in the Southwest in that period. The original narrative was maintained as much as possible, including Ludolf Gratama's style of prose. Editorial annotation was kept at a minimum. The photographs accompanying the text were taken by the Gratamas themselves. The text of the manuscript is put in parentheses, while the editorial comments are provided in italics.

Redskins: Travel through Arizona, New Mexico, Indian Territory, Utah (1928)

In Phoenix and the surrounding area the Gratamas received their first impression of the living conditions of the Indian population.

The Apaches

"Apache" is a collective name for several culturally related groups who lived a semi- nomadic lifestyle which included hunting, gathering, trade and low intensity agriculture. They were feared for their raids on neighbouring tribes and white settlers. In the nineteenth century armies of both Texas, the United States, and Mexico fought against them in what is called the Apache Wars (1849-1886) when the Native people resisted forced relocation to Indian reservations, broken treaties, and disputes about traditional Apache Indian lands. One of the most well-known Apache leaders, Geronimo, finally surrendered in 1886.

4 Family archive Gratama; Drents Archief; no 296.

Apache grandmother with grandchild (Drents Archief; photo nr. DA 652.1).

"The most beautiful part of Phoenix' surroundings was still waiting for us... The road took us first along Tempe Mesa, through the barren desert, where people had behaved as hooligans and chopped away everything that grew. Luckily, the government interfered and founded the National Papago Saguaro Monument which protects nature. A little further away we saw the desert when it's most beautiful. In addition to what the Mexicans called guards of the desert (*Cereus giganteus*), the tall Saguari cacti, that give the whole landscape a certain look and sometimes grow to 10 meters high and look with their side arms like macabre lamps, we saw various cacti with red and yellow flowers, such as the prickly pear and *cholla* and *ocotillo* (candle bush), and the our broom resembling mesquite which has yellow flowers as well. The aforementioned *Cereus giganteus* can become 300 years old. We now followed the Superior Highway and approached the increasingly impressive rocks of the Superstition Mountains, to the Indians a sacred mountain range that has played a significant role in their history, of the Apaches especially. Here in the canyons some bloody conflicts have occurred, among the Indians themselves and with the American troops that were sent to subjugate them. We visited an Apache village, a camp consisting of domed white cotton tents that looked shabby. We were received with great suspicion and thought it best to stay for only a short while. Once there were many Apaches, comprised of the Tontos, San Carlos, Coyoteros, Chiricahuas and Mohaves. All were cruel rapacious tribes and very much feared. During the last decisive battles with American troops they defended themselves bravely under Geronimo's command, refused to surrender and were nearly killed to the last man. Their numbers have decreased significantly, as they were unable to adapt to a more

Mr. and Mrs. Gratama on the way to the Grand Canyon (Drents Archief; photo nr. DA 666).

sedate lifestyle. They maintained their bad reputation and are known as horse thieves. A few of them still live in the canyons of the Superstition Mountains. In the last few years people have started to breed buffalos in this area."[5]

Grand Canyon

Another important theme of the American Grand Tour was pristine nature. In the Northeast of the United States the Niagara Falls were the major destination and in the Southwest the Grand Canyon was considered one of the highlights of the journey. Of old, Indians were considered to be one with nature with the result that visits to wonders of nature in the Southwest were often combined with visits to Indian settlements.

"It was already dark when we reached our destination, the Grand Canyon. It was bitterly cold, besides we were on a high altitude and further north. The El Tovar Hotel that is completely constructed of timber made a very cosy impression. The fire in the hearth provided a pleasant ambiance. The lobby and rooms are decorated in a rustic style."

"The next morning we rushed to see the wonder of the world that nobody has been able to describe well. This is no surprise. It's too grand, too imposing. Imagine a chasm, 160 km. long, 26 km. wide and nearly 2 km. deep whose faces show many colors that, as if by magic, change according to the position of the

5 All the Gratama quotes stem from the manuscript and are translated as literally as possible. When certain passages sound offensive or incorrect to contemporary readers, please keep in mind that the manuscript was written in the 1920's-1930's and that the Gratama's could have been misinformed or misunderstood the information they were given.

Hopi dancers performing at the Grand Canyon (Drents Archief; photo nr. DA 680).

sun. You think you're looking down on another planet. The rock formations down below are whimsically shaped and give lots of room to the human imagination and they were christened with names. It is moving and unreal. It is captivating all hours of the day. A walk along the edge of this magic land brings surprises without interruption. Not just down below where you can see the wide Colorado River that looks like a thin line that already ran 2700 km. through 5 states. In and above the canyon eagles hover close to their nests that are built on inaccessible peaks with their young clearly visible. The whole area surrounding the Grand Canyon is a nature reserve in which the animals are protected. The antelopes, who are usually so skittish, eat from your hand. On the other side of the canyon stretches a purple colored mesa with the black mountains in the far distance. This mesa is practically virgin territory and difficult to enter. There are no roads, just a few trails that are known to Indians and hunters. Thousands of deer, many bears are found there, as well as cougars, and in such high numbers that the government offers a reward for the killing of the latter species. With the result that in 4 years time, 500 were submitted."

Trading posts

The Gratamas were most interested in the aboriginal inhabitants: the Rio Grande Pueblos, the Zunis, the Hopis and the Navajos. Like before in Polynesia they made a serious effort to interact with local Native peoples, especially Mrs. Gratama. The couple seemed to have enjoyed visiting trading posts. The manuscript provides many detailed accounts of the colourful characters they encountered at these establishments in the semi-arid deserts. Trading posts also provided opportunities to talk to Indians.

"After an hour we arrived at the Little Colorado Trading Post, situated along the river with the same name. In such a trading post, of which there were several in Indian Territory, an important part of Indian life takes place. These shops are controlled by the Agent or Superintendent who is appointed by the government. Here, the Indians can sell their products such as wool, or exchange it for necessities. You can see horse saddles, barbed wire, tools, candy, tobacco and all kinds of groceries. They can also pawn items for money. You can see silver jewelry decorated with turquoise and beautifully colored blankets that are offered for sale when the pawns aren't claimed on time."

"Since not only the Navajo reservation is near, but the Hopi reservation as well, Tuba City Trading Post is very interesting for us. Here the interests of both tribes are concentrated. All day long you can see the Hopi and Navajo Indians, often with their *squaws* (women) arrive on their little horses and the men do their business while the *squaws* immediately enter the shop of the trading post to look at jewelry. Among both the Hopis and Navajos skilful silversmiths are active. They predominantly make silver and turquoise objects. The *squaws* love it, but the men also wear beautiful and heavy belts. It must be very difficult for them that when times are hard, such as bad crops, they cannot claim their pawn at the trading post and it will be sold instead. As soon the men have exchanged their wool and the women their colorful woven blankets for necessities or groceries, the men gather in a circle to chat. They smoke a pipe when they are doing that. My wife loved to join and to talk them about anything she thought would interest them. On all occasions someone could interpret. Suspicious as they are, not without reason, regarding what they have endured from American whites, it was obvious that in the beginning they did not really enjoy this. When they were reassured, it was a nice moment when one of them got up to shake my wife's hand as a sign that she had gained their trust. The Agent of the trading post was so surprised that when the first time he saw it he wanted to take a picture. In his long career it had never happened before that Indians permitted a white woman to join them. Eventually they allowed my wife to sketch one of them."

Indian Boarding Schools

The keen interest of the Gratamas in the places and peoples they visited is exemplified by their visits to places often avoided by other travellers, such as Indian Boarding Schools. They went to these schools in Phoenix and Tuba City. The Dutch couple was shocked that such institutions existed and criticized boarding school methods and the irreparable damage it caused to native cultures.

"We were surprised to find a school in Tuba City where the government's policy has been to take the children away from their parents for several years to teach them the American language, hygiene, white customs and modern agriculture and convert them to Christianity. The officials who take the children away don't have an easy time. Often, the parents don't want to give their children away and

Children at morning roll-call at Tuba City Indian School (Drents Archief; photo nr. DA 674.2).

hide them. The result of this education is disappointing to both parties. The adoption of American habits makes them unsuitable for the primitive life that made them happy. The best thing an Indian girl can hope for when she leaves Indian Territory is to become a housekeeper. When she returns to her tribe, she finds it difficult to adjust herself to her old life. Her tribal members often think that she feels superior to them, especially when she attempts to change food preparation and eating habits."

"At Tuba City we saw in the morning the little ones gather in front of the school to salute the American flag. Near the school is an auditorium for Indians where performances take place. The décors were remarkably well painted considering that this Indian had not been to school for 24 years. The Navajos and Hopis are very intelligent, artistic races by the way. We had a great time around the fire at the Trading Post last night. We heard all kinds of interesting facts. For example, the administration of justice is in hands of the Indians, however an appeal to the Agent of the Indian Territory is permitted. Jail is considered as something humiliating and terrible; they wouldn't last a few years. That's why it is alternated with forced labor on the roads. It is curious to observe that prisons are open and inmates could escape. The reason that they don't is that they will be caught anyway and that their sentence will be increased. In contrast with what we thought before we were told that when you get Indians to know better they are remarkably upbeat and have a great sense of humor. They will never beat each other up. Swear words don't exist in their language. Immorality is rare but there are some prostitutes. Indian children are very obedient, their parents don't mete out corporal punishment. The missionary who had told us this offered to take us to the Hopi reservation."

The Hopis

Many travellers journeyed to the Southwest of the United States to see 'unspoilt' Indian peoples. East coast Indians were no longer considered interesting as they were largely assimilated into the dominant white culture and had lost their exoticism. In the Southwest the Indian peoples were still relatively authentic. Especially the Hopis attracted many visitors because of the isolated location of their villages on the mesas, their beautifully decorated pottery, the intriguing hair-do of unmarried girls and last but not least, their ceremonial dances. The Snake Dance in particular drew many spectators. The Hopi villages were the first pueblos *the Gratamas visited, together with the missionary and a Hopi guide.*

"First we arrived at Moencopi. The Hopis are what one calls *pueblo*-inhabitants, which means that they live in houses, in contrast to the Navajos. These houses have a special construction. They are like layered homes built terrace-wise. The ground level cannot be entered through doors, but with ladders from the terraces. Because of security reasons. The rooms are square and built of stone or *adobe* and wood. Many families live in one house. The villages have a particular look due to their construction. The Hopis are farmers and familiar with irrigation. They grow corn, cotton, beans and learned from the Spaniards cattle and chicken breeding. Hunting is still done with bow and arrow, except for rabbits when they use some type of boomerang. As craftsmen they excel in basketry weaving and since contact with whites they are silversmiths as well. The tribe consists of several units that are subdivided into clans. These Totem-clans consider themselves blood-relations because they share the similar totem animal. They don't marry each other. After marriage a husband moves in with his wife,

Mrs. Gratama with Hopi children (Drents Archief; photo nr. DA 674.1).

and the children belong to the tribe of the mother. As an extraordinary favour we were allowed to visit the *kiva* (underground temple), accessible with a ladder. It has a round shape and an earthen bench. Masks and dried animal skins were hanging on the wall. Snakes are kept here, but we will talk about that later. In this place the wise men of the tribe meet and take their important decisions in accordance with their laws. Of course in the presence of the priest and *cacique* (chief) who conducts the ceremonies. The latter are often married; the villagers contribute to their subsistence."

The Pueblo Indians

The Pueblo Indians are culturally related to the Zunis and Hopis and live in twenty-one villages along the Rio Grande River in the state of New Mexico. The villages are famous for their beautiful painted pottery that already drew the attention of tourists in the 1920's. As museums advised potters on white taste and quality demands, the women adapted their work and were able to sell more wares at better prices.

"Our next stop was Acoma, one of the oldest Indian villages in New Mexico. Like a vision it was situated on top of an approximately 100 m. high rock. The village itself is very picturesque, because of the three storey houses with their terraces. As the rock itself is completely barren, the inhabitants need to descend to the plain to work their fields. It must have been quite an effort to build the houses and the mission church with its side buildings. Even the earth for the churchyard was taken up. Here we were given the impression of life like it was a few centuries back. Prior to visiting the villages, one has to ask permission from the governor, who turned out to be a decent man, in contrast to the villagers

Pottery sellers at Santa Clara pueblo (Drents Archief; photo nr. DA 730.3).

who were rather hostile, probably because of the great isolation in which they lived until very recently when there was only a barely passable path up the rock. The old mission church contained the painting of Joseph that caused quite some trouble and nearly led to animosities between Acoma and nearby Laguna. This was given by a Spanish king to the mission. As it performs miracles it is considered sacred. The Indians say that in case the crops are in danger of withering the painting from the church is carried around. Acoma never has crop failures but nearby Laguna has."

"Our first destination was Santo Domingo a nearly original Indian *pueblo* (village) with a very conservative population, that doesn't allow outsiders to see their ceremonies and dances. Their special dance is the Buffalo Dance. As it was Sunday, it was rather difficult to find the governor to ask permission to enter the *pueblo*, although we had already seen a lot before we found him. Both the *pueblo* and the villagers were very picturesque. The blankets they wear are colorful, a dirty yellow and orange and their skin color red which is not the case with all Redskins. Most of them were dour and very suspicious. Photography was difficult and later we heard of cases that the cameras were snatched away and destroyed. Curious are the *kivas* (temples) that are round, but rise high above the ground and no white man may enter. The *pueblo* has several houses with multiple storeys. With the brightly colored population on the terraces it was a view never to forget. We visited a few houses that were spacious and clean. In one of them an old *squaw* was busy baking bread that they call *matzé*. She dipped her fingers in liquid dough and spread this out over a hot rock and took it up immediately with her other hand and the bread was ready. It is similar to the bread the Israelites use. The church, on the Rio Grande River that often floods, is built in the old style but the Indians have not forgotten to add their own designs to the decoration."

Travel conditions

Part of the attraction (and for others the nightmare) of the Southwest was the fact that travellers could easily go off the beaten track. Roads were infamously rough and comfortable hotels sparse.

"We spent this night in Gallup, for the first time in ages, in a hotel with some comfort. The town itself offers very little and we used it only as a starting point for our car tours. From here we visited Chaco Canyon, which was made a National Monument because of the ruins. The tour itself is 320 km. long of which a large part through Indian Territory with very bad roads. Sometimes the road was not even a trail, but more like a trace. It took us an hour and a half to cover 10 km. of road."

"While we took in the landscape, a Navajo with his *squaw* on the back of his horse rode past, at about 100 footsteps from us. Continuing our way, we met another Navajo who herded his flocks of sheep and goats, permitting us to

Mr. Gratama enjoying a picnic with friends and driver (Drents Archief; photo nr. DA 711.2).

Gratama, driver Jack Young and Indian guide (Drents Archief; photo nr. DA 674.3).

photograph him. Then followed another Navajo camp where the inhabitants ate cooked mutton with bread after which we didn't see anything for hours on end. The car laboured through tracks that were so deep that we feared that the gas tank would get damaged because of the rocks that lay between. Eventually we reached the San Juan River that we crossed over a wooden suspension bridge that looked terribly shaky and reached the Mexican Hat Trading Post where we rested and picnicked."

"Our purpose was to visit the Gran Quivire National Monument, but had to leave the highway to follow a trail for 125 km. The trail didn't look promising due to the awful rains last night. We barely drove 5 km. before we got stuck in a pool of slippery mud. We proposed to abandon our plan altogether as we could see the clouds gathering in the sky. Our driver and his helper thought that we would be alright if we put snow chains on the back tires. After 35 km. we got stuck again. A thunderstorm made things worse. When after three hours the mud was dug away from the axles the engine refused. Meanwhile the sun set. We decided to look for a ranch to see if we could get anything to eat over there and possibly find shelter."

The Navajos

The Navajos are a nomadic people whosince the arrival of the first Europeans, the Spaniards, lived in conflict with whites for a long time. The situation deteriorated quickly when their traditional homelands came under the control of the American government in the nineteenth century. The most dramatic moment in this history is the "Long Walk" when in 1864 thousands of Navajos were forced to walk five hundred kilometres to Fort Sumner where they, together with other tribes, were interned in camps. Crop failure and bad storage management caused severe starvation. In 1868 the Navajos were assigned their own reservation on traditional lands.

"A medicine man (an Indian priest who cures illness as well) who had to be in Kayenta where we intended to spend the night, joined us as a travel companion. His name meant 'he who sings to sleep'. Before he stepped in the car he smeared some pollen that he kept in a little purse on his forehead and tongue. We could smell his presence, a pity that he hadn't taken a sweat bath beforehand. At Red Lake, a lake that as the name suggests looks red, we got out and entered the little trading post. There were no Indians, probably because of the cold and nasty weather. The road took us along lonely rocks, called Elephant Feet, that clearly resemble elephant legs. We went past many Navajos. The Indians are nomads and move with their herds of sheep and goats from one meadow to the other. We visited such a camp that was located near junipers and pine trees. When the Navajos saw us with the medicine man they had more trust in us because they usually are not so fond of the *pelicanas* (whites). We visited one of the *hogans* (huts) that are made of wood and *adobe*. Sometimes they are square, sometimes round. The diameter I estimated at approximately 4 meters. A blanket covers the entrance! The floor is covered with sheepskins where they sleep at night. In the middle a fire was burning, with a rabbit roasting. The smoke escaped through a hole in the roof."

"We also saw a sweat lodge that didn't differ much from those of the Hopis. Near the camp was an enclosure of a low fence, called a corral in which the sheep and goats are kept at night. In another camp there was a celebration planned and a sandpainting made in front of a medicine man's hut. The fine sand is

Navajo hogan (Drents Archief; photo nr. DA 691.1).

Navajo shepherd near Shiprock on the Navajo Indian Reservation (Drents Archief; photo nr. DA 687).

made by grinding colored rocks. The depictions are completely symbolic and are religious in nature. We didn't understand the correct meaning although clearly discernible were swastikas, clouds, a rainbow and star figures that depict corn plants. Swastikas symbolise the four directions. Our medicine man explained to us that tobacco smoke from sacred pipes mean rain clouds and that with the beginning of the earth, the sun was put up in the sky with a rainbow. The

Navajos and Apaches, both nomadic peoples, belong linguistically to the Déné or Athapascan."

Chaco Canyon

Chaco Canyon is one of the most important archaeological sites in the Southwest. The site consists of a complex network of ceremonial centres of which Pueblo Bonito is the largest. They are still mainly accessible through oldroads. Chaco Canyon was completely abandoned in the thirteenth century. The inhabitants of these centres are considered to be the ancestors of the contemporary Pueblo *peoples. They share important cultural traits such asarchitecture, pottery and* kivas, *the subterranean ceremonial chambers.*

"After passing Crown Point where the administration buildings of the Eastern Indian Reservation are located, we arrived in the wild nature of Chaco Canyon where many ruins are to be found of which Pueblo Bonito is the most important. It contained 1200 rooms and is assumed to have been inhabited by 150 people and is the largest prehistoric ruin in the Southwest of the United States. It was a *pueblo* or community house, carved in a rock in the shape of the letter D. The materials for construction such as wood needed to have been transported from great distances. Several generations must have lived there as below the ruins other structures have been found. The walls on the inside are well finished and several are even plastered. The building order is completely different from that in other places, including the *kivas*. Some have large measurements. The Hopis use six support beams for the roof; one for every direction (north, south, east, west, above and below). Here you find sometimes eight or even more beams. The interior is also different. In the surrounding areas more ruins can be found, of which Del Aroyo is completely uninvestigated and ChetroKetl partially. According to a very knowledgeable source, the archaeological service has been aware of her tasks since a few years. Vandals have ruined much. The people that go 'souvenir hunting' damage a lot as well."

Zuni

In 1539 four Spanish sailors were shipwrecked on the Texan Gulf coast. After their return to New Spain (Mexico) they told fantastic stories about the 'Seven Cities of Cibola' that contained incredible treasures, including gold. Encouraged by the wealth of the Aztecs in Mexico and Incas in Peru, the viceroy of New Spain sent a group of scouts to these mythical cities, but they were ambushed at Zuni. A few escaped and recounted in Mexico City that they had seen the cities in the distance and that the houses were built of gold, silver and turquoise. The military expedition that arrived at Zuni discovered that the stories were not true. Nevertheless, the Spanish conquered Zuni.

"The Zuñi Indians differ from the others and speak a completely different language and marry mostly each other. The older part of the village is built against a hill and has built terraced three storey houses like the Hopis, that can only be entered by ladders and are easy to defend. However, the new houses consist of one storey with fairly large rooms. We were invited to enter. The people are friendly and hospitable and happy. The *squaws* (women) are pretty but on the short side. They busy themselves with the weaving of their clothes and blankets that are embroidered for the dances and ceremonies with vibrant colors such as red, yellow and green. The men wear a kerchief around their heads and have earrings and necklaces of turquoise. On and between the houses there are little ovens of *adobe* in which bread is baked and pottery fired. They are very skilful at pottery. The shapes and painted decorations are very beautiful. The base color is a beautifully warm red. Their *kivas* (temples) are completely different from those of other Indians and have a square shape. Their little gardens look like big waffles of which the little squares are cultivated. The little dams contain the water that is poured in from pots. Planting is accompanied by ceremonies. A stick with eagle feathers is put in the ground then."

Epilogue

The manuscript of the American part of the Grand Tour ends rather abruptly but appropriately with the three Grand Tour themes: nature, culture and history. Gratama concludes his journal as follows:

"For travellers who love nature, Arizona and New Mexico are an Eldorado. Nowhere else in the world you will find such a variety and natural phenomena. They [Arizona and New Mexico] have an atmosphere that a land with an ancient culture simply has. The Indians with their quiet bearing, even when they travel on foot or on horseback, belong to the impressive and often overwhelming landscape. They, who have seen and lived through it like my wife and I, will never forget it. The memory of these two states will stay with us for ever."

References

Chambers, E. (2010), *Native Tours: The Anthropology of Travel and Tourism.* Long Grove, IL: Waveland Press Inc.

Glass, A. & A. Jonaitis (2010), *The Totem Pole: An Intercultural History.* Seattle, WA: University of Washington Press.

Gratama, L.R. (1931), *Onder de Bewoners der Betooverende Zuid-Zee Eilanden.* Met illustraties van J.H. Gratama- Schultz van Haegen. Amsterdam: Allert de Lange.

Hovens, P & M.G. van der Hooft (2010), Van Drenthe naar het Wilde Westen. De Grand Tour van Ludolf Gratama en Johanna Schultz van Haegen door Indiaans Amerika (1928); in: *Nieuwe Drentse Volksalmanak* 127:1-27.

Jasen, P. (1995), *Wild Things: Nature Culture and Tourism in Ontario 1790-1919.* Toronto: University of Toronto Press.

Peter, H. (2000), Geloof, Onderwijs en Cultuur, circa 1807-1902; in: H. Gras (ed.), *Geschiedenis van Assen*: 270-273. Assen: van Gorcum.

Phillips, R.B. (1998), *Trading Identities: The Souvenir in Native North American Art from the Northeast, 1700-1900.* Seattle, WA: University of Washington Press.

Sears, J.F. (1989), *Sacred Places: American Tourist Attractions in the Nineteenth Century.* New York: Oxford University Press.

West, P. (1998), *The Enduring Seminoles: From Alligator Wrestling to Ecotourism.* Gainesville, FL: University Press of Florida.

Casino Tourism in Northern New Mexico

Pueblo "Indian" Casinos as Capitalistic Ventures in a Traditional Setting

Susanne Berthier-Foglar

The New Mexican Pueblo Indians (Pueblo Nations) have a long history of surviving on the margins[1]. The dire condition of the land is attested by the wish of the first colonists to go back to Mexico. The banks of the Rio Grande are productive agricultural land but the surrounding high altitude desert is barren. Famine affected both colonists and Pueblo Indians and a Franciscan friar declared that "any Spaniard who gets his fill of tortillas feels as if he has obtained a grant of nobility" (Simmons 1991:158). The Spanish colony survived, aggregating the existing pueblos into larger units, acculturating them through the placement of a church as the vector of Spanish culture by Franciscan friars. The closeness of the contact between Pueblo and Spanish cultures, as well as the intrusiveness of the church, and the indigenous refusal to abandon their religion, led to the secrecy of most traditional native rituals. Secrecy, or the "Iron Curtain" in the words of Pueblo anthropologist Edward Dozier, is still one the main characteristics of the Pueblo today and is effective in protecting indigenous culture against contemporary tourist encroachment on the Pueblos (Brandt 1980:123-125, 131-132).

The Pueblos are still located on the original land grants obtained from Spain. They do not encompass the total surface of indigenous land before conquest but they form the core of Pueblo land today and have, in the past decades, been extended through purchase by the Pueblos or other acquisitions. Therefore Pueblo Indians do not live on 'reservations,' *i.e.* residual land where tribes were relocated to in order to avoid clashing with the advancing mainstream population during the conquest of the West. Like all Indian Nations in the United States they claim sovereignty which takes on a more significant meaning for the 19 New Mexican Pueblos on the land of their ancestors (Cohen 1982).[2]

1 The term "Indian" in this article is construed to be non-derogatory and is used according to local New Mexican semantics. Pueblo may refer to the people (tribes/ Nations) or their villages and towns, called Pueblo by the Spanish Conquistadors. The people are referred to as "the Pueblo," and the villages as "the Pueblos".

2 The sovereignty of Indian Nations has been extensively analyzed by Felix Cohen in his *Handbook of Federal Indian Law*, first published in 1941. The 1958 edition is to be avoided as it has been expunged of pro-Indian material during a period of federal backlash on the policies implemented under Franklin Delano Roosevelt.

The Pueblos form enclaves of several hundred to a few thousand people in Northern New Mexico, where the surrounding mainstream society is composed of Hispanics, often the descendants of the Spanish settlers, and Anglo-Americans. Cities close to the Pueblos, Albuquerque and Santa Fe, provide jobs, bring in tourists, and increase the risk of identity loss through integration with a multicultural mainstream. Each Pueblo is a distinct "Nation", more precisely a "domestic dependent Nation" in the words of the Supreme Court under John Marshall (Deloria & Lytle 1984:16-17). The concept of dependency entails necessary interaction with the mainstream, above all in economic matters, and the Pueblos have embraced a limited form of tourism and a lucrative casino economy.

However, they also wish to maintain elements of their traditional culture that form the basis of their social cohesion. This article discusses how tourism has evolved since the Territorial period, how the Pueblo have taken touristic developments into their own hands, how they have adapted to the ambient economy by entering the gaming industry, and finally how they use the discourse of cultural tourism as a marketing tool. The author of the article has conducted field work on the subject of Pueblo economy and integration in mainstream society since the 1990s, focusing more specifically on their tourism and casino economy between 2000 and 2014. To respect the Pueblos' wish for secrecy concerning their internal affairs, only the public side of their touristic ventures has been researched.

Tourism in Indian country: evolution and adaptation

Tourism in Indian country started during New Mexico's Territorial period (*i.e.* before statehood in 1912) when the railroad reached the Rio Grande Valley in 1880 and was extended further to the West (Bryant 1974:62). Tourists and anthropologists traveled with relative ease to an exotic domestic destination. Along the line entrepreneur Fred Harvey built hotels, the "Harvey Houses", capitalizing on the local culture and hiring a young designer, Mary Colter, to establish her mark in a style that came to be known as Pueblo Revival. Harvey also brought in Native craftspeople to demonstrate their skills to the travelers and to sell their crafts. The Pueblos adapted to the market, producing items for domestic decorative purposes in accordance with the current fashion (Bsumek 2003:119; Lidchi 2005:41-42). While the new style of objects produced did not influence Pueblo life, wage work did and tribes within the reach of railroad stops saw their traditional agricultural subsistence economy gradually modified by the monetary economy of arts and crafts. The revival of traditional crafts had an overall positive effect on Pueblo self-esteem as seen in the example of Maria Martinez, the San Ildefonso potter, who revived the ancient black-on-black style copying shards found in archeological digs. She became an inspiration for countless followers who furnished the growing market of Indian crafts (Parsons

1939:1118). Thus, in the early decades of the 20th century, with the advent of a steady influx of tourists, a major evolution occurred in the way Pueblo set the boundaries between themselves and the mainstream. The late 20th century casino industry appeared as an outgrowth of these developments.

Tourism became a major source of income for the tribes in the early statehood period. Outside income changed the way ceremonial societies were perceived and has "disintegrated Pueblo patterns of behavior" in the 1930s (Parsons 1939:1143). However, despite the grim predictions, the Pueblos survived and have adapted to tourism without being overwhelmed by the newcomers. After the first phase of tourist invasion of the Pueblos in the 1920s and 30s when tour busses could be seen parked on the Pueblo plazas during ceremonies, the intrusiveness of outsiders was kept in check. The wall of secrecy surrounding Pueblo beliefs and ceremonials has a long history dating back to the colonial rebellions of the 17th century, the Pueblo Revolt of 1680, as well as the lesser, and often forgotten ones (Weber 1999:3-18; Espinosa 1998). During these rebellions, bicultural individuals who could choose sides played an important role. The same phenomenon exists today on a different level with Pueblo leaders who are involved in ceremonial societies while being business leaders in mainstream New Mexican society.

Pueblo secrecy, and their absolute refusal to proselytize, have often been commented upon (Brandt 1980:123). Travel journals and early New Mexican narratives show the determined wish to refuse the outside gaze from an early period onward. Even a visiting U.S. Army Captain who toured the Pueblos in the 1880s was physically prevented access to a kiva, even "lifted out" and "thrown out" (in his own words) when he tried to enter by force (Bourke 1884:19-24). This pattern is repeated consistently. Ethnologists Elsie Clews Parsons and Franz Boas, visiting Laguna Pueblo, probably in the 1930s, to see a specific ceremony were told it was delayed, and when they intended to stay in the Pueblo as long as need be they were locked in a room with a window covered in sackcloth and a guard at the door (Parsons 1939:940). Thus, the tourist "gaze" (Urry 1990:1-4) is a characteristic that reaches back to the mid-19th century in Pueblo territory, if one considers the touristic phenomenon in the contemporary sense.

Since the 1930s the Pueblos have managed a situation where the fashion of primitivism, paralleling the rising industrialization of the United States, has increased the arrival of tourists to their ceremonies. While tourists have visited sites of cultural interest since the 18th century "Grand Tour" of Europe by young British aristocrats, the primitivist cultural tourists of the 1930s were "seekers" (Rothman 2003:8) in quest of the authentic, supposedly uncorrupted cultural artifact belonging to a pre-industrial society.

Without packaging their tourist activities, without even claiming them to be held in favor of tourists, the Pueblos have managed to blur the notions of backstage and front stage. The backstage of a tourist destination is where the authentic life of the Natives happens and the front stage is what is shown to the tourists (Goffman in McCannell 1989:92). The quest for the authentic is part of the tourist experience, especially in the context of primitivism. For McCannell, a core belief of the tourist in non-Western societies is the notion that the Others are "outside of historical time" (1989:77) giving weight to the primitivists' wish to escape the industrialized present (Jacobs 1999:59-60). The "backstage," where the real life of the visited peoples takes place thus becomes an important destination.

Refusing the gaze and controlling the outsiders' gaze and his access to the "backstage" has been Pueblo policy in the last decades. The power to show and the power to hide, the "displayed withholding" (Lawlor 2006:62), as well as the possibility to close off a Pueblo and to regulate tourist activity within the village on opening days have a positive effect on tribal self-esteem (Berthier-Foglar 2010:382-390). Pueblo policy in matters of Pueblo closure is an effective antidote to the negative effects of tourism which is after all "an inherently extractive industry" that utilizes human resources, in this case the visited peoples, as a recreational experience (Bryan 2003:142). Moreover, in recent decades the Southwest has become "the panoramic dreamscape of the region" (Rothman 2003:4) and Native American tribes have capitalized on the situation by entering the new field of the gaming business.

This study on casino tourism draws upon the theories of cultural studies, postcolonial studies, tourism studies, and Native American studies with a viewpoint "from the outside," *i.e.* by a European scholar who has done extensive fieldwork in the Southwest but who has not experienced Native American culture from the inside as an individual growing up in a Native context would have. The theoretical framework for the study follows Hollinshead's analysis of history, heritage, and identity as constructs in a post-modern context. He posits history and heritage as social truths, and their "aggregated social narratives" produce a potpourri of styles that define post-modernity (Hollinshead 1997:170-183). Moreover, culture is used here in the broad sense defined by Raymond Williams (1985:90) as a "particular way of life [...] of a people, a period, a group".

Casinos as a new alternative for tourism revenue

In the 1980s Native American tribes "discovered" their right to develop gaming institutions on tribal land. The rationale was that tribes are under federal jurisdiction, and not state jurisdiction, and that there was no federal legislation against gaming. The courts decided in favor of Indian gaming as they did not wish to handicap struggling tribal economies (Nash 1999; Clarkson & Sebenius 2011: 1074-1075). While the first gaming institutions were bingo halls, tribes soon moved into more complex operations. Spurred into action by a situation that needed to be controlled, Congress passed the Indian Gaming Regulatory

Act in 1988 (IGRA), establishing three classes of gaming, from traditional social gaming (Class I), to bingo (Class II), up to casino-style gaming (Class III), including slot machines, roulette and other table games.

When the New Mexican Pueblos realized that a new business sector was open to them, many hastily set up gaming halls. The main inequality arose from geography. Tribes close to large cities or located on a main thoroughfare had a better chance to make their business plan work than those in remote and sparsely populated locations. New Mexican Pueblos located along Interstate Highway I-25 hastily set up makeshift structures resembling industrial buildings or large tents to accommodate the new activity. Today there are 13 Pueblo casinos and when driving from Isleta, in the South, to Taos, in the North, one encounters an Indian casino, on the average, every 20 minutes.

Gaming is presented by Native Americans as a traditional social activity. Creation stories of many tribes abound with supernatural beings who acquire or lose possessions through gambling, who are mischievous and irrational (Clarkson & Sebenius 2012:1069-1070; Nash 1999). However, the purpose of the cosmic gamblers in creation stories seems to be didactic, teaching humans that through irrational actions they can lose what they have, including spouses. In pre-IGRA discussions and hearings Tribes have claimed that commercial gaming was the logical outgrowth of their traditional beliefs and their traditional activity of organizing social chance games. However, the paradigm of recreational gambling, as part of a contemporary leisure activity, is very different from traditional Native American gambling in the context of a social gathering with the purpose to strengthen social cohesion.

It seems that the cosmic gambler was called upon to justify, post-fact, the mushrooming of casinos and convey a moral aura to an activity considered sinful by some segments of the American mainstream population. From an economist's viewpoint, impoverished tribes set up businesses not to honor a supernatural being but to jump on the bandwagon of an economic activity that draws visitors and produces income without impinging on the life of the Native community. The tribal opinion about the casinos of the early days of Indian gaming was: "Build it and they will come" (IG 2013).

The fact that both Interstate Highways I-25 and I-40 bisect Pueblo land without cutting through the territories of the pueblo villages themselves seemed, all of a sudden, a great asset. The first aesthetically unappealing gaming halls with the single function of housing gaming infrastructure were placed on Pueblo land as far as possible from the dwelling areas themselves. The newness of the ventures, the upbeat economic period of the 1990s, the presence of young retirees with money and time on their hands, all made for a favorable situation for the gaming industry. From the point of view of the tribes, or their economic advisers, the idea was to have the gaming tourists spend their money within the casinos without invasive physical intrusiveness, following thus the practice of Indian gas stations and their smoke shops, a historic feature on Indian land, low-key, non-glamorous establishments attracting customers with tax-free tobacco and gas, selling cheap tourist trinkets and providing jobs and a steady income for the tribes. Commodification of tribal life is thus minimized, limited in fact to the use of the tribal name and exhibition of tribal arts and crafts production. The tourist impact and "experience" is thus kept under control in the words of McKercher and du Cros (2002:28-31, 36).

The Indian Gaming Regulatory Act of 1988 included a provision for a compact between tribes wishing to enter into Class III (Casino-style) gaming and the state in which they are located. These compacts had to be accepted by the Secretary of the Interior. The rationale behind these compacts is the legal impossibility for a state to tax a business on Indian land and the notion that it is "fair" that Class III casino tribes participate in the state budget as the incoming tourists would use the state's infrastructure. Negotiations for the compact proved difficult in the absence of a track record and the 1995 compact between the Governor of New Mexico and the Pueblos was rescinded at the request of the state legislature wishing to be involved in the negotiations.

The 1997 compact requested the Pueblo to pay 16% of the net win[3] to the state as "revenue sharing." The amount seemed extremely high and the Secretary or the Interior, Bruce Babbitt, considered it "well beyond Congress' intent." With harsher words, the Governor of Pojoaque Pueblo, Jacob Viarrial, called it "extortion" (Babbitt 1997; Viarrial 2003:1). He argued that his Pueblo finances tribal programs with casino revenues – after-school programs, scholarships, cultural preservation, expansion of the tribal buffalo herd, infrastructure and law enforcement (Viarrial 2003:6) – transforming "sin money" into socially acceptable funding that would be reduced if the tribe has to pay 16% of revenue sharing to the state. Claiming that their sovereignty was being trampled upon the tribes stopped their payments to the state in 2000. A new compact was renegotiated in 2001 giving smaller casino operations a better deal. It was signed by all the Pueblos in 2001 except Pojoaque who waited until 2005 to sign their compact.

The economic impact of casino income for the tribes as well as for the state is undeniable and the "revenue sharing" statistics for New Mexico speak for themselves: in the first quarter of 2014 (ending March 31, 2014), the state of New Mexico received $17,228,447 from 14 New Mexico tribes, 11 of which are Pueblo. Over the years the figure is consistent, oscillating between $16 and 17 million per quarter in the 2012-2014 period, between $15 and 16 million per quarter in the 2008-2011 period (State of New Mexico Gaming Control Board). While it is customary for tribes in the United States to emphasize the lack of revenue of their casino economy (Glover 2003), it is not the case in New Mexico where the lowest net win in the first quarter of 2014 was slightly over

3 "Net Win" is the amount wagered on gaming machines, less the amount paid out in cash and non-cash prizes won on the gaming machines, less State and Tribal Regulatory Fees. "Net Win" is not the net profit of the casino. (Source: State of New Mexico, Gaming Control Board 2014).

$1,9 million for the Pueblo of Taos with a small casino, and the highest net win in the same period was over $40 million for the casino resort of the Pueblo of Sandia. These sums fund the tribal governments and badly needed services for a Native population with an employment rate under 46,3% (Fogarty 2014; Lawlor 2006:133).

The primary aim of the tribal casinos is for the general (*i.e.* mainstream) population to spend their dollars on a commercial project that will benefit the tribe. It also means jobs with a preference for tribal members or Native Americans. However, an applicant has to be qualified and tribal, or Native, preference is only granted in the case of an equal qualification. The Pueblo of Sandia enterprises, managing the Sandia Resort and Casino, employ 1300 area residents, 10% of whom are Sandia tribal members, and 90% from other communities, including other tribes.

It is legally impossible to prevent tribal members from playing in a casino. Lawlor attests the unease of tribal leaders when asked about Acoma members using the tribe's Sky City casino (2006:151). In every Pueblo casino Native Americans are patrons along mainstream customers and addictive gaming is an issue dealt with on tribal and state levels. However, the positive effects seem to overshadow the negative side of gambling and non-directive interviews have evidenced the pride of the Pueblos in their "own casino," in the words of a beaming young woman in traditional Pueblo garb who corrected herself adding "the casino of my tribe". She then proceeded to order a bowl of chili "because it is really good here" thus implying that tribal food culture is to be found in the casino. In an unexpected setting, cultural tourists can experience tradition.

Indian casinos and cultural tourism

The first gaming wave was not linked to an appreciation of Native American culture on the part of the customers. It must be said that Native Americans themselves were eager to avoid any link between the gaming halls and their culture. Moreover Pueblos have never given in to dressing up casino personnel in Indian garb, whether fantasy Indian garb, with fringes and feathers, or traditional historic attire. Croupiers and hospitality personnel in Pueblo casinos wear the professional clothes of their trade without signaling that they are part of a tribally owned business.

The first wave impromptu structures were replaced in the late 20th century by architecturally designed buildings in Pueblo Revival style surrounded by landscaped grounds. The fact that gaming might not always be the main driving force of the new economy was also taken into account and the larger casinos became destination resorts in themselves with an increasing diversification of their attractions often including golf courses and a wide range of places to eat and drink.

Isleta Casino (photo by the author).

Restaurant fare ranges from fast food to gourmet, following the upscaling trend of the American foodie scene. Do Native American casino restaurants differ in this respect from non-Native owned and operated establishments? In matters of native food, the benchmark is the food court of the Museum of the Native American Indian in Washington which opened in 2004. Customers navigate with their trays among the self-serve isles of the restaurant, each isle representing a geographic area of the Americas, with the chefs preparing the food in their center and displaying the dishes on the periphery. While the general flavor of the restaurant falls between exotic and traditional, new ingredients, and new dishes signal innovation.

In the Pueblo casino restaurants Native names are used more often than native ingredients. Sandia has its P'a Shur Deli, Kowira Grill, and Thur Shan Buffet; Pojoaque's Buffalo Thunder has its Mica and Red Sage Restaurants; there is a Tiwa restaurant at Isleta. New Mexican food is already foreign by mainstream American standards. Its major ingredients, corn, squash and beans, have been staples for pre-contact Native Americans and are widely used in colonial inspired dishes with spices brought from Spain, or from Northern Africa. Contemporary New Mexican food is exotic enough for the travelers and a bowl of chili with tortillas signals otherness, especially if eaten in a locale decorated with the trappings of Pueblo Revival architecture. For Ezequiel "Zeke" Perez, Casino

New Mexico flag.

Manager at the Isleta Resort & Casino, this type of food is traditional food as it "can only be found in New Mexico" (Indian Gaming 2014:52).

The Pueblo casinos of Northern New Mexico signal their difference, even if is sometimes through the "conventional motives of Indianness" (Lawlor 2006:146) that stem from the wish of the tourist boards to perpetuate the utopian vision of a state where three cultures coexist as equal partners. The notion of a tri-cultural New Mexico dates back to the first decade of the 20th century when the Territory of New Mexico was about to gain statehood and a new flag was sought to replace the military looking provisional flag. The new flag that was chosen represents the Zia sun symbol, loosely copied from a Zia Pueblo jar by Dr. Mera, a local physician interested in Native American culture. The stylized face of the sun and the four groups of perpendicular radiating lines are in red and the background saturated yellow. When the design was submitted its creator mentioned that it was of Pueblo Indian inspiration and the colors were the red and gold of Castile (U.S. Department of Commerce 1999:128-129). While the flag represents a state the United States, its design and colors symbolically stand for the two other peoples of New Mexico. While the use of a Pueblo design on a U.S. flag can be seen as a wish to integrate Native Americans into mainstream society it can also be construed as colonial misappropriation of Pueblo culture. Pueblos were forced to accept the inclusion of their identity in New Mexico's marketing policy.

The history of tourism on Pueblo land shows that the tribes gradually distanced themselves from the tour operators intruding on their ceremonies. In true Pueblo fashion this was done in a low-key mode, with ceremonies being staged without the knowledge of outsiders or in locations unknown to them. And if ceremonies are closed to outsiders it is generally done without publicity. The Pueblos, due to their long history of contact with Euro-American invaders, have perfected their secrecy policy while giving the public something to see and experience something considered unique (Lawlor 2006:62). Since they do not advertise themselves as tourist attractions, visitors have to do their own "research" to find the specifics of a feast day or an open ceremony. The cultural

Isleta pueblo (photo by the author).

Taos (photo by the author).

tourist comes for history, heritage, a place, and its people (Smith 2003:29) and is expected to understand rules of conduct, to pay camera fees, and at times entrance fees. The tourist also has to find the location as Pueblos never have signage. The tourist comes to witness ceremonies that take place without a timetable or a host to explain what the viewers see. Questions to the locals seem unwelcome, and often one is made to feel that it is not proper to ask for details.

The only example of a touristic and well visited pueblo is Taos, a UNESCO World Heritage site with regular opening hours, except for unscheduled closures due to internal pueblo affairs such as funerals. The Taos casino is located on the access road. However visitors of the Pueblo do not mention plans to stop at the casino, or prefer not to speak about them. Gambling has after all a negative image in the United States.

It is difficult to determine the influence of cultural tourism on the attendance of casinos. Is the pull factor of casinos strong enough to attract customers to any location, with or without culture? Since almost every advertisement for Pueblo casinos mentions the ancient culture of the people who own the facility, it is believable that culture plays a part in the advertising. The discourse of casino architects certainly mentions culture. The Pueblos provide decorative themes for casino architecture: the pattern of rain-cloud steps and lightning arrows, the colors of adobe, turquoise and coral, the *viga* (rough-hewn beam) ceilings, the typical fireplaces and their masonry benches. For Thalden-Boyd-Emery, architects of the Buffalo Thunder Resort at Pojoaque, the whole design of the building is reminiscent of the organic growth of a traditional adobe construction while the general quality of the construction is in line with the specifications of Hilton, managing the resort. One of the partners of the architectural firm, Chief Boyd is Cherokee and he explains in a video on the firm's website that there is no such thing as a generic "Indian" architecture due to the multiplicity of cultures. The firm has worked with over 50 tribes and the projects "have incorporated expressions of the tribes' culture, traditions and heritage." Moreover Buffalo Thunder is decorated with more than 700 pieces of Native American artwork commissioned for this project (Thalden-Boyd-Emery n.d.). Boosting the visibility of Native artists and transforming the casino resort into an art gallery creates artistic authenticity in line with the Santa Fe Indian market, an event bringing over 175,000 people, definitely cultural tourists, to Santa Fe every August.

The link between cultural tourism and casinos can also be seen in the choice of objects in the casino gift shops. Usually a few high end items are found among an array of traditional and more affordable tourist goods, "affordable mementoes" (Lidchi 2005:41) signifying the Southwest and Indianness. Moreover, the perceived archaic quality of Indian crafts functions in the tourist experience as a primitivist "antidote for modern anxieties" (Mullin 2001:132).

Hyatt Regency Tamaya Resort (photo by the author).

Another example of a cultural themed resort is the luxurious Hyatt Regency Tamaya Resort on Santa Ana land, on the banks of the Rio Grande, north of Albuquerque, managed by Hyatt under Pueblo supervision. The cultural tourist has a Pueblo casino a few miles away, the Santa Ana Star. Tamaya is the ancient name of Santa Ana Pueblo who owns the infrastructure and who outsources the management to Hyatt. The managers have to cooperate with a council of five accomodationist pueblo members for decisions ranging from the placement of trails and golf course fairways, to plantings and decoration to ascertain their appropriateness in relation to Pueblo culture. For Jerry Westenhaver, Managing Director of the resort, the cooperation between the conservative Santa Ana Pueblo and a high end hospitality business has not been easy (Westenhaver interview 2008). Neither has the role of the Pueblo council been an easy one as they have to interact with conservative Santa Ana hardliners who wish, for example, to close the resort at specific times of the year for important Pueblo rituals. As closure is incompatible with the management of a hotel, a compromise has been found. Two additional days of vacation are given to every staff member, to be taken up whenever they wish, on Pueblo feast days, or at any other time, so as to avoid accusations of favoring one religion over another.

The scenery of cultural tourism becomes evident upon arrival at Tamaya. The last miles of the access road from the public highway are narrow and winding in a way that seems unrelated to the topography. At first it may seem that the curves of the road match the placement of the holes of the resort's golf course. However, the

Bronze sculpture representing a Pueblo farmer by Sharon Fullingim, Tamaya Resort (photo by the author).

real reason is the wish of Pueblo elders to avoid places with special significance for clan members (Erlanger 2007). The website of the resort emphasizes the sacredness of the location of the golf course "winding through and around 20 ancient cultural sites" where an "ancient cave [is to be found] next to the 15th tee box" and an "abandoned horse corral off the 17th fairway" (Tamaya Resort). However as is always the case in matters of Pueblo secrecy it is not considered appropriate to request information about the ceremonial role or the clan ownership of specific "places of interest." The cultural tourist wants to know that ancient culture infuses the location and to add to the general feeling of antiquity the landscaping of the grounds and the hewn timber fences are reminiscent of National Park aesthetics and have been chosen in accordance with the Pueblo council.

Are the customers of the Tamaya Resort cultural tourists? In a sense, yes, as many visual and textual elements of the resort are related to the "culture and history of the Tamayame," the ancient name of the inhabitants of Tamaya, now Santa Ana Pueblo (Tamaya Resort n.d.). The architecture of the resort is inspired by Pueblo Revival, the whole resort claims to be the replica of an ancient pueblo, and within the structure, where the pueblo plaza would be, the walls of a large roofless kiva, resembling Chaco Canyon's Great Kiva at Chetro Ketl, encase a swimming pool. The adjoining spa offers beauty treatments with exotic names. In the first years of the hotel they were named after the places where the Santa Ana lived before their present location, *kashe k'atreti, kwisste puu, paak'u* and *tamaya,* today they have been altered to more mainstream spa terminology: spirit path, three sisters salt scrub, ancient drumming. It is unclear whether the Santa Ana wished to discontinue the ancient names or whether the spa customers were unable to pronounce the Santa Ana Keres language.

In a New Age perspective a spa treatment comes close to cultural tourism, especially when the whole array of cultural traits of the resort are taken into account: the museum-like setting of the lobby, the traditional activities from bread-baking to storytelling, the marketing discourse of the hotel centered on Pueblo tradition (Shepherd 2001), and the bronze sculptures of ancient Pueblo farmers adorning the entrance courtyard to the lobby. However, the upscale Tamaya Resort with its quiet expanses of naturally landscaped grounds and the majestic flow of the Rio Grande surrounded by the cottonwood *Bosque* (*i.e.* riverside forest) clashes with the nearby Santa Ana Star Casino with its clanking slot machines and mall-like *muzak* (Lawlor 2006:42). The physical link between the Tamaya resort and Santa Ana's Star Casino is a free shuttle for resort customers who wish to gamble. The resort management, Jerry Westenhaver and Allen Shull, then financial director, are aware that the interests of the gaming customers and the resort customers may clash but the resort caters to tourists, some of them cultural tourists, who stay at Tamaya because of the resort's attractions, but who also want to pursue an interest in gambling (Berthier-Foglar 2010:385-387).

While hard-core cultural tourists balk at visiting Indian casinos there is gliding scale in cultural tourism. The placement of Native artwork, historic artifacts and vintage photographs in most Indian casinos as well as the presence of a curator for their management indicates that the rationale behind the visibility of Native culture goes beyond interior decoration. Culture, and more precisely the lower end of high culture, is definitely part of the branding of Indian Casinos. While the term 'branding' may seem incongruous when speaking of culture, the Southwestern "Indian Country" is marketed through a discourse about ancient culture. The cultural experience of the visitor may not go far beyond the acknowledgment that the discourse exists and that the tourist has validated its existence though his presence. As a matter of comparison the city of Santa Fe boasts an open-air opera, a type of entertainment catering in the United States to the cultural elite. For the non-opera-going tourist public the presence of the opera adds glamour and prestige to the destination. In the case of Native culture, the fact that the casino hospitality businesses have a dominant and very visible cultural theme is thus significant. It seems that while mildly addicted gamblers do not care about their gambling environment, tribal managers want to transform the casinos into upscale destination resorts for tourists with at least an appreciation for cultural tourism.

The only casino that does not visibly attract the cultural tourists is Laguna Pueblo's *Route 66*. As its name implies, it is located on the historic highway, now I-40 and draws upon an antiquated road imagery harking back to the 1950s. It has, however, a small exhibit room at the main entrance devoted to traditional

Laguna's Route 66 casino (photo by the author).

high quality crafts showcased in the manner of museum exhibits like a downscaled version of an exhibit in the Indian Pueblo Cultural Center in Albuquerque.

On I-25 (and South-North highways along the Rio Grande, 84 and 68 from Santa Fe to Taos):
Isleta Gaming Palace (Isleta Pueblo)
Sandia Casino (Sandia Pueblo)
Santa Ana Star Casino (Santa Ana Pueblo, the Hyatt Regency Tamaya Resort is close to the casino)
San Felipe Casino Hollywood (San Felipe Pueblo)
Camel Rock Casino (Tesuque Pueblo)
Cities of Gold Casino (Pojoaque Pueblo)
Buffalo Thunder Casino and Resort (Pojoaque Pueblo)
Santa Clara Hotel Casino (Santa Clara Pueblo)
Big Rock Casino (Santa Clara Pueblo)
Ohkay Casino Resort (San Juan Pueblo)
Taos Mountain Casino (Taos Pueblo)
On I-40 (East-West):
Dancing Eagle Casino (Laguna Pueblo)
Sky City Casino (Acoma Pueblo)

Table: the 13 Pueblo Indian casinos in Northern New Mexico.

Conclusion

Casinos are part of the attempt of Northern New Mexican Pueblos to achieve economic independence. While casinos are rooted mostly in global popular culture with the overpowering imagery of slot machines, table games, and mainstream entertainment, the Pueblo have managed to introduce a discourse of their own, affirming their independent existence. From the least Indian themed casino, Laguna's Route 66, with only one museum quality display room of historic artifacts, to Pojoaque's Buffalo Thunder's with its 700 original artworks by Native artists, all of the casinos present a vibrant Pueblo culture remaining creative despite the encroachment of mainstream America. Moreover, the gift shops represent a retail outlet for local craftspeople, offering customers a choice of trinkets, crafts, or blue-ribbon style artistic creations. Almost all the new casinos have been built according to Pueblo inspired architecture. While they function for the recreational needs of the surrounding mainstream society, they also represent more than an economic endeavor as they render visible the success of the tribes enabling the creation of a wide variety of jobs, including managerial positions. They also help funding projects that are beneficial to the tribe rather than paying individuals a lump sum.

The advertisement discourse aimed at cultural tourists is prevalent in high end resorts, a finding which is consistent with cultural tourism in general. While gaming is often considered in a negative light by American society, it has a positive effect on Pueblo economy, all the more so since the larger Pueblo casinos branch out into broader touristic ventures offering non-casino attractions such as spas, golf courses, and theater stages. Despite the negative side of gambling addiction affecting tribal members and the general public, Native American casinos contribute to the financial well-being and self-esteem of the tribes and to the economy of the state.

References

Babbitt, Bruce (1997), *Statement of the Secretary of the Interior Bruce Babbitton the New Mexico Gaming Compacts.* Washington, DC: Department of the Interior.

Berthier-Foglar, Susanne (2010), *Les Indiens pueblo du Nouveau-Mexique. De l'arrivée des conquistadorsà la souveraineté des nations pueblo.* Bordeaux : Presses Universitaires de Bordeaux.

Bourke, John Gregory (1884, repr. 1984), *Snake-Dance of the Moquis : One of the Fullest Accounts of HopiRituals Ever Recorded.* Tucson: University of Arizona Press.

Brandt, E.A. (1980), On Secrecy and the Control of Knowledge: Taos Pueblo; in: S. K. Tefft (ed.), *Secrecy: A Cross-Cultural Perspective*, 123-146. New York: Human Science Press.

Bryan, W.L. (2003), Appropriate Cultural Tourism – Can it Exist? Searching for an Answer. Three Arizona Case Studies; in: H. K. Rothman (ed.), *The Culture of Tourism, the Tourism of Culture. Selling the Past to the Present in the American Southwest*, 142-163. Albuquerque, NM: University of New Mexico Press.

Bryant, K.L. (1974), *History of the Atchison, Topeka and Santa Fe Railway*. Lincoln, NE: University of Nebraska Press.

Bsumek, E.M. (2003), Exchanging Places: Virtual Tourism, Vicarious Travel, and the Consumption of Southwestern Artifacts; in: H. K. Rothman (ed.), *The Culture of Tourism, the Tourism of Culture: Selling the Past to the Present in the American Southwest*, 118-139. Albuquerque, NM: University of New Mexico Press.

Clarkson, G. & J. Sebenius (2011), Leveraging Tribal Sovereignty for Economic Opportunity: A Strategic Negotiations Perspective; in: *Missouri Law Review* 76 (4):1046-1112.

Cohen, Felix S. (1941; repr. 1982), *Handbook of Federal Indian Law*. Charlottesville, VA: Michie Bobbs-Merrill.

Deloria, Vine J. & C.M. Lytle (1984), *The Nations Within: The Past and Future of American Indian Sovereignty*. New York: Pantheon Books.

Erlanger, E. (2007), Hyatt's Award-Winning Tamaya Resort Honors a Proud Tradition; in: *Golfing Magazine*: http://www.publinksgolfer.net/.

Espinosa, M.J. (1988), *The Pueblo Indian Revolt of 1696 and the Franciscan Missions in New Mexico: Letters of the Missionaries and Related Documents*. Norman, OK: University of Oklahoma Press.

Fogarty, M. (2014), Native NM tribal area employment under 50 percent; in: *Albuquerque Business First*: http://www.bizjournals.com/albuquerque/.

Glover, V. (2003), Casinos Don't Help Most Indians; in: *Social Education* 67 (5):M14.

Hollinshead, K. (1997), Heritage Tourism under Post-Modernity: Truth and the Past; in: C. Ryan (ed.), *The Tourist Experience*, 170-193. London: Cassell.

IG (2013), 'Ask the Experts,' in: *Indian Gaming* 23 (12):39.

Jacobs, M. D. (1999), *Engendered Encounters: Feminism and Pueblo Cultures, 1879-1934*. Lincoln, NE: University of Nebraska Press.

Indian Gaming (2004-2014), *Indian Gaming: The National Magazine of the American Indian Gaming Industry*. Monthly magazine; Liberty Point, WA: Arrowpoint Media.

Lawlor, M. (2006), *Public Native America: Tribal Self-Representation in Museums, Powwows, and Casinos*. New Brunswick, NJ: Rutgers University Press.

Lidchi, H. (2005), Guilty Pleasures. Selling Indian Arts and Crafts in the American Southwest; in: *European Review of Native American Studies* 19 (1):35-44.

Marshall, J. (1945), *Santa Fe: The Railroad That Built an Empire*. New York: Random.

McCannell, D. (1989), *The Tourist: A New Theory of the Leisure Class*. New York: Schocken Books.

McKercher, B. & H. du Cros (2002), *Cultural Tourism: The Partnership Between Tourism and Cultural Heritage Management*. New York: The Haworth Hospitality Press.

Mullin, M.H. (2001), *Culture and the Marketplace: Gender, Art, and Value in the American Southwest*. Durham: Duke University Press.

Nash, D. (1999), *Indian Gaming*: website: http://www.findlaw.com/.

Parsons, E.C. (1939), *Pueblo Indian Religion*. Lincoln, NE: University of Nebraska Press.

Rothman, H.K. (2003), Introduction: Tourism and the Future; in: H. K. Rothman (ed.), *The Culture of Tourism, the Tourism of Culture: Selling the Past to the Present in the American Southwest*, 1-11. Albuquerque, NM: University of New Mexico Press.

Shepherd, S. (2001), Capitalizing on Culture and Gaming; in: *New Mexico Business Journal*. Webpage visit 12/12/2008 (ceased publication).

Simmons, M. (1991), *The Last Conquistador: Juan de Oñate and the Settling of the Far Southwest*. Norman, OK: University of Oklahoma Press.

Smith, M.K. (2003), *Issues in Cultural Tourism Studies*. New York, Routledge.

State of New Mexico Gaming Control Board (n.d.), *Tribal Revenue Sharing*. http://www.nmgcb.org/tribal/revsharing.html.

Tamaya Hyatt Resort (n.d.), Webpage: http://www.tamaya.hyatt.com/.

Thalden/Boyd/Emery Architects (n.d.), Webpage: http://thaldenboydemery.com/.

Urry, J. (1990, reprint 2002), *The Tourist Gaze*. London, Newbury Park: Sage.

U.S. Department of Commerce (1999), *Regarding Issues Surrounding Trademark Protection for the Official Insignia of Federally-and/or State-Recognized Native American Tribes.* Transcript of Proceedings. U.S. Department of Commerce Patent and Trademark Office. Albuquerque, NM : U.S. Department of Commerce Patent and Trademark Office.

Viarrial, J. (2003), Statement of Jacob Viarrial, Governor of the Pueblo of Pojoaque, State of New Mexico, before the Committee on Indian Affairs, United States Senate, Concerning Difficulties of Negotiating Revenue Sharing Agreements With the State of New Mexico and Use of Gaming Revenues By the Pueblo; Washington, DC: U.S. Senate.

Weber, D.J. (1999), Pueblos, Spaniards, and History; in: D.J. Weber (ed.), *What Caused the Pueblo Revolt of 1680?*: 3-18. Boston: Bedford/St. Martin's.

Williams, R. (1985), *Keywords: A Vocabulary of Culture and Society.* New York: Oxford University Press.

One Type of Boundary[ies]

Native American Jewelry and Santa Fe Indian Market

Bruce Bernstein

In scholarly and popular discourse it is frequently stated or implied that change to Native arts are adaptations to the non-Indigenous world of travelers, souvenir seekers, and art collectors. This has widely resulted in the Native art collected being from a special class of objects produced for art collectors and tourists. Moreover, these objects are more often than not, separated from Native exegesis about their meanings and functions. As a result of settlement and governmental programs, Native peoples are often left with little but to be inventive in finding work and funds, including the playing out of conquers' fantasies about primitive peoples. These insidious, persistent, and damaging preconceived notions and the trinkets, tourist art, and performances put on for outsiders all seem to be constructed, contrived, and maintained because of the colonizers. But on the other hand, Native people may also welcome some of the changes to art forms brought about by tourism and the Indian art market: tools improve art production and new materials and influences expand creativity. While there is little doubt about the oppressive way dominant society has acted toward Native peoples there are nonetheless many ways that Native people can and do make sentient decisions in what they make for outsiders.

What follows is the another side of the story, how people from the San Geronimo tribe[1] in the American Southwest build, maintain, and defend the Native American art market, particularly as it surrounds production of Indian jewelry and participation in the renowned Santa Fe Indian Market. A recent round of discussions with jewelers has provided clarification of just how and to what lengths they will go to maintain their definition of authenticity, as it pertains to individual jewelers as well as a class of art and craft producers. As this study illustrates in the face of touristic and anthropological celebrity, a number of San Gerominos continue to be active strategists and ingenious cultural politicians.

There is also an assumption that tourism is imposed on passive and powerless people and this invariably brings a loss of agency to those who are the focus of the tourist gaze. While tourism has certainly transformed and challenged the lives of people in many locales such global assumptions about the passivity

1 This is a pseudonym. No further description of San Geronimo is provided to protect their privacy.

of indigenous people vis-a-vis globalizing forces are problematic. In these conversations, authenticity eventually becomes part of the conversation: who defines and maintains authenticity. While Indigenous people's jewelry production is helping to maintain culture and its functions, visitors may see these actions through a nostalgic lens; buying to sooth their desire to shelter the natives (and themselves) from twenty-first century influences.

Here, I pursue a more nuanced understanding of authenticity to better understand its workings. I argue that by considering jewelry in such an expanded field develops a deeper understanding of Native art production as a set of intercultural aesthetic and functional decisions. In addition, jewelry is particularly ripe for closer examination because it is made both for Native use and to sell to non-Native people. It is no surprise then that the jewelry subtext, too, is ready for a closer reading and analysis since as jewelers address one issue they may in fact be using it as mis-direction. By playing to non-Native generalities and sentimentalities the jewelers can control discourse. It is within the subtext of this discussion that the truest meanings of Southwest jewelry may be identified. Additionally, this mis-direction is intended to build and sustain a boundary around the discussion's ownership. As a result jewelry and the discussions that surround it are continually crossing and erasing artificial boundaries of utilitarian/art and made for sale/made for home use, as well as art and craft distinctions that may chimerically guide the non-Native interpretation and understanding of Native made art.

We think of globalization as hegemonic in its spread of western goods and ideas around the world. Until recently, many anthropologists, curators, art historians, and collectors dismissed the authenticity of tourist art, the art made by indigenous people (MacCannell 1989). According to Phillips and Steiner (1999:10) scholars were reluctant to consider objects authentic unless they were functional, "made for home use." It follows then, to suggest that Native American art producers may have little or no interest, or authority, in maintaining an ethnic art market. Often, these markets, too, are part of a colonialist structure, part of patron-client relationship that defines much of Indian peoples' relationship with the non-Indian world over several centuries. In what follows I demonstrate how imposed definitions of authenticity can come to be adopted and used by a Native community in its own self-identification and how the embrace of inauthentic materials are enabling Southwest tribes to commoditize and simultaneously continue their own art traditions. Moreover, the sardonic truth of the matter is that the tables are being turned on the non-Indian, on the very people who inevitably believe they are the dominant party in the relationship. As discussed below, it is really the Other keeping the Other.

The Southwest Indian Jewelry Market

Santa Fe is one of the largest art markets in the United States.[2] Native arts in particular are a dominant part of this market, whether historic Indian art sold in galleries and art fairs[3] or the infinite varieties of Native arts produced by local tribes; Indian people from other parts of North American who moved to the region because of the vibrant Indian art scene; and the Institute of American Indian Arts, the preeminent Native arts college that has producing Indian artists since 1962. Within this group are the Indian or Native jewelers. Jewelry made from silver and turquoise is widely identified as Southwestern Indian jewelry and widely recognized with Navajo and Pueblo peoples and their cultural arts, today any American Indian tribal member from anywhere in North America might be identified as an Indian jeweler.

A distinctive factor of Southwest Indian jewelers is that they make jewelry for their own use and to sell to non-Indians. People wear jewelry every day as well as in the numerous dances and ceremonies that punctuate the calendar. Unlike fifty years ago, being a jeweler today is usually a fulltime occupation rather than something one does to supplement an income or farming. In the Southwest there are many categories of jewelers, mostly distinguished by quality of craftsmanship, which, in turn, is reflected in prices. While most produce the relatively less-expensive jewelry easily identifiable as Southwestern and Indian, there is an elite class of jewelers who are highly individualized, and usually more expensive.[4] The most distinguished jewelers might sometimes make a high-end

---

2 "The New Mexico Department of Cultural Affairs commissioned report, *Building on the Past, Facing the Future: Renewing the Creative Economy* quantifies the current economic impact of arts and cultural industries in New Mexico and identifies challenges and key opportunities. The study, conducted by the UNM's Bureau of Business and Economic Research (BBER), reveals a $5.6 billion impact on the state's economy and challenges business, government, and non-profit sectors to harness strengths and address key shortfalls to fully realize economic potential.
Arts and cultural industries in New Mexico enjoy a national reputation that is far beyond the state's size or economic standing. Narrowly defined, these industries employ 43,031 persons in New Mexico, equal to 1 of every 18 jobs in the state (5.5%). More broadly defined, including persons employed in cultural tourism, art and cultural education, and industries linked to the unique culture and heritage of the state, the arts and cultural industries employ 76,780 persons, equal to nearly one in ten jobs (9.8%) in the state. That is more than the state's construction and manufacturing industries combined" (http://www.newmexicoculture.org/about/cultures-impact accessed on April 6, 2015).

3 Santa Fe has a vibrant gallery scene that includes all types of art. While the total number of Native art galleries has dropped due the recent recession and changing collector acquisition patterns, there are still a significant number of permanent, quality galleries. These galleries continue to mount exhibition sales for the artists they represent. The Indian art market is generally divided between historic and contemporary Native art, galleries reflect this division, as do private and public collections. During August there are presently two large antique American Indian art shows where a few hundred dealers from throughout the US set up. Thousands of people attend these sales events. Mobile devices, email, and social media make Native artists continually available, where once phones were scarce and Indian Market was the one time of year one might meet some Native artists.

4 In recent years there is an increasing number of laudatory books on some of these jewelers: Cirillo (2008); S. Dubin (2002, 2014); Pardue (2007); Bahti (2008); Schaaf (2003, 2012, 2013); and Struever (2005). The mix of commerce and scholarship influences who is and who is not written about; see M. Dubin (2001) and Lidchi (2015).

and low-end product, the type of jewelry produced and subsequently purchased discriminating between tourist, collector and art collector, bringing into play a hierarchical scale of connoisseurship linked to class. Here, discussions will focus on the less individualized forms, the middle and lower price jewelry. However, whether expensive or cheap souvenir all purchasers are concerned with authenticity; specifically defined as being made by an Indian person.

Tourism in the American Southwest increased in the late nineteenth and early twentieth century and with it an interest in the areas first residents (Lidchi 2015; Weigle 1989). Collecting souvenirs began with the first visitors, but items specifically directed at tourists existed by 1880 (Batkin 2008).[5] In response to this demand, new tools as well as sheet silver and pre-cut cabochons became widely available, along with new design iconography and forms. Of course there were trends and souvenir items that rankled the purists, but these were primarily social class distinctions because while new or non-traditional items such Navajo serving sets and place settings were encouraged, tourist knick-knacks such as small spoons and snuffboxes were not. "Oliver LaFarge objected to the type of workshop run by [Santa Fe based trader, Julius] Gans and worked to preserve the 'primitive' and 'traditional' character of production methods by establishing 'standards of genuineness' and a governmental run Indian Arts and Crafts Board in the 1930s" (Bsumek 2008:36). By the 1920s buyers made the distinction by paying more for "pawn" or heavier jewelry than the newer-style, lighter tourist-oriented products.[6] Historic jewelry is sometimes viewed as more authentic because it is associated with the past when a truer and more authentic Indian jeweler might work without the distractions of tourists and traders. In the past, there was some use of non-Native materials such as early plastics, phonograph records and car battery casings too, until recently derided in the Indian arts market for their inauthentic use of materials. Fortunately, exhibitions and publications are more properly contextualizing the creative use of these materials (Kline 2015).

By the 1920s to help satiate the demand for Indian jewelry, manufacturing businesses were established (Bsumek 2008:190-207; see also Batkin 2008). Small and large shops, the establishments used assembly line production: several jewelers, sometimes Native and sometimes not, working together, each person performing one step in making of the item: cutting, shaping, setting the stone, polishing. The quality of stones varied quite substantially and the sheet silver thinness was unmistakable. The designs and therefore the finished look of the

---

5 The region's art tourism and Indian jewelry is been well documented by Batkin (2008); Bernstein (1999, 2012); Brody (1971; 1998); Bsumek (2008), and Mullin (2001).

6 Pawn is a system of using jewelry as loan collateral primarily associated in the pre-1970 Navajo reservation era where local people would pawn their jewelry to trade for necessary goods during the winter months, purchasing it back once spring lambing and shearing season earned the owners cash. For more about traders see McNitt (1962); Willow Powers (2001); Southwest Indian Development (1968). Traders' accounts of the pawn system can be found in Kennedy (2009) and Hegemann (2004).

Navajo silversmith demonstrating at the Gallup Inter-Tribal Ceremonial, ca. 1930. The myth of the solitary jeweler working alone is reinforced in this staged demonstration and photo-opportunity (courtesy of the Library of Congress, LC-USZ62-99523).

jewelry is identifiable and is mostly unambiguously different from handmade pieces. Many village-based jewelers also employed albeit smaller but nonetheless assembly line processes. The critical difference in identifying authenticity was the knowable Indian jeweler as compared a faceless manufacturing business owned by non-Natives in Gallup, Albuquerque, Santa Fe, Phoenix and Denver.[7] The authenticity of materials is more rarely mentioned, most likely because there were sufficient amounts of turquoise and silver for all. Nineteen-thirties US governmental programs were the first to try and provide a consistent way to differentiate authentic handmade jewelry from the jewelry produced by manufacturing techniques. For the first time, the names of jewelers provided authenticity.

This was perhaps the last time the market was so proscriptive for its makers. Beginning in the 1960s, Hopi jeweler Charles Loloma through his inventive jewelry encouraged the use of diverse materials (Struever 2005). Following on his work, over the next two decades there was an expansion of new materials considered acceptable for use in contemporary Indian jewelry but not for traditional Indian jewelry (Monthan 1975; Cirillo 2008; Pardue 2007). Since that time, what Native jewelers make has exponentially grown, incorporating

7 Many well-known jewelers worked in these businesses too (see: Bsumek (2008); and Batkin (2008).

influences, tools, and materials from around the world. Nonetheless, descriptions of an item being traditional or non-traditional and contemporary or traditional persist.

Finally, a deeply insidious and negative type of jewelry is infiltrating the Southwest and continues to drive change and undermine the authority of Indian people about their art form: the fakes and imitations made overseas and sold through a multitude of stores in Gallup, Phoenix, Scottsdale, and Santa Fe. These businesses consistently undercut the prices possible for any handmade article, taking sales from Native jewelers. These gift stores began appearing in Santa Fe in the late 1990s and today more than eighty of these gift shops surround Santa Fe's historic plaza. Business practices are difficult to discern, but many if not all of the stores are owned by just a few people and primarily operated by chain-smoking, aggressive young men from the Middle East. The stores are brightly lit and overflowing with goods and mirrored walls and cases filled with foreign made jewelry and pottery, most in imitation of Southwest Native arts and crafts.[8]

Southwest Indian Jewelry and Santa Fe Indian Market

Traditional jewelry is defined by the use of time honored materials and manufacturing techniques, and, increasingly, certain forms and styles. Silver, turquoise and coral are widely considered to be the traditional materials. There is also a long tradition of using shells in Southwest jewelry; coral however is a relative new comer, being adapted from the Spanish by the late eighteenth, early nineteenth centuries. The use of silver is also not aboriginal to the Southwest. Turquoise however is unique to the American Southwest and for many millennia has been used by it indigenous peoples. Southwest Indian silver smithing is initially based on blacksmithing technologies, Navajo and Zuni men being the first to work in silver (Adair 1944).[9]

This is a living art form and no set of written rules govern the making of Indian jewelry. However, the US Government and other advocate organizations have tried to protect the commerce of Indian jewelers from the counterfeiters and non-Indian imitators (Bsumek 2008:190-207). The United States government agency the Indian Arts and Crafts Board (IACB) puts out a set of guidelines but primarily about the marketing of authentic Indian arts: "Under the Indian Arts and Crafts Act of 1990 (P.L. 101-644), as amended, it is illegal to offer or display for sale, or sell, any art or craft product in a manner that falsely suggests it is

8 This insidious problem continues to grow. Local and state government demonstrates little resolve to support Native people and their indigenous products from these foreign counterfeits. http://alibi.com/news/44863/Faux-Native.html and http://legalnewsline.com/news/215748-new-mexico-ag-targets-fake-native-american-jewelry, accessed April 4, 2015.

9 See John Adair's 1944 *Navajo and Pueblo Silversmiths*. Although others have written about the origins of silversmithing in the Southwest, Adair's original fieldwork and interviews remain the most authoritative source.

American Indian produced, an American Indian product, or the product of a particular American Indian Tribe." Under Federal law, "Authentic Indian art and craft" means any art and craft product, including traditional or contemporary, that is made with Indian labor.[10] Unlike the IACB, Indian Market has sought to define and canonize what is Indian jewelry. Beginning in the 1970s these rules became lengthier and more detailed; attempting to sanctify what is and is not considered Indian made jewelry, as well as guidelines for interpreting authenticity. All of the Indian Market rules focus on items being hand-made.

Globalization has brought to the Native jewelry world a plethora of materials and techniques. In addition, there is an increasing use of plastic imitation material or block, and pre-made, pre-drilled beads. Most, if not all of these materials and technologies are far beyond the boundaries of iconic turquoise and silver and the overriding emphasis on the handmade. In New Mexico jewelry supply houses stock literally hundreds of styles of pre-made, pre-drilled beads and precious and imitation stones. Some jewelers purchase these components and merely assemble them to make Indian jewelry. But more virulent is the numerous block or plastic materials sold as turquoise or other stone substitutes. These are nothing more than colored sand and epoxy. It is of course cheaper and easier to work with. A long time jewelry supplier told me "It is like slicing bologna." He continued, people now "purchase plastic and stones because they are turquoise and orange colored" rather than because they are made of coral or turquoise. To continue, it is also a matter of economics. A piece of block is less than $100 and can, for example be made into about 120 pairs of earrings while real turquoise might be over $2000 for the same amount and make about 40 pairs of earrings.[11]

A unique and direct result of Southwest tourism and interest in Native cultures is the Santa Fe Indian Market.[12] The Southwestern Association for Indian Arts (SWAIA) is the 95-year old parent organization that most famously plans, develops and stages the world-renowned Santa Fe Indian Market each August. One hundred and fifty thousand people attend the Market, enjoying the work of over 1000 artists as well as multiple venues for film, literature, food, music, fashion, and traditional clothing. Fourteen city blocks around the city's historic core are filled with artist booths and stages. It is a time of year that also includes hundreds of gallery and museum openings, fundraisers and benefits for all kinds of Indian organizations, and private and public parties. In

---

10 http://www.iacb.doi.gov, accessed March 31, 2015. "The Indian Arts and Crafts Board (IACB) promotes the economic development of American Indians and Alaska Natives of federally recognized Tribes through the expansion of the Indian arts and crafts market. The IACB provides promotional opportunities, general business advice, and information on the Indian Arts and Crafts Act to Native American artists, craftspeople, businesses, museums, and cultural centers of federally recognized Tribes. Additionally, the IACB operates three regional museums, conducts a promotional museum exhibition program, produces a *"Source Directory of American Indian and Alaska Native Owned and Operated Arts and Crafts Businesses"*, and oversees the implementation of the Indian Arts and Crafts Act."

11 Personal communication, Jeff Lewis, Trade Routes Collection, May 2009.

12 See Bernstein (2008 and 2012).

Indian Market 2009. Tens of thousands of people come to the annual August event specifically to purchase Southwest Native jewelry. Customers have confidence that they are buying authentic jewelry because of the oversight provided by SWAIA (photo by the author).

the booths at Indian Market is the remarkable array of who Indian people are today. There are some booths that have five to six generations of self-taught, legacy or traditional family members and right next to it might be a university-trained artist. An extraordinary part of the Market is that it is all first person voice: artists represent and sell their own work. It is the proverbial cacophony, unbridled, unedited, and free and open to the public. Indian Market does not make rules for any other markets other than its own two-day annual event. Nonetheless, Indian Market has an enormous effect on the Indian arts market, most notably, jewelry. People use and quote Indian Market rules both real and imaginary. The rules are not created in a vacuum. Indian Market creates rules in reaction to what jewelers do. It can take as long as two years from the time a new idea or art form is seen at Indian Market to be sanctified by its rules.

Each artist is vetted or juried into Indian Market. Artists are required to submit images of recent work that is then vetted by a panel of experts and their peers for authentic use of materials and manufacturing.[13] Non-allowable

13 As a way to understand the heightened tension about who is allowed into market and who is not, allow me to provide two examples. In the mid-2000s a jeweler appeared on the scene who used computerized cad drawings and new (to Indian Market) metals such as stainless steel and titanium. The legions of Indian Market faithful decried his participation because he was not an Indian jeweler. He is enrolled member of an American Indian tribe and therefore an Indian as defined by the United States Government. For this reason he was allowed into Indian Market. There is no lessening of outrage from the traditionalists that claim he should not be participating in Indian Market. However, his followers and collectors claim him as antidote to the stultifying rules that hold Indian people in a paternal death-grip, forcing them to live in the past. Another jeweler was rejected from the Market because it was widely rumored that he employed Mexican silversmiths to help him produce his jewelry. Experts claimed that no one could make so much jewelry without assistance.

Customers purchasing jewelry at Santa Fe Indian Market, 1994. The table includes only handmade and natural turquoise jewelry. Because of the time and effort it takes to make this type of jewelry, the vendor's table is not over flowing with merchandise (courtesy of SWAIA).

materials are very few except the use of plastic imitation materials and mass production techniques such as centrifugal casting. Aesthetics is rarely mentioned. If accepted for participation the exhibitor agrees to abide by the rules of the Market. To ensure that exhibitors are following the rules and that customers can trust their Indian Market as authentic, during the Indian Market event, every booth is evaluated. Jewelers' booth evaluations focus on materials, particularly plastic imitation turquoise and pre-made or manufactured beads and other jewelry components. It is a tedious process but intended to protect the integrity of the Market and to help educate and ensure buyers they are purchasing genuine and authentic Indian arts. In addition, booth evaluation can be contentious because of its basic assumption: "Is what the exhibitor selling authentic Indian art?" Market's employees and volunteers are placed in an intermediating role. If a jeweler uses a cheap, substitute material, for example, and it turns a wearer's wrist or neck a purple or blue or the blue stone disintegrates soon after purchase, buyers might think Indian jewelry as cheap and inauthentic and/or the Indian Market as place of deceptive business practices.

Indian Market justifies its rules by suggesting that they protect integrity and quality in jewelry. But the reality is that these plastic and pre-made materials are increasingly being included by Indian Market jewelers in their handmade work. Certainly one could make a case that jewelry making today is an evolving, living art form; therefore, nothing like these newer materials were available forty or fifty years ago when Indian Market rules where first written down. With globalization the pace of change is also continually increasing. Some rules are more malleable than others. For example, Southwest jewelers for centuries have hand-drilled their beads, so in the Indian Market definition of twenty-first century jewelry there is a requirement that hand drilling continues. However, it makes no difference if they are drilled with a pump-drill, hand drill, or a power drill, they just need to be drilled by the artist. This rule also ignores that some hand-drilling is done on contract for a jeweler, or the shell material might be imported from the Philippines. Does having someone else make your beads that are then incorporated into the piece constitute assembly? Since the beads are hand-drilled, aka traditionally made, this practice receives nothing more than a wink.

Indian Market rules dictate the materials and techniques that artists may use in producing work to be sold at Indian Market. Rules are about craftsmanship and material rather than aesthetics. Today's rules allow most jeweler's techniques and materials. However, as recently as thirty years ago the rules were highly proscriptive with a list of "Allowed" and "Not-Allowed" materials being researched, compiled and modified each year by a committee known alternatively as the Standards or Indian Market committee. From about 1975-2005, primarily three individuals who were board members and volunteers presided over these discussions for SWAIA. At first the rules were highly restrictive, allowing few natural stones other than turquoise. However, as interest in Indian jewelry expanded and access to materials changed, authenticity became a topic of heated discussion. The Committee's work primarily focused on stabilized turquoise, which at first designated a poor quality turquoise stone with an epoxy binder. But today there are many varieties of stabilized turquoise; some using the lowest quality stone, which when combined with increasingly sophisticated technology can produce deceptively natural looking stone. In addition, the use of stabilized turquoise is driven by turquoise becoming scarcer. Some mines are tapped out except for this lower quality stone.[14] Further, as other natural stones became more and more available the rules were adjusted to accommodate them. There is a natural assumption that all of the jewelers can tell the differences of the quality of stone available to them, along with begin able to distinguish the different types of stabilized turquoise. The highly proscriptive Indian Market rules persisted for thirty years until the organization's staff deemed all materials allowable doing away with lists and fraught conversations of authentic and inauthentic,

14 Interest in turquoise has risen along with its scarcity. The jewelry market over the past twenty years has begun to emphasize the source of turquoise to accent its authenticity. Books on the subject seem to be proliferating: Lowry and Lowry (2010); Emmerling and Arndt (2011); Osburn (2012); McBrinn and Aschulter (2015).

Indian Market 2009. This Native vendor is not an Indian Market exhibitor, but is set up adjacent to the annual market to give the impression that her booth is part of Indian Market and therefore selling authentic and Native made jewelry. The booth includes no Native made jewelry and all of the turquoise is blue plastic or poor quality stabilized turquoise (photo by the author).

Window display of one of Santa Fe gift shops selling Indian-style jewelry. The necklaces were probably made in Asia or the Middle East. The ceramic figures too, are copies of hand-built Pueblo pottery (photo by the author).

contemporary and traditional, and innovative and traditional.[15] However there were two rules not dropped -rules prohibiting the use of manufactured or plastic based Block, in imitation of turquoise and coral; and the use of pre-drilled beads and jewelry components.

Evidence: Interrogating Authenticity

To assure quality and compliance with rules every artist in Indian Market is monitored beginning with requiring artist applications and concluding with photographs of every artist's booth at Indian Market.[16] The increasingly widespread use of pre-made components and use of plastic imitation materials was viewed as undermining the quality and integrity of Indian Market artists resulted of an especially intensive 2009 artist review process. In this review the use of pre-made beads and block came under closer scrutiny. Additionally, staff wanted to signify Native made jewelry from the counterfeits being sold in some Santa Fe stores.

As one step in this process, a meeting with jewelers was organized to assess these issues and how rules might be adjusted to better reflect current day jewelry making. Through inclusion of the practitioners, the meeting was intended to be educational; it was expected that the tone was to be amongst peers, a learning environment. But regardless of hours of preparation the meeting turned antagonistic and heated in a very short amount of time.

In 2009 when these discussions took place there were 370 Indian Market jewelers. Following a review of the booth photographs taken at that year's Indian Market of all jewelers 80 were selected to attend a mandatory meeting because of their obvious use of pre-made and/or imitation materials.[17] Sixty of the 80 jewelers who received notices were from San Geronimo.[18] No tribe was singled out to receive these notices; however, given the preponderance of stone and cut

15 These rules were heavily modified and then dropped over a three-year span, 2008-2011. Changes were part of a larger organizational shift to better represent the exhibitors as they are rather than as nostalgia and SWAIA Indian Market might imagine them to be. It was a simple and straightforward trajectory. Artists would use materials all year except for Indian Market; Market merely needed to catch up with the jewelers to understand the sense it made to drop this highly restrictive set of anachronistic rules. The shift to representing modern jewelers was facilitated by removing nostalgic-driven artists who participated in the organization Indian Market committee.

16 The evaluation of an exhibitor's work is as old as the Market itself. In the first years, every piece was evaluated before it was placed on indoor exhibition tables. Once the event moved outside, curators and anthropologists walked down the row of artists, reviewing all work, and placing a small sticker or stamp on the work that met the rules of the Market. The art police were created in the 1970s to go booth to booth. They would report back to the committee following Indian Market. Digital photography allowed a new and more accurate way to evaluate booths. Initiated in 2009 every participant's display was imaged and reviewed by staff and artist peers.

17 This was not a capricious review, but a number of experts including artists, curators and jewelry suppliers reviewed the images. Block can be obvious to spot due to its even and intense blue coloration while other materials are more difficult to distinguish. The 80 jewelers included obvious violators and potential problems.

18 This is a pseudonym. No further description is provided to protect their anonymity.

stone, and drilled stone used by the San Geronimos they were more susceptible to use of these manufactured materials.

The meeting was held in a local hotel meeting room. About 100 people from San Geronimo attended and about ten SWAIA staff, board and volunteers also were there. SWAIA was told that "San Geronimo jewelry is a handmade product; the handmade beads are 100% original to the continent.... [and that] These people bring nothing but the best." The meeting continued in a downward trajectory, "...it is always San Geronimo that is being singled out and flagged when it is other tribes who are mimicking [copying] San Geronimo." These other tribes who borrowed and are making this jewelry clearly could not know or follow the same principles as us [San Geronimos]." To add credibility to their claim, village members suggested that "San Geronimos are the original: we were at the first Indian Market, [we] invented jewelry making in the Southwest.... In the face of great adversity, San Geronimo has worked to maintain their traditions."[19]

Quieter individuals stated that using these plastic and pre-made materials "is an issue and you need to help us," insinuating that some jewelry supply dealers were responsible since they are the ones supplying the materials. Others in the room picked up this idea, "Outsiders make this difficult; we trusted outsiders and showed them our traditions. In return they sold us fake materials and took our jewelry making process.... We... are just trying to defend and uphold our traditions while others take these shortcuts. Then we San Geronimos must defend ourselves against these others, in the face of these others, when we have done nothing wrong.... It is wrong to target San Geronimo, we are a proud people. We know our culture and we abide by the rules."

Following the meeting, SWAIA's Director of Artist Services observed that the "most dedicated did show up for the meeting, while the most serious violators had not contacted SWAIA," suggesting that some well understood that the use of plastic and pre-made parts is not acceptable in Indian Market. He made the additional observation that not everyone spoke at the meeting: "the most vocal [at the meeting] didn't even receive letters." Although the letters have been mailed to individuals, the content of the letter was shared more broadly throughout the tribe. From comments at the meeting it was clear it was discussed with the tribal government and that this matter was being interpreted as an affront to the tribe. One tribal councilman attended the meeting; his attendance was assumed because he received a letter because of his use of plastic block. Interestingly, the letters had the right effect on the worst violators who did not show up for the meeting, or apply for Indian Market over the next few years.

19 All quotations from the meetings are from meeting transcripts in possession of SWAIA and notes by the author.

The meeting ended more positively than it began; the most constructive outcome being the scheduling of a follow-up meeting the next week. The follow-up meeting was less formal; no further correspondence or invitations were sent. Only six San Geronimo people attended the next meeting, most from San Geronimo believed the matter to be closed; they had united and successfully defended themselves from what they perceived to be false accusations.

The six San Geronimo women who came to the second meeting had all attended the previous week's meeting. They came on their own, without tribal leadership permission; therefore they represented only themselves and not the village.[20] Cultural proscription is that women should not discuss San Geronimo with the outside world. Although jewelry is public and made for the outside world, nonetheless, talking about any cultural aspect to non-tribal members is absolutely forbidden, particularly by women. In addition, representing themselves was a violation of the secrecy and insular manner in which the tribe is run and maintained.

Significantly, it was revealed during the second meeting that one of their officials was planning a meeting to develop a response to SWAIA,[21] making the women's presence as tribal members ever the more perilous. This official was one of the jewelers who received a letter; so his motivation to call the meeting might be further interrogated. At the larger meeting, which he attended, he belligerently declared that he made every bead used in his necklaces. All the while whispers could be overheard in the room from the other San Geronimo jewelers that this man "had never made a coral bead in his life," and "that he couldn't made a bead to save himself." Rivalry between people and families can be rife in the tribe. Jewelers frequently speak poorly of other jewelers' materials or manufacturing techniques (or lack thereof) in order to differentiate their work as authentic and not inconsequentially, better their sales.

Analytically, one could suggest that San Geronimo divided into at least two factions over the issues brought up by SWAIA. One group denied any culpability and refused to take any responsibility, relying on anger and loud voices to make their point. The other faction worked more quietly, conversationally demonstrating an understanding of the rules and a comprehension of why SWAIA is intent on enforcing them. These were largely along gender lines. The men, led by the tribal official as mentioned above were predominantly belligerent. As it turned out the meeting being called by the men was to be an "official" meeting intended to displace and deflect blame to the principal turquoise and coral supplier to the tribe, a non-Indian. In contrast, the women who attended the committee meeting demonstrated some acquiescence and admission of violating the standards, as well as a desire for more information.

20 The norm in these situations is that permission must be granted from the tribal government to speak to non-tribal members. In addition, because the jewelers were being asked to talk about something cultural they were required to have the proper permission from their government.

21 No tribal response was received by SWAIA.

The Indian Market Committee had selected a non-Indian woman jeweler as moderator for the meeting with the jewelers. She quickly lost control of the meeting, voices and tempers escalating. The Native committee and Board members stood with their backs against the walls on the sides of the room, seemingly enjoying watching their appointee stumble and unintentionally offend the Native jewelers. But soon Native board and committees began voicing their opinions, at first appearing in solidarity with the other Native people in the room. However, soon these SWAIA representatives were arguing with San Geromino jewelers about what constitutes authentic Indian jewelry with the threat that they would be "thrown out of Indian Market unless you follow my…I mean, our rules".

Almost all jewelry production is focused on sales to non-Indians and broadly published in books and articles, which is in contrast to their usual persona of cultural conservatism and endogamy. In addition, sales buy community members' cars, TVs, and other modern conveniences. San Geronimo sales are very much dependent on selling their jewelry as authentic or the most Indian of all jewelry. A well-respected second generation Indian arts dealer tells me stories about how San Geronimo women who sell on the streets of Santa Fe feign their ignorance of English, all the time chatting with friends in English on their cell phones.[22] One experiences the posturing of sales to fit the notions of potential customers while maintaining their self-proclaimed role as proprietor and protector of the authentic.

Discussed here is not an art form created to satisfy tourists or the need for developing a means to enter the broader cash-based economy. Rather, Southwest jewelry is a several thousand-year-old tradition that is continually remade through new forms and materials. It is no surprise that new materials are being incorporated. The purpose of this discussion is not to lament the introduction of these new materials. Rather, the purpose here is to report on their use and sometimes mis-representation of their use as something unchanging and traditional. For some jewelers there might be a total denial of their use, others claim that their suppliers (non-Natives) have deceived them.

The jewelers may seem at cross-purposes with themselves. Unkindly, the meetings demonstrated that they are constructing and helping in maintaining authenticity standards and widely circulated definitions of Indian jewelry that are based on false information. Also clear is that some of the jewelers take a shortcut to maintain an appearance of authenticity, believing that most consumers do not know the difference. Our conclusion here, however, is more inclusive, the jewelers understand their market: buying from a Native person is the primal and most critical act in maintaining authenticity.

22 Personal communication, September 2009.

There is no culprit or sucker in this story; this is not about "got-you," or a revealing exposé but rather one of descriptive ethnography to understand a deeply nuanced and layered interaction sphere. Perhaps this is a narrative of desirability and access, and maintaining a viable market share. In addition, the San Gerominos know their customers and are acting on this to not lose their market share. When approached by the outside they adamantly stand their ground because only San Geronimos are permitted to describe San Geronimo.

In actuality, considering Native made jewelry as authentic, tribal, or primitive is a nonstarter. It is an antiquated bit of thinking just as would be the use of the word "hybridity" because, quite simply, everything in living cultures is a combining of ideas, forms, and materials. At a recent public ceremony I noted jewelry, made of plastic materials worn by many of the dancers, while clothing adhered to long-used standards of materials (cotton and wool).[23] The use of cotton in Southwestern ceremonialism is well documented because of its association with fertility and its metaphoric symbology of clouds. The color turquoise too has deep cultural values and meanings and it may be startling to see blue plastic look-alike turquoise replacing turquoise stone. What we do not know is how, potentially, the use of color can maintain inner meanings.

The SWAIA participation in both meetings included artists and Indian art experts who serve on Indian Market's rules committees. The committee's artist members in particular are largely among a group that believes that Indian Market should return to its origins and be more traditional. One committee member from Jemez said, "too bad, they brought this on to themselves." He and another committee member from Ohkay Owingeh continued to bemoan the jewelers' lack of traditionality and how their work was "no longer Indian art." By being brash, singling out, and removing violators from the Market they intended to demonstratively exhibit that as the members of Indian Market board and committee their views of authenticity were immutable and more accurate. And, again, if exhibitors refused to abide by rules and their unwritten subtext of maintaining authenticity, then they would be removed from participation. Native committee and Board members believed it their responsibility to uphold and defend traditional Indian art. Moreover, these two board and committee members were part of a faction that over a period of a decade sought to control every aspect of Indian Market. They are a bit like creationists or absolutists, believing in an unassailable and timeless definition of tradition, defined by historic artwork and forms only. At play is the definition of authenticity, which

23 Comparing cotton with wool embroidery dance regalia and jewelry seems a pertinent example. Cotton was once grown and woven into cloth by people but today cotton cloth used for dance kilts and mantas is almost exclusively made in factories and purchased. Perhaps people decried this change, but documentation suggests because of the gradualness of the change it did not produce as much critic (see Kent 1983). On the other hand perhaps this example suggests something different; because although the materials changed the essential designs on these garments have not changed in nearly one thousand years.

meaning is followed and, following that, who then defends authenticity. Of the SWAIA representatives in attendance they were the loudest and most vocal.

At both meetings, people wanted to know if all San Geronimo jewelers received the letter and why their tribe was being targeted. They then began to press that there were other violators in Market and they too needed to be investigated. They didn't need to say it out loud but the correct assumption is that they were now complaining about Navajo people and their jewelry. Again, while on the surface the discussion was about rules, it was actually a discourse on who is more traditional than whom. As mentioned above, San Geronimo people took the position that they are the original Indian Market families and they are the preservers of Native-made jewelry for Indian Market. In addition, by singling out Navajo people they were using the position of Pueblo people more generally as the first Indian Market participants and Puebloan concerns about Navajo craft people's proclivity to replicating other tribal art forms. In this way the San Geronimo use their reputation for conservatism to distinguish the work of their community members.

San Geronimo words and posture toward the outside world serves them well. San Geronimo is vigorously insular. By drawing boundaries around their culture and physical world, outsider perceptions have little effectiveness. It doesn't matter that San Geronimo people were prohibited by their own government from participating in the first decades of Indian Market when they claim to have been the first Indian Market participants. In place of objective facts they have engaged words as boundaries, constructing an impermeable world of tradition to uphold their version of authenticity. Being called out for taking shortcuts and replacing traditional materials with fake materials (plastics) is clearly an affront to their constructed persona. The fact that members of their tribe make the jewelry means it is Indian made and needs no further parsing. If they were disallowed from participating in Indian Market, SWAIA would be saying they were not Indian or Indian-enough to participate in Indian Market. Additionally, Indian Market is an outside entity, always perceived to be non-Native in its work and function, regardless of the composition of Indian Market staff, board, committee and volunteers it is never an "Indian" organization.

The Results: Two Parts Authenticity, Two Parts Tradition and a Pinch of Reality

Indian Market is a wonderfully large and visible project that is blamed for any variety of ills including keeping the "Indian" in Indian art. Indeed, many believe that Indian Market created and maintains the Indian art ethnic boundary. Just recently, a potter was quoted as saying that she "needed to get out of Indian Market to be free to create." These are nothing but self-imposed borders, imaginary boundaries that create and maintain the specialized market that is Indian art. The truth is that this potter wanted to sell to a new market and wanted to differentiate herself as being perceived as producing Indian pottery. She believed to do so meant she needed to leave the comfortable confines of Indian Market. Even those artists who don't want to be part of this ethnic art enclave too often describe their work in contrast or opposition to tradition by using such terminology as non-traditional or contemporary. Like the San Geronimo jewelers she is using Indian Market to define herself.

Indian Market is a community, artists and their families come together once a year in a giant gathering that is cooperative and collaborative in the boundaries drawn around the artists and their Market from the outside work. It is a powerful boundary too. Two days each year, Native people are on center stage in the middle of the city that defines a region that they lost to Spanish and American greed, government, disease and warfare.

Money serves as a lubricant: an estimated 18 million dollars' worth of art is sold in two days. There are many different questions that frame the boundary question. Is Indian Art still authentic when made for and sold to non-Indians? How does making something for sale change anything? Is it art or craft, low or highbrow; and just who is an Indian today? The idea that Indian Market is restrictive or a boundary is both truism and contrived; SWAIA and the Market are a convenient scapegoat for most anything having to do with Native produced art. The truth of the matter is, Indian Market artists represent themselves and do whatever they wish. This is not a derisive comment but truthful because it is their Market and there would be no Market without the artists.

SWAIA's rules about tradition are intended to protect and preserve an authenticity, what is widely implied to be a set of art practices that pre-date European settlement, having been practiced from time immemorial in an unchanged fashion. Regardless of our discussion here, traditional arts in the Native world continue because they are necessary and possess a positive value as culture bearers and standards; material examples of how culture is to look and be performed. Traditional art continues because tradition works; for tradition to work it needs to continually change and adapt. But what does happen when traditional style arts are made primarily for consumption by the outside world?

Art and traditional art are continually moving targets to describe: when does tradition begin, when does it stop, and why are some things traditional and others not? Indian Market is a vast, complex, and nuanced cultural renewal and renovation site. We can only conclude here that there is unassailable permeability and malleability of boundaries; particularly in the Indian art market where they are convenient and forever changing. Despite Indian Market staff and volunteers best intentions, ultimately and compellingly the artists are the authorities. The tradition and authenticity brokers are the artists, not Indian Market.

Additionally, there is a dizzying set of boundaries at play in any discussion about what is Native jewelry. Yes, artists can use authenticity as a sales device. People, collectors as well as artists, love to imagine today's artists are sitting in their ancestors' chairs, working in the same exact fashion. This is not possible.

Today's Santa Fe is ringed with over 80 gift shops selling imitations of Native American made jewelry and pottery. These stores rely on the century long campaign of associating Santa Fe, tourism, and Native Americans (photo by the author).

No one mines his or her own turquoise any longer. Everyone buys their stones from a supplier; everyone uses electrical equipment; everyone uses store bought tools; everyone works at night under electric lights; everyone sells their work for money; and the principal buyers are non-Indians. Authenticity and ethnicity in the art and crafts marketplace is used to divide and separate. And understanding tradition is something deeper and more meaningful than authenticity; it is about a continuity of cultural values and principles rather than products of these time-honored processes.

Ostensibly, Indian Market rules are based upon an ancient set of principles observed and recorded, ensuring buyers that they are buying authentic and traditional Indian jewelry. Authenticity used with Indian art can have a pejorative connotation, suggesting that Indians need to remain somewhere in the past, someplace before, someplace more Indian than Indians appear today. By its very definition the Indian Market seems a perfect vehicle for bordering and dispensing ethnic art; but instead it unspools worlds of limitless and unrecognized horizons and narratives.

The issues of authenticity are tortuous and are further muddled with the numerous perceptions of traditional; stated colloquially, what is and what is not Indian, as well as whom is more Indian than whom. These distinctions are not

WITHOUT RESERVATIONS

Cartoon by Ricardo Cate (Kewa: Santo Domingo Pueblo) from "Without Reservations" series (courtesy of the artist).

ethnic monikers but rather are played out through art making within the highly hierarchical world of Native artists and arts. In portions of this world, being more authentic by using more traditional tools and materials can be a positive attribute. These are the types of conversations that artists use to broker their version of authenticity.

The San Geronimos fall outside Graburn's (1976:1) "Fourth World" because although fitting his description of peoples in the minority they maintain considerable power and authority. In addition, this is not a study of changing arts or one of emerging ethnicity, modifying identities and commercial and colonial stimuli (Graburn 1976:2) but rather one of active identity and cultural maintenance, construction and fortification. Jewelry production is part of a continuum; not a choice of accommodation or a departure from real or perceived traditional materials and manufacturing techniques. Moreover, San Gerominos are not attempting to change tastes through introduction of new materials but rather are telling us that their jewelry is unchanged. Jewelry is produced from the primacy of San Geronimo cultural backdrop; jewelry is a diacritical mark of their ethnic or cultural identity, a vehicle of self-representation before an external public.

References

Adair, J. (1944), The Navajo and Pueblo Silversmiths. Norman, OK: University of Oklahoma Press.

Batkin, J. (2008), The Native American Curio Trade in New Mexico. Santa Fe, NM: Wheelwright Museum of the American Indian.

Bahti, M. (2008), Silver and Stone: Profiles of American Indian Jewelers. Tucson, AZ: Rio Nuevo.

Bernstein, B. (1999), Contexts for the Growth and Development of the Indian Art World in the 1960s and 1970s; in: J. Rushing (ed.), *Native American Art in the Twentieth Century*: 57-74. New York and London: Routledge.

Bernstein, B. (2008), The Booth Sitters of Santa Fe Indian Market: Making and Maintaining authenticity; in: *American Indian Culture and Research Journal* 31(3): 49-79.

Bernstein, B. (2012), *Santa Fe Indian Market: A History of Native Arts in the Marketplace*. Santa Fe, NM: Museum of New Mexico Press.

Brody, J.J. (1971), *Indian Painters and White Patrons*. Albuquerque, NM: University of New Mexico Press.

Brody, J.J. (1997), *Pueblo Indian Painting: Tradition and Modernism in New Mexico, 1900-1930*. Santa Fe, NM: School of American Research.

Bsumek, E. (2008), *Indian Made: Navajo Culture in the Marketplace, 1868-1940*. Lawrence, KS: University of Kansas Press.

Cirillo, D. (2008), *Southwestern Indian Jewelry: Crafting New Traditions*. New York: Rizzoli.

Dubin, M. (2001), *Native America Collected: The Culture of an Art World*. Albuquerque, NM: University of New Mexico Press.

Dubin, L. (ed.) (2014), *Glittering World: Navajo Jewelry of the Yazzie Family*. Washington, DC: Smithsonian Books.

Dubin, L. (2002), *Jesse Monongya: Opal Bears and Lapis Skies*. New York: Hudson Hills Press.

Emmerling, M. & J. Arndt, (2011), *Art of Turquoise*. Layton, UT: Gibbs Smith.

Graburn, N. (ed.) (1976), *Ethnic and Tourist Arts: Cultural Expressions from the Fourth World*. Berkeley, CA and London: University of California Press.

Hegemann, E. (2004), *Navaho Trading Days*, Albuquerque, NM: University of New Mexico Press.

Kennedy, J. (2009), *A Good Trade: Three Generations of Life and Trading Around the Indian Capital Gallup*, New Mexico. Bloomington, IN: Xlibris.

Kent, K. (1983), *Pueblo Indian Textiles: a Living Tradition*. Santa Fe, NM: School of American Research.

Kline, C. (2015), Depression Jewelry: *El Palacio*, 120 (1):47-53.

Lidchi, H. (2015), *Surviving Desires: Making and Selling Native Jewellery in the American Southwest*, London and Norman, OK: British Museum Press and University of Oklahoma Press.

Lowry, D. & Lowry J. (2010), *Turquoise: The World Story of a Fascinating Gemstone*. Layton, UT: Gibbs Smith.

MacCannel, D. (1989), *The Tourist: A New Theory of the Leisure Class*. New York: Schocken.

McBrinn, M. & R. Asltshuler (2015), *Turquoise, Water, Sky: Meaning and Beauty in Southwestern Native Arts*. Santa Fe, NM: Museum of New Mexico.

McNitt, F. (1962), *The Indian Traders*. Norman, OK: University of Oklahoma Press.

Monthan, G. & D. Monthan (1975), *Art and Indian Individualists: the Art of Seventeen Southwestern Indian Artists and Craftsmen*. Flagstaff, AZ: Northland Press.

Mullin, M. (2001), *Culture in the Marketplace: Gender, Art, and Value in the American Southwest*. Durham, NC: Duke University Press.

Osburn, A. (2012), *Turquoise: Jewel of the Southwest*. El Dorado, CA: Nevada Gem.

Pardue, Diana (2007), *Contemporary Southwestern Jewelry*. Layton, UT: Gibbs Smith.

Phillips, R. & C. Steiner (1999), *Unpacking Culture: Art and Commodity in Colonial and Postcolonial Worlds*. Berkeley, CA and London: University of California Berkeley Press.

Powers, W. (2001), *Navajo Trading: The End of an Era*. Albuquerque, NM: University of New Mexico Press.

Schaaf, G. (2002), *American Indian Jewelry I: 12–Artist Biographies*. Center for Indigenous Arts and Culture: Santa Fe.

Schaaf, G. (2012), *American Indian Jewelry II: A-L–Artist Biographies*. Santa Fe, NM: Center for Indigenous Arts and Culture.

Schaaf, G. (2013), *American Indian Jewelry III: M-Z -Artist Biographies*. Santa Fe, NM: Center for Indigenous Art Studies.

Southwestern Indian Development (1968), *Traders on the Navajo Reservation: A Report on the Economic Bondage of the Navajo People.* Window Rock, AZ: Southwestern Indian Development.

Struever, M. (2005), *Loloma: Beauty is His Name*. Santa Fe, NM: Wheelwright Museum of the American Indian.

Weigle, M. (1989), From Desert to Disney World: the Santa Fe Railway and the Fred Harvey Company Display the Indian Southwest; in: *Journal of Anthropological Research* 45 (1): 115-137.

Economic Development and Self-Representation

An Example of Tribal Tourism on the Northern Plains

Markus H. Lindner

In July 2014 the Standing Rock Sioux tribe decided to terminate its tourism program and to terminate the contract of the long year tourism director who had held that position for many years.[1] The reason for the measure was simple: the tribe had run out of funds and had to find options to make cuts to the budget. This decision by the tribal government seems to illustrate the opinion of many scholars and businesspeople that tourism is just about monetary investment money or the creation of jobs. This does not take into account that tourism provides also an ideal opportunity for self-representation.

When I began research on tourism on this reservation in 2002 my goal was to investigate the relationship between hosts and guests on this most northern Lakota Reservation on the border of North Dakota and South Dakota (Lindner 2007). Since I had worked on the famous Lakota leader Sitting Bull and the Hunkpapa band before, I decided to spend time with their descendants at Standing Rock instead of going to the Pine Ridge Reservation where most research on the Lakotas has been conducted since the late 19th century.

The story begins before the time when North Dakota got a boost to its economy because of oil fracking. Being situated in a region with the lowest number of leisure visitors, only few tourists spent time on the reservation, situated far removed from any large scale tourist attraction. I encountered a tribe that was preparing for the Lewis & Clark Bicentennial (2003-2006). The people responsible tried to invest the available funding in projects that were expected to be sustainable instead of short termed. Projects of other institutions along the so-called Lewis & Clark Trail impacted the tribal planning and integrated the initiatives at Standing Rock to the national commemoration. Tribally operated projects were usually referred to as "tribal tourism" and often depended on cooperation with or funding by federal or state programs. The representatives mostly understood their activity as a communication tool. "Tell our own story" is a phrase that was heard in many places as a main goal since then, not only in the Upper Missouri region.[2]

1 The Tourism Office closed on January 30th, 2015. The Visitor Center remained (SRTO 2015).

2 When talking to the people of "Experience Hopi", a private tourism organization on the Hopi Reservation (summer 2015) exactly the same phrase was used to indicate the importance of tourism projects.

Being interested in material culture as well I discovered that there were few arts and crafts on offer for tourists, especially in comparison to other places and regions. Only later I realized that it was a museological view that shielded my eyes from all the other manifestations of tourist material culture that surrounded me, such as brochures, road signs or historical monuments. All these can be incorporated into the analysis of tribal tourism.

A glance into the story of tribal tourism on the Standing Rock Indian Reservation will contribute to the clarification of this concept. Where applicable comparisons will be made with other tourism developments, especially in the American Southwest, one of the major regional destinations of tourists. The local situation and the fairly recent emergence of tourism enterprise on Standing Rock provided an opportunity to learn from experiences in other parts of North America and to develop new ideas, geared to local conditions. It also provided a glimpse into contemporary Native American political and economic life.

History of tourism on Standing Rock

After the Wild West was "pacified" Americans wanted to see the natural wonders of the West. Tourism increased rapidly in the late 19th and early 20th century. The Yosemite, the Yellowstone and the Glacier National Parks became major attractions, and Native Americans often worked as tour guides or sold arts and crafts in or near the parks. Usually Native Americans were not a primary reason to visit such a place. Nevertheless, visitors expected their presence as they constituted a significant part of the popular image of the Wild West. However, the Native populations of the parks were sometimes forced to leave by the federal authorities as they were regarded to disturb the natural environment (Keller & Turek 1998:xi, 21-22). Much of the early tourism development in the U.S. was related to the construction of transcontinental railroads between 1860 and 1890. In the beginning travelers felt offended by poor Native Americans begging and selling arts and crafts at railway stations. This attitude changed in the early twentieth century and the railway companies began to pay Native people for performing dances. These entrepreneurs also became involved in selling Native arts and craftsas souvenirs, and organized so-called Indian Detours to bring tourists to Indian pueblos in the Southwest.

The Standing Rock Sioux were hardly affected by these developments. They were far removed from major tourist attractions. However, to some extent they experienced some occasional tourism. The German explorer and naturalist Prince Maximillian zu Wied-Neuwied visited the Northern Plains and the Sioux in 1832, accompanied by the Swiss artist Karl Bodmer. The famous Lakota medicine man Sitting Bull and his people had been visited by adventurous travelers in the 1880s before and shortly after the "Ghost Dance Craze." The reservation was more frequently visited by tourists on their way to the Yellowstone National Park after 1912.

When some Lakota and people from the border town of Mobridge dedicated the Sitting Bull Monument in 1953 it was located directly on Highway 12. Today the memorial is about 4 miles south of the new highway which opened in 1962 after the flooding of Lake Oahe (YTA n.d.b.; photo by the author, 2004).

The Good Roads movement had reached South Dakota two years before. It promoted the construction of new roads to attract tourists. One of the private associations emanating from this idea was the Yellowstone Trail Association. It built a transcontinental road to the National Park and U.S. Highway 12, that crossed Standing Rock from east to west. It became part of the original so-called Yellowstone Trail (YTA n.d.a; Lee 1989:203-208). The Missouri River bridge in the southeast corner of the reservation was one of the few possibilities to cross the stream.

Travelers who preferred to take the train to go west took the same route. They had to stop at the railway station in the border town of Mobridge on the east bank of the Missouri River, which was a regular stop on the Pacific Coast Extension of the Chicago, Milwaukee, and St. Paul Railroad since 1906. Attached to the depot was an exhibition area where some Sioux performed “twice a day, for the benefit of the passengers on the ‘Olympian’ and ‘Columbian’ passenger trains” in the mid-1930s (photo description Klein Museum, Mobridge).

In contrast to the Pine Ridge Reservation where the Sun Dance was commercialized in the late 1960s (Bolz 1986:216; 2000:11-12), this ceremony was not revitalized at Standing Rock before the 1970s and has not become a tourist attraction. The first tribal attempt to promote tourism on the reservation was the construction of the Land of Gall Inn, a hotel between Mobridge and the reservation town of Wakpala. Opened in 1972 it was particularly promoted during the centennial of the Standing Rock Reservation one year later (Allard 2005, email).[3] Even being somewhat successful in its early years the inn went bankrupt around 1978 and the Area Youth Treatment Center came to occupy the facility. During the same time the Standing Rock Sioux Tribe, in cooperation with the Bureau of Indian Affairs, developed a Recreation Development Potential Plan. This led to the planning of cultural centers and boat ramps for Lake Oahe, created by the damming of the Missouri river in the 1950s. Only the boat ramps were actually built.

During the 1980s little happened with regards to tourism development. In 1992 the tribe followed the trend to engagement in the gambling industry. The first establishment to open on the Standing Rock Indian Reservation was the Prairie Knights Casino in North Dakota. It was followed by the smaller Grand River Casino close to Mobridge, South Dakota. In 2001/2002 an event center and a hotel were added to the Prairie Knights Casino. The hotel of the Grand River Casino opened in 2004. This was two years after both casinos had taken over management of camping sites and boat ramps on the shores of Lake Oahe from the U.S. Corps of Engineers. These sites were frequently used by people for fishing on the lake.

Not included in the tribal tourism planning was hunting tourism although it already existed on the reservation. The Cheyenne River Sioux Tribe south of Standing Rock used hunting opportunities as one of the major attractions to promote tourism on their reservation. Its tourism office saw unspoilt nature and its wildlife as the strength of their land base. The northern reservation only offered a short hiking path close to the Prairie Knights Casino to visitors, that became the "Lewis & Clark Legacy Trail" in 2006 (SRTO 2006). This reflects the "absence of ecotourists" and the lack of interest in this aspect by current visitors (Hearne & Tuscherer 2007:13).

More important for the development of "tribal tourism" was a decision in June 1999 when Tribal Council Resolution No. 243-99 permitted Sitting Bull College to undertake activities that were not primarily related to teaching. This permission included economic and especially tourist activities:

> "WHEREAS, Sitting Bull College sees cultural tourism as a viable means of promoting both the Dakota/Lakota culture and economic development; and
>
> WHEREAS, Sitting Bull College is building a cultural resource center and is jointly funding with the Standing Rock Sioux Tribe a proposal for a scenic byway; [...]

3 The Oglala Sioux Tribe opened a visitor center with a camping facility, restaurant and souvenir shop in the same year (Bolz 1986:141).

> NOW THEREFORE BE IT RESOLVED, that the Standing Rock Sioux Tribe does support Sitting Bull College in seeking funding for other cultural, education and economic development endeavors and pursuant to its Charter, Sitting Bull College shall continue to deliver annual reports, budget and audit findings to the duly elected Tribal Council" (TCSRST 1999).

Following this permission the college began to discuss opportunities and risks of tribal tourism openly. The former manager of the reservation's radio station KLND, Dennis Neumann, was one of the organizers of public and internal meetings: "We advertised [...] to have the public coming to talk about plans and planning for how tourism would be conducted on Standing Rock. There were elders there, there were young people there. There was a good range of people...We did some brainstorming and created [...] ideas and talked about what some of the things were that people liked about the notion of creating tourism and some things about what they want to avoid, what sort of pitfalls and traps there might be, things that they weren't comfortable with in terms of tourism" (Neumann interview, 2004).

In addition to the radio station the Tribal Tourism Partnership Initiative (TTPI) became a cooperation partner. This was a two year program at the United Tribes Technical College in Bismarck, North Dakota. The college is a collaborative institution of the five reservations in North Dakota. The TTPI program was funded by the U.S. Department of Labor. This was reflected in the mission statement: "United Tribes Technical College Tribal Tourism Partnership Initiative provides an intertribal forum and educational programs that promote the economic, social and cultural advancement of American Indians" (TTPI 2002).

The original focus on economic questions and professionalism was expanded by the second program director of the TTPI, Karen Paetz, who thought that it was important to control tourists. She added four other important goals of the program:

1. „have our own people telling our own story"
2. „dispelling the stereotype and misconceptions"
3. „We are not reenacting our culture – it's alive"
4. „We do not disappear – we are still here" (Paetz interview, 2002).

The program was one of the possibilities to exchange knowledge and experiences about tourism on reservations. The Three Affiliated Tribes from the Fort Berthold Reservation had the most experience in tourism in North Dakota. Amy Mosset was the tourism director of the reservation who became also one of the leading Native people involved in the Lewis & Clark Bicentennial.

The second cooperative link was, and still is, Standing Rock's membership in the Alliance of Tribal Tourism Advocates (ATTA), an intertribal non-profit organization in South Dakota that has been promoting tribal tourism in South

Dakota since the 1990s. ATTA is the place where the different tribes meet to exchange ideas and develop plans. The organization is geared to cooperate with the tourism department of the state. Both networks involving both states played an important role in implementing tourism projects on Standing Rock.

In his study of tribal tourism the German geographer Bertram Postner points out that the implementation of tourism projects cannot work on a reservation without acceptance by the host community (2002:147). This was also the case at Standing Rock. In cooperation with the initiators the first official tourism conference was held on the reservation in May 2002. This meeting was broadcasted by Radio KLND, the radio station of the Standing Rock and Cheyenne River Indian Reservations. When I arrived on the reservation only a short time later I met a lot of people who were very sceptical about tourists. However, public discussions like this tried to change that attitude. About 75 guests and speakers participated in the conference that brought together people from Standing Rock and other localities to promote the idea of tourism.

It was a common theme to emphasize the possibility to teach visitors about culture and history from the Lakota point of view to correct stereotypes and combat prejudices. The protection of sacred sites was stressed as one of utmost concern and urgency. In fact, a statement of Brant Kary, at that time economic development director at Standing Rock, shows that the focus tended to shift away from the economy: "Tourism is a chance for us to teach, not so much to make money, but first to teach" (Kary 2002, Standing Rock Tourism Conference).

Preparing for the Lewis & Clark Bicentennial

In 2002 the situation at Standing Rock was impacted by the fact that the Bicentennial of the Lewis & Clark Expedition (1803-1806) was only two years away. William Clark and Meriwether Lewis were famous as they had led the first official expedition – called Corps of Discovery – to find a transcontinental route of travel to the Pacific Ocean. The federal government and the organizers of the national event forecasted that millions of travelers would follow an improved Lewis & Clark Trail along the original route. John Beheler, the first program director of the TTPI, announced that Standing Rock had to be prepared for about 30 million travelers between 2003 and 2006 (Beheler 2002, Standing Rock Tourism Conference). The National Council of the Lewis and Clark Bicentennial called it a "critical opportunity for all Americans to reflect upon the many timeless social issues faced by the expedition that are still relevant in today's society – tolerance and non-discrimination; teamwork; non-violence; and protecting and preserving the environment" (NCLCB 2003).

The role of Native Americans was important. As they criticized the idea to celebrate an event of colonialism, the official wording became "commemoration" instead of "celebrating" (NCLCB 2004). This differentiation was important and even critics like Karen Paetz (2002 interview) regarded it as an opportunity to tell tourists about Native Americans, their cultures and their survival. Another positive expectation, not only of Native Americans, was the sustainability of the investments made for the event: "Long after visitors go away, and they have forgotten most of the Lewis and Clark story, they will remember the quality of their experiences on the Lewis and Clark Trail. These will have a great deal to do with human contact, and not much to do with the American history" (Jenkinson 2002:1).

The Scenic Byway

Such promise motivated not only the Standing Rock Reservation but also other reservations in the Dakotas and beyond to initiate programs to attract visitors. One of the most important projects was the creation of a National Native American Scenic Byway. Not directly connected to the Lewis & Clark Bicentennial, it was an addition to a scenic byway that was created on the Lower Brule Reservation in South Dakota in 1996. Its planning is one the examples of the integration of Native life into U.S. American life and vice versa. It was realized by Leasure and Associates, a company from Utah specialized in tourist projects. After finishing it on Lower Brule the company offered to create a plan for Standing Rock. The tribe decided that the college was the place to work on this project (Leasure & Associates 1998:1-2).

The Conceptual Development Plan of 1998 was not written by the company alone, but tribal members were very much involved. The historical section tells the history of the place and of the Lakotas, and was written by Ladonna Allard, a trained historian and tribal member. She played an important role in the whole process and later became the Tribal Tourism Director. The plan states that the byway can create income and economic development on the reservation. It also mentions the possibility to teach and talk about Lakota culture and history. This argument was used before and became even more important later. To resolve existing doubts within the Lakota community it is pointed out that "the byway will enable the tribe to direct where visitors travel and how the Lakota/Dakota culture is presented to them" (Leasure & Associates 1998:4).

The concerns of the people were not based on actual experiences with tourists, but on experiences from other regions of the U.S., especially the Southwest, where different forms of so-called visitor etiquette were developed since the early twentieth century to protect villages and their inhabitants from misbehaving tourists. Talking to people I realized that their main prejudice was that all tourists were be digging for bones in graves on the banks of the Missouri. According to Tribal Archeologist Byron Olson this was not true (Olson 2002, interview). Mark White Bull, Management Specialist of the tribe, saw the problem in the fact that "the people are not used to the concepts of tourism" (2002, interview). Even if it is hard to know how strong the faction of opponents really was, the control of tourists became one of the main issues, as Ladonna Allard (2002, interview) pointed out: "I would [...] say we have people who are very scared of tourism. We have people here that look at it as a violation of culture, and my position is, I am trying to teach that it will not violate our culture if we do it in a good way. That's why we've developed the scenic byway and keeping people on the scenic byway. We don't want people travelling to our sacred lands and traditional gathering spots."

When the scenic byway opened in 2002 it connected most of the places tourists would like to see during their visit: Sitting Bull's grave, the Sitting Bull Monument, the casinos, and the Standing Rock Monument. The Conceptual Development Plan had included additional attractions like a Sitting Bull Historic Center, a Prairie Knights Interpretive Center, and a replica of Fort Manuel Lisa, but only the latter was under construction at this time. The fur trade fort from the 1810s was important for the bicentennial as it is said that Sacagawea, the Shoshone guide of the expedition and best-known Native American woman from history, had died there.

Visitors

While the scenic byway existed regionally and just waited for federal recognition, tourists crossed the reservation regularly. Tribal chairman Charles W. Murphy (2002, Interview) noted that they usually just stopped at one of the casinos or at the two Sitting Bull sites: the Grave of Sitting Bull in Fort Yates, ND and the Sitting Bull Monument west of Mobridge, SD at the border in the southeast of the reservation.

The latter was also one of the few places for the researcher to meet tourists; but even there they were usually in a hurry and not open for longer interviews. Most of them stated to have some interest in Lakota culture, but none of them really did anything to learn about it, except stopping at the monument, because "it was on the map" (Cindy 2002, pers. com.). Most tourists enjoyed the "amazing" plains (Bob & Shirley 2002, pers. com.) or the "real pretty country" (Cory 2002, pers. com.) In contrast, some found the same a "waste land" not worth to come back to (Ronda 2002, pers. com.).

None of the tourists was longer on the reservation than necessary to cross it, and it was never a travel destination. Some people just drove the Lewis & Clark Trail, while others were on their way to Yellowstone National Park. Only one family stayed longer and got in touch with people on the reservation. The couple from California was not on a vacation trip but their daughter participated in a healing ceremony of a Lakota medicine man. But even these two were staying outside the reservation and spent their time fishing on Lake Oahe (Bob & Shirley 2002, pers. com.).

Tourists with some interest in the Native people, in general Europeans, usually stopped at the radio station KLND where they were welcomed as warmly as I was on the first day of my fieldwork. The station invited people on air to take a

The Standing Rock Wacipi was the only powwow on the reservation with signage on one of the main roads. While the painting of the dancer was already in poor condition in 2002, it was destroyed a few years later (photo by the author, 2002).

break there, and some people used that opportunity. Usually, these travelers were on a more extensive tour through Lakota country, visiting not only Standing Rock but also the Black Hills and the Pine Ridge Indian Reservation.

Exceptional was a group of five women and three men from Catalonia and one Italian. The tour was organized by a Spanish travel agent and guide who was specialized in such tours. They camped south of the reservation border on the Cheyenne River Reservation and stayed for about a week in South Dakota. They all were keenly interested in Native Americans. Visiting the radio station was one of the major activities. Guided by Vaughn Three Legs they wrote down whatever he told them about contemporary Lakota life, not only about the radio station. They listened to stories about everyday life, history and religion and took countless photographs, demonstrating the typical *tourist gaze* (Urry 1996). It was obvious that they enjoyed having direct contact with Lakota people and culture. They were very unhappy when they realized that they could not buy any souvenirs from the radio station as the room with the mugs, pins, caps and other merchandising was locked on that occasion.

It was no surprise to meet the same group again at one of the local powwows on the reservation a couple of days later. At this event the group passionately watched the dances and ceremonies. They were enthusiastic about the fact that they were told to come into the circle.[4] Being very interested in Lakota culture a major problem for the group was their insufficient mastery of English. At KLND the tour guide had translated, at the powwow he explained a little bit, but almost nobody of the group was able to get in touch with the local population.

Powwows were one of the few opportunities to see tourists and Lakotas interacting to a certain degree. Usually the number of interested visitors was low and they did not really receive negative attention from their hosts. At giveaway ceremonies they received gifts like everybody else, and if they were willing to talk to people they did. Even visitors with cameras who acted immodestly and unfriendly were tolerated.

My own experience at a powwow in Little Eagle provides insight into pseudo-negative attitudes towards visitors. I was looking for a seat on the white painted, shaded seats for the spectators that surrounded the dance arena. I took a space next to an old man, greeted and sat down. The situation was uncomfortable as he was obviously not very happy to have a stranger sitting there. He asked me a lot of questions showing his rejection. I told him that I was working on tourism and tourists but he remained negative in attitude. It was hot that day and I offered some water to him. He enjoyed it and only a couple of minutes after our first "Hello" he became very open and talked freely and friendly.

This little story is exemplary of my experiences. If somebody proved skeptical at first, he or she could be very friendly and hospitable as soon as it was realized that the stranger was open-minded and interested. However, this did not change the general attitude towards tourists. Joan D. Laxson (1991:368) observed a similar phenomenon in the American Southwest. Here tourists are not called "tourists" anymore when they do not fit into the negative stereotype. In this case Pueblo Indians often call them "Whites." However, there was no official encouragement by the Standing Rock Sioux Tribe to get in touch with tourists. If such interethnic exchanges happened it was by chance or because individuals were personally interested.

The Lewis & Clark Bicentennial at Standing Rock

During the Lewis & Clark Bicentennial in South Dakota in 2004 I did not encounter the negative attitude anymore. Possibly because the continual information campaigns had an impact or because nobody was affected by tourists directly. Except for the opening of Fort Manuel Lisa and new signage for the not yet nationally recognized Native American Scenic Byway the situation had not much changed in general. Even the number of travelers seemed not to be very different from two years earlier. More important was the fact that in 2003

4 What they expected did not happen as long as I followed the powwow, even some of them gave me their cameras in expectation of the event.

the tribe had surprisingly decided to hire a tourism director. It is unclear why the tribal government changed its mind after they had given the responsibility to the college initially.

Unfortunately, the working conditions for the first tribal tourism director were quite poor and she eventually failed. The tribe did not support the low paid job with any additional funding, not even for traveling, except for some funds from the Office of Economic Development. Even if it is not clear what the expectations of the tribe were, it is obvious that these did not correspond to those of the director who wanted to establish relationships with visitors. She planned to give information, to have signage, to print brochures, to advertise. Since she did not see how to do this without any support she resigned and the tribe had to find a new person to fill the position after only six weeks (Bear Catches 2004, interview). It required five job advertisements until Ladonna Allard was hired in 2004. Being well experienced because of her involvement in the tourism projects of the college she had much more power to change things, as economic development director Brent Kary pointed out: "Finally Ladonna came. And I think the big reason that it's working with Ladonna now is because of her commitment and her passion. She's had been doing this for free anyway. So, for her this is a 9 dollar an hour raise. Where anybody else feels like they're being underpaid, she feels like 'I'm getting paid for now'. So, she's willing to do it for the price, because she believes in it, she wants to do it and it's her passion in life" (Kary 2004, interview).

Although tourism was a tribal task now, the development of the Scenic Byway was still part of the college's responsibilities in 2004. Pam Ternes who was in charge there was a friend of Ladonna Allard, and this created new opportunities. As the position of the tourism director had been vacant for a year, the saved money could be used for a program. Brant Karywas sure that it was most important to help private people to open businesses for tourism, but the political and economic situation was constricting: „We're set up closer to socialism as a tribe than we are to capitalism: The tribe owns everything, it's expected to run everything, it pretty much controls everything. So we're a lot closer to communism and socialism than we are to capitalism. As Indian people and enrolled members we expect the tribe to do things, as Non-Indian people here in the region they expect tribal government to do things, as a tribal government they expect to do things, as a state, as a federal government you will get the tribal government to do things. That's socialism" (Kary 2004, interview).

On Memorial Day 2004 Fort Manuel Lisa opened next to the small town of Kenel with its 200 inhabitants. While some tribal members expected that "Fort Manuel could really be a money maker" (Bear Catches, 2004 interview), most people "looked at it as an opportunity to have an attraction of something that they could actually talk about in a cultural way with people. And meet and greet people in a sense that in a way would be more of a cultural and human relations kind of interaction rather than a concession to earn money. And I think in that

Fort Manuel Lisa at Kenel, South Dakota with a visitor group from Sitting Bull College (photo by the author, 2004).

respect they've created something that has the potential for that: of creating an interpretive and informational narrative that they can give to people who come through there" (Neumann 2004, interview).

It had never been in doubt that economic success was important, and the expectation was that the replica fur trade fort would create new jobs, and become an outlet from which to sell local arts and crafts, thus contributing to the development of the town (Neumann, interviews 2002, 2004). That the number of visitors was very low that first summer[5] was not only a result of the lack of advertising, but also of the number of travelers in general, which had not really increased despite the Lewis & Clark Bicentennial. However, the community was happy with the project and planned additional attractions like a prairie walking path, wagon tours, etc. Nevertheless, the fort never became a real money maker, and was destroyed during a storm in early 2010. It has not been back in operation since as the town lacks the funds to rebuild it.

The material culture of tourism

In an introduction to the study of material culture Christian Feest (2006:249) urges that cultural anthropologists while they are doing field studies should also focus on stationary material culture like buildings and everything else that

5 The numbers were about eight a day (Thompson 2004, interview) or 300 in total in 2004 (St. John 2006, email).

cannot be easily transferred (in)to a museum. Maybe we should regard the reconstructed Fort Manuel Lisa as material culture of the Lakota or of Kenel. When it comes to tourism the study of material culture usually is limited to souvenirs and arts and crafts, but being on the reservation it is obvious that it is much more.

We have seen that the majority of the Lakota people regard tribal tourism not so much as an economic opportunity, but as an opportunity to meet and greet people, and to tell their own story about their culture and history. They did not want to leave that to Euro-American historians, anthropologists or tourism agents. However, the souvenir and arts and crafts "industry" did not play a major role in this tourism concept at that time.

Since 2005 the Alliance of Tribal Tourism Advocates (ATTA) has been planning the large "Hé Sapa Black Hills Center for Northern Plains Indian Arts and Performance" in Rapid City, South Dakota. Being in an off-reservation town but close to one of the major Interstates, this venue is scheduled to include space for performances, cultural interpretation, and arts and crafts: "Honoring the spirit and cultural heritage of the Plains Indian tribes, Rapid City's new HéSapa Black Hills Center for Northern Plains Indian Arts and Performance will capture the character and spirit of a proud people, and explore their past, present and future through a diverse array of interpretive offerings, dance, oral history, art and crafts" (ATTA 2012a).

The financial planning for the venue includes funding by tribes in the region, the Rapid City council, and private sponsors. Funding was secured in January 2015 when the Shakopee Mdewakanton Sioux Community and the Oglala Sioux Tribe guaranteed financial support (Chasing Hawk 2015). ATTA will partner with the United Tribes Technical College "as they carry with them a consistent history of sound management and providing educational and technical educational opportunities for students." This cooperation is planned to create a "Native educational institution in the Black Hills" (ATTA 2012b:4) in addition to its function as tourist attraction.

Tourist constructions like the Hé Sapa Black Hills Center are proof of the will of Indian people for autonomous cultural and historical interpretation, and show that external self-representation and internal education are frequently combined in tribal initiatives. This is also the case for the cultural centers on reservations. They often serve as visitor centers, museums, and venues for cultural and social gatherings. Depending on their concept they can be a meeting point or a place to teach visitors (Mauzé 2003:514). Sometimes they confer a very specific message, like the Mashantucket Pequot Museum and Research Center that opened in 1998 and is very much focused on demonstrating historical continuity of the tribe (Bodinger de Uriarte 2003:550).

As the relationship between visitors and hosts is often complicated these institutions can also work as a welcome sign to travelers, like the Makah Cultural and Research Center at Neah Bay in Washington State (Erikson 2003:523,526).

At the same time such centers can be used to establish a degree of control over tourists, and manage their movements. The Zuni Pueblo Department of Tourism recommends to "check-in at the Visitor Center to receive an orientation, obtain current information, schedule tours, purchase photo permits" (ZPDT n.d.). What seems like a good service also helps to keep visitors away from protected sections of the pueblo.

With the tribal visitor center that opened in May 2013 the Standing Rock Sioux Tribe also created a location where a small collection of artifacts, photos, books, and such provide information about the tribe and the reservation to visitors. Like others it is a place where tourists can stop and get in touch with their hosts. The interpretational focus of the tribal tourism office had also resulted in road signage with explanations at places of interest along the Scenic Byway and electronic information desks at the tribal casinos.

When doing fieldwork I was interested in the question which souvenirs tourists were purchasing in the region, if they did at all. In reality, there are not many possibilities to do so, even today. The main places to buy souvenirs close to or on Lakota reservations are tribal or mission museums and cultural centers, the Five Nations Store in Mandan, North Dakota, and Prairie Edge Trading Co. & Galleries in Rapid City, South Dakota, the Klein Museum in Mobridge, and the two casinos on the Standing Rock Indian Reservation. Other major galleries and museums selling arts and crafts are in Mitchell, Sioux Falls and Vermillion, South Dakota, and at the tourist attractions of the Black Hills, particularly at the Crazy Horse Memorial. I visited many of these places but want to focus on the two tribal casinos on the Standing Rock Reservation. Contrary to other Lakota casinos both have gift shops with every kind of typical commercialized souvenir like mugs, caps, pens, T-shirts, and so on with the logos of the casinos. But at the same time both shops also sell arts and crafts from the reservation: star quilts, bracelets, key chains, ear rings with glass beads and porcupine quill, baby moccasins, and so on.

Charles Archambault (2004, interview), sales director of the Prairie Knights Casino, stated that the casino shop does "pretty significant business ..., but if you look over there [to the shop], it isn't much the artwork that we sell versus the mass produced products: T-shirts, things with Prairie Knights Casino logo." The ignorance of tribal arts and crafts by the gambling public fits the prevalent view of Archambault and other casino managers that their casinos should not be marketed as something "Indian" or "Lakota" but just as a gambling establishments (*cf.* Berthier, this volume). Tourist activities on the reservation were not relevant to him, and asked about intercultural interaction and communication between visitors and guests, he said: "Our guests are very respectful [to] our people when they come here. ... They relate to us in a very business sense. ... It's never a cultural type of thing" (Archambault 2004, interview).

Despite this approach both casinos are communicating and marketing Native American or Lakota culture in a modest way. Like casinos of other tribes they include murals or other contemporary art by Native artists. It is not always easy to detect the relationship between features of the building and its interior design to traditional culture, except for paintings and sculptures by Indian artists as interior decoration. The casino shops do offer a modest number of arts and crafts. And even commercial products like mugs, caps or jackets can be message bearers. As souvenirs they remind the owners of their visit to the casinos, and the logos may remind them that they were on an Indian reservation (*cf.* Berthier, this volume).

The privately operated Klein Museum which is only about one mile outside the reservation also sells arts and crafts of varying quality. It offers Lakota pottery from the Black Hills and art prints by Hunkpapa artist Del Iron Cloud. However, it also includes glass bead products and other commercial merchandise from China. Diane Kindt (2004, pers. com.), the curator of the museum, told me that tourists do not buy handcrafted souvenirs very often, and in most cases these artifacts may "only" be souvenirs for most visitors, even if they incorporate the message that Lakota people are still around.

Not much arts and crafts are sold to tourists on or close to Standing Rock, but it is important for the makers to have places where they can go to sell their work if they need that income. The Klein Museum and the Grand River Casino buy arts and crafts often without the aim of profit but more with a view to support the local craftspeople. This has also been true for other places like some of the missions on other reservations. Peter Strong, the director of the Red Cloud Heritage Center on the Pine Ridge Reservation told me that the large collection of the museum was not so much a result of the drive to collect but of buying whatever somebody had offered when he or she needed money (2010, pers. com.).

Kathleen Ann Pickering (2000:53, 128) remarks that this kind of business is not generating much income. The arts and crafts are not specifically made for tourists but also for the local community that uses star quilts for ceremonies and beadwork for powwow regalia or as everyday jewelry. These kinds of customers do not have much money to spend. Therefore prices stay low locally. They only rise if an artist is able to sell to institutions or stores in Rapid City, South Dakota or Mandan, North Dakota, in other cities or even in Denver, Colorado. The lack of capital makes an advance on commission work necessary in order to be able to buy the raw materials.

Typically, arts and crafts are produced in microenterprises by household producers. They are very flexible and can join ceremonies or powwows whenever they choose. Often craftsmen and women have seasonal jobs in the summer time and produce crafts during the winter season (Pickering 2000:20-21, 56). While smaller arts and crafts like beadwork or moccasins usually are made individually, the creation of other things can impact and include the whole family of an artist.

Baby Star Quilt, Mary Ann Helper 2002. While others use quilting machines, Mary Ann Helper is sewing and stitching her star quilts by hand in the middle of her home. Like her mother she is usually, but not always, tagging her quilts on the back (collection of and photo by the author, 2015).

Pickering (2000:61) states that "the household is a collective, integral economic unit, producing together, consuming together, and transmitting necessary skills and labor from one generation to the next."

When I ordered my first star quilt on the Standing Rock Reservation, Mary Ann Helper, who had learned making such quilts from her mother, changed the living room into a working space. Her husband and the whole family had to help cutting the fabric diamonds that were needed for the quilt.

In the 1980s Mary Jane Schneider wrote that Kiowa tourist items were "those which are easily and quickly made, require little outlay in materials, and have a fairly rapid turnover" as there was "a difference in status and training between those who produce for non-Indian consumption and those who produce for Indian consumption" (1983:238-240). This is not automatically true for the Lakotas in the beginning 21st century, even if it may be true that tourists tend

A selection of tourist material culture from Standing Rock that is not arts & crafts (collection of and photo by the author, 2015).

to buy lower priced objects which may of less quality. Arts and crafts as material culture are usually not only produced explicitly for tourists but also for internal consumption as has been pointed out. They are also sold and bought as souvenirs for tourists but they are not very important for the marketing of a reservation as a travel destination.

Other contemporary material culture seems to be much more important to support tribal tourism and its conception. Like the offices of other tribes the Standing Rock Tourism Office was responsible for a much tourism related material. In the case of Standing Rock it is brochures with information about the Scenic Byway and the reservation, a visitor center, computer terminals with relevant information, printed and online maps, and the interpretive signage along the National Native American Scenic Byway, and internet representations. All these information and marketing tools are important elements of contemporary tourist material culture at Standing Rock. These belong to the life at Standing Rock and they have an important function: they can guide visitors through the reservation, and through them the people of the reservation have the opportunity to tell their own story. I would commend more research on this kind of self-representation. The selection of logos (here the "Standing Rock", "Sitting Bull", and the tribal seal), the selection of topics, and the way the information is gathered, edited and published would provide insight into economic and cultural life on a reservation.

Conclusion

More than a century ago, American travelers "discovered" Native Americans and their cultures as tourist attractions in the Southwest. Travelers interpreted the sedentary Pueblo tribes as more or less civilized. Tourists and collectors appreciated their art, and visitors crowded ceremonies in such numbers that tribes had to close them for guests. That they were able to do this proves that Native Americans were not helpless victims of this development. They were able to minimize the negative impact of tourism while they tried to retain the economic advantages. Throughout the decades they have been able to adapt tourism to their daily lives. Long experience has resulted in different kinds of visitor etiquette, restriction and prohibition of photography, or degrees of control of tourists' movements within Indian communities.

In other parts of North America the situation has been different. The development of "Indian tourism" in the southwestern United States more than 100 years ago was also related to the new interest in nature and the wilderness. The sedentary Pueblo cultures created a strong contrast to the hostile Plains tribes popularly known from the Indian wars of the 1860s and 1870s. Even the image of the latter changed positively in the late 19th century after the campaigns of the federal army resulted in the settlement of the last hostile Indians on reservations. During this period Blackfeet and others began to play an important role in national parks. One hundred years later the situation changed again and the reservations and the people on the Plains and Pacific Northwest themselves came into focus with the Lewis & Clark Bicentennial.

The (erroneous) expectation to see millions of travelers crossing the reservations made it necessary to prepare for this event. In the beginning it was understood as an opportunity for local economic development, but within a short time-period the attitude changed into anon-economic perspective. What became important was the use of tourism as a possibility for self-representation. The Standing Rock Reservation is a particularly good example. In the 1990s the tribe had no interest in tourism and transferred the responsibility for this subject to Sitting Bull College. The tribal government did not spend any money until it changed its mind in 2003. Outside and inside pressure made it necessary to get involved. Activities of the Alliance of Tribal Tourism Advocates, of the United Tribes Technical College and other institutions, advertising campaigns of the States of North and South Dakota, and the whole Lewis & Clark Bicentennial created momentum that was grasped by both the college and Economic Development Director Brent Kary.

Having learned from the experience in other regions of North America, the community was involved into the process of implementation. The protection of the land was one of the first issues to talk about. Economic questions very soon became unimportant in relation to the opportunity to tell the tribal cultural and historical story. This is also reflected in the fact that the casinos have not played any role. Whatever has been built up reflects this approach of self-representation, even Fort Manuel Lisa. But when the tribe closed the tourism office in 2015 it demonstrated that self-representation is not only a question of the will of the people, but also of budget.

References

ATTA (Alliance of Tribal Tourism Advocates) (2012a), *The Legend Lives...* http://www.attatribal.com/the-legend-lives.

ATTA (Alliance of Tribal Tourism Advocates) (2012b), *He' Sapa Black Hills Center for Northern Plains Indian Arts and Performance.* http://archive.rcgov.org/sc20130325/VF032513-03-ATTA/Rapid%20City%202012%20Vision%20update-2.pdf.

Bodinger de Uriarte, J.J. (2003), Imagining the Nation with House Odds: Representing American Indian Identity at Mashantucket; *Ethnohistory* 50 (3): 549-565.

Bolz, P. (1986), *Ethnische Identität und kultureller Widerstand. Die Oglala-Sioux der Pine Ridge-Reservation in South Dakota.* Frankfurt/New York: Campus.

Bolz, P. (2000), The Lakota Sun Dance between 1883 and 1997: the Outlawing and Revival of a Cultural Symbol; in: T. Claviez, Thomas & M. Moss (eds.), *Mirror Writing: Re-Constructions of Native American Identity*: 1-22. Glienicke/Cambrich: Galda + Wilch.

Chasing Hawk, E. (2015), Tribes Donate to Cultural Center: He Sapa Center Becoming a Reality; in: N*avajo Times*, 13 January, 2015; webpage: http://navajotimes.com/wires-wp/index.php?id=1580932200&kid=FyZXAFiNSd9e1EB3.

Erikson, P.P. (2003), Welcome to this House: a Century of Makah People Honoring Identity and Negotiating Cultural Tourism; *Ethnohistory* 50 (3): 523-547.

Feest, C.F. (2006), Materielle Kultur; in: H. Fischer & B. Beer (eds.), *Ethnologie. Einführung und Überblick* (5th ed.): 239-254. Berlin: Reimer.

Hearne, R.R. & S. Tuscherer (2007), *Stated Preferences for Ecotourism Alternatives on the Standing Rock Sioux Indian Reservation* (Agribusiness and Applied Economics Report 601). Fargo, ND: North Dakota State University, Department of Agribusiness and Applied Economics (http://purl.umn.edu/10005).

Jenkinson, C.S. (2002), *A Lewis & Clark Chapbook: Lewis and Clark in North Dakota.* Bismarck, ND: The North Dakota Humanities Council.

Keller, R.H. & M.F. Turek (1998), *American Indians and National Parks.* Tucson, AZ: University of Arizona Press.

Laxson, J.D. (1991), How 'We' See 'Them': Tourism and Native Americans; in: *Annals of Tourism Research* 18 (3): 365-391.

Leasure & Associates (1998), *Conceptual Development Plan for an Extension of the National Native American Scenic Byway; Prepared for the Standing Rock Sioux Tribe.* (unpubl.; archive of the author).

Lee, S. (1989), Traveling the Sunshine State. The Growth of Tourism in South Dakota, 1914-1939; *South Dakota History* 19(2): 194-223.

Lindner, M.H. (2007), *WayuíeskaOíglake: Eine Fallstudie über den Beginn des Tribal Tourism auf der Standing Rock Indian Reservation.* Frankfurt am Main: Universitätsbibliothek (http://publikationen. ub.uni-frankfurt.de/volltexte/2007/5128/).

Mauzé, M. (2003), Two Kwakwaka'wakw Museums: Heritage and Politics; *Ethnohistory* 50 (3): 503-522.

NCLCB (2003), *Press release,* National Council of the Lewis and Clark Bicentennial; 3 December 12, 2003; archive of the author.

NCLCB (2004), *Press release,* National Council of the Lewis and Clark Bicentennial; July 9, 2004; archive of the author.

Pickering, K.A. (2004), *Lakota Culture, World Economy.* Lincoln et al: University of Nebraska Press.

Postner, B. (2002), *Tourismus auf Indianerreservationen. Wirtschaftliche Entwicklung auf den Indianerreservationen im Westen Nordamerikas unter besonderer Berücksichtigung des Tourismus.*Trier: GeografischeGesellschaft.

Schneider, M.J. (1983), The Production of Indian-use and Souvenir Beadwork by Contemporary Indian Women; *Plains Anthropologist* 28 (101): 235-245.

SRTO (2006), *Events,* Standing Rock Tourism Office; webpage: http://www. standingrocktourism.com/eventsView.asp?ID=23 (checked October 24, 2006).

SRTO (2015), *Untitled,* Standing Rock Tourism Office; Facebook post, January 21, 2015; https://www.facebook.com/StandingRockTourism)

TCSRST (Tribal Council of the Standing Rock Sioux Tribe) (1999), *Resolution no 243-99* (June 3rd, 1999). (Archive of the author).

TTPI (2002), *Untitled*; Information Brochure of the Tribal Tourism Partnership Initiative; Bismarck, ND: United Tribes Technical College (archive of the author).

Urry, J. (1996), *The Tourist Gaze: Leisure and Travel in Contemporary Societies.* London: Sage.

YTA (n.d.a): *History of the Yellowstone Trail*; Yellowstone Trail Association (webpage: http://www.yellowstonetrail.org/yt_history.htm).

YTA (n.d.b): *South Dakota, detailed map 5, Waltworth*; Yellowstone Trail Association (webpage: http://www.yellowstonetrail.org/SDe.pdf).

ZPDT (n.d.): *Celebrate Our Past; Understand Our Future*; Zuni Pueblo Department of Tourism (webpage: http://zunitourism.com/visiting_zuni_pueblo.htm).

Quoted interviews, pers. comments, talks, and emails:[6]

Allard, Ladonna Brave Bull: 7/16/2002 (Ft. Yates, ND), 02/14/2005 (email to Markus Lindner)

Archambault, Charles: 8/23/2004 (Ft. Yates, ND)

Bear Catches, Deanne: 8/22/2004 (Kenel, SD)

Beheler, John: 5/21/2002 (Standing Rock Tourism Conference)

Kary, Brent: 8/19/2004 (Fort Yates, North Dakota), 5/21/2002 (Standing Rock Tourism Conference)

Kindt, Diane: 8/29/2004 (Mobridge, SD)

Murphy, Charles W. 7/26/2002 (Fort Yates, ND)

Neumann, Dennis J.: 8/24/2004 (Bismarck, ND)

Olson, Byron: 8/12/2002 (Fort Yates, ND)

Paetz, Karen M.: (White Weasel Woman): 8/14/2002 (Bismarck, ND)

St. John, Sterling: 08/20/2002(Ft. Yates, ND), 9/7/2004 (Fort Yates, ND), 3/23 2006 (email to Markus Lindner)

Strong, Peter: 07/30/2010 (Pine Ridge, SD)

Thompson, Jerold: 8/20/2004 (Kenel, SD)

White Bull, Mark: 7/30/2002 (Fort Yates, ND)

Tourists (anonymized):

Cindy, 8/24/2002

Bob and Shirly, 7/19/2002

Cory, 8/24/2002

Ronda, 7/19/ 2002

6 The Standing Rock Tourism Conference was recorded by Radio KLND. Copies of the recordings are in the archive of the author.

Native American Objects, Tourism and Museums

A De-Reterritorialized View

Maaike de Jong and Alexander Grit

Introduction

This chapter addresses exhibition and stewardship issues raised by culturally sensitive and sacred Native American items in European ethnographic museums. It reflects on questions of representation raised by museums' displays of indigenous objects. Native objects are often portrayed as specimens of 'primitive craftsmanship', historical artifacts or examples of rudimentary science or ecological conservation. These representations neither comprehend nor show these Native American objects' distinct cultural and spiritual significance. Traditionally, museums have a strong object-centered approach. In more recent times museums are increasingly faced with market pressures. Governmental and corporate funding has decreased significantly during the economic crisis and museums need to generate more income on their own. Some institutions believe blockbuster exhibitions are a way to survive the crisis, while others focus specifically on the development of their museum as a tourist attraction within the urban or regional market of travel and tourism. Both approaches are not mutually exclusive of course and might even strengthen each other. It indicates the complexity of curating exhibitions that depict the cultural and spiritual significance of the objects, while at the same time offering accessible exhibitions that are attractive to a wide arrange of visitors. Moreover, it offers opportunities to rethink museum representations of indigenous artifacts and how they are displayed.

In a globalized world museums also increasingly face confrontation with the peoples whose cultural heritage they curate. This chapter looks at issues related to the uprooting of culturally significant items, including assertions of ownership by Native groups. Different approaches to representing sacred and cultural sensitive objects are examined. A best practices model is proposed based on consultations with Native Americans, dialogues that crossed continents and cultures. Co-curations with Native American groups were also considered. This best practices model seeks a new balance between indigenous peoples' legitimate claims and museums' formal missions.

This chapter specifically addresses the exhibition "The Plains Indians: Artists of Earth and Sky" staged at the Musée du quai Branly in 2014. This case study is used to explore the processes of de- and reterritorialization of Native American objects exhibited in museums. Analysis of the case study deals with what James Clifford called different "contradictions and tensions" in the contemporary museum world (2007:1), specifically focusing on the contradictions between the stewardship of culturally sensitive and sacred Native objects and the demands of the tourism industry. These contradictions are analyzed by using French philosophers Gilles Deleuze and Félix Guattari's discourse on processes of deterritorialization and reterritorialization. These processes can be broadly understood as movements producing change: "deterritoriali[z]ation indicates the creative potential of an assemblage. So to deterritoriali[z]e is to free up the fixed relations that contain a body all the while exposing it to new organizations" (Parr 2005:67). When deterritorialization takes place, so does reterritorialization: "territories are not fixed for all time, but are always being made and unmade" (Macgregor Wise 2005:79).

The conclusions suggest a different philosophically inspired discourse for discussing the issues at stake, enabling different dialogues regarding European museums' displays of Native objects. Informed by this discourse, future exhibits could represent multiple meanings of culturally sensitive and sacred Native objects, developing a philosophically inspired 'syntax of dialogue', while maintaining visitor value for institutions. This chapter is based on qualitative research, including literature research, exhibition visits (2014), and interviews with Native American political and spiritual leaders in the 2006-2014 period.

Museums, Tourism and Native Collections

Tourism and museums have a long and complex relationship. Initially, during the Middle Ages, objects brought back from the Holy Land and other relics were in the possession of wealthy private collectors and monasteries. Later on, in the sixteenth century, objects of interest brought back from far away countries were placed in the cabinets of curiosity of noblemen, entrepreneurs, and scientists. Some of the earliest public institutions that focused on collecting included the British Museum (1753) and the Louvre (1793). From the start these early museums were intertwined with tourism. Witz describes how "histories of the development of public museums and mass tourism are inextricably bound together." It is no coincidence that some of the first package tours undertaken by the Thomas Cook organization in the mid-nineteenth century were trips to the Great Exhibition in London. This Great Exhibition set in place the key discursive practices of the modern museum (Witz 2006:128). By the end of the 19th century there where, according to Nason, several types of cultural exhibitions in museums. One of the main kinds of museums Nason talks about is the ethnographic/geographic type that lends itself to the viewers 'traveling' through the cultures. It allowed "the ordinary museum visitor to take his studies pretty much as he would take them in traveling from country to country" (Nason 2000:36).

Museums still serve as 'surrogates of travel.' Tourism and the museum industry are co-dependent variables that should collaborate to create profitable exhibits (Kirshenblatt-Gimblett 1998:151). Meanwhile, the continuing economic restraints as explored by Kratz and Karp (2006) emphasize a need to combine educational value with entertainment value. However, a museum cannot create a tourist attraction by focusing on entertainment at the sacrifice of its mission and educational values. Business concerns emphasizing visitor volume have led to significant restructuring in the museum and heritage sector. This change caused repercussions for management structures, staff organization, exhibitions, marketing, community relations, and far more. As Kratz and Karp observed, "While museums and heritage professionals and institutions everywhere grappled with funding shifts, the specific mix of funding and sources of support available and the nature of those shifts varied considerably across the globe and across institutions – the full range of sources might include governmental bodies, foundations, private donors, corporate funders, public-private partnerships, and income-generating enterprises such as entry fees, shops, restaurants, and IMAX theaters" (2006:14).

Despite the changes, 'surrogates of travel' remains a major function of museums. Museums have even become destinations in themselves in the world of international travel (Witz 2006:128). In general, museums are often conceptualized as engaging tourist attractions that are popular, high traffic areas. Kreps (2003) shows that appealing to tourists can be achieved without sacrificing quality. Accurate knowledge of aboriginal customs acquired by museum visitors helps minimize stereotypes. Profits from tourism also promote the acquisition and development of ethnographic collections by western museums.

Native American political activism led to the passage of legislation and repatriation policies in the USA. Tribes never had the opportunity to curate their own cultural objects because these things were often taken from them without their consent. Maybe, it's more attributable to the fact that after indigenous peoples' activism on the issue, museums became more willing to listen, co-operate, and co-curate to source communities. This changed power discourse has resulted in a growing involvement of Native communities with museums. According to Kirshenblatt-Gimblett (1998) Native groups assume responsibility for the care, access, proprietorship, and interpretation of exhibits of their culture, lifestyles, and objects. A new generation of exhibition experts, teams of curators work together with Native source communities and proactively tend to the stewardship of cultural property, its presentation and interpretation in museums. These developments have implications for the tourism business, which often used a modernist approach to presentation of object with labels such as 'science', 'history', 'art', 'music' and other categories. These categories were generalized and void of spiritual or religious connotations, or frame indigenous medicine men, rituals, and sacred artifacts as 'superstitious'. Now, due to practices of co-curation and communication with Native source communities, an additional view has emerged, one that focuses on the uniqueness of an object's spirituality whose cultural value becomes available through its translation by the cultural producers.

Pine and Gilmore's concept of the 'experience economy' in which they bring forward that "An experience occurs when a company intentionally uses services as the stage, and goods as props, to engage individual customers in a way that creates a memorable event" (1998) helps explain the contemporary relationship between museums and tourism. Museum visitors seek entertainment value which leads to the restructure of museums to accommodate audience demands. This restructuring for tourists is necessary for museums to meet their financial needs in this economic crisis. Clifford (2007) notes how the Musée du quai Branly strives to become a cultural hub of art, ethnography, antiquities, and other exhibits that appeal to diverse backgrounds and populations. Adjacent to the Eiffel Tower the museum is situated in a prime tourist area. However, Clifford argues that a failure to attract proper support could make it 'just another theme park' rather than a compilation of innovative scholarly programs that reflect past, present, and continuing histories. He notes that this failure could thus transcend the project's intended identity, producing instead an institution representing the contemporary specifically including its 'impurities and inconsistencies.' The correct combination of tourism, economic activity, and events drawing attention should raise the needed revenue to make the museum interesting and of intrinsic value to potential visitors.

Peers and Brown (2003) advocate stronger collaboration practices in which native community members are active in the creation of the exhibit and co-create the final product with the museum. Sharon MacDonald proposes more intense collaborative processes involving community members, specialist designers, museum designers, subject specialists, and other consortium participants. According to Sleeper-Smith (2009) collaboration reflects the creativity and decision-making underlying the exhibit. MacDonald (2004) contends that through collaboration a curator presents a view that transcends that of Western dominance, instead reflecting the varied and mutual voices that helped create the exhibit. A collaborative process of creating exhibits also furthers the museum's goal of a multidimensional staff representing different and even contentious perspectives.

With this sensitivity in mind, it is important to remember what these artifacts mean to the people from which they originate. Gurian (2004) argues that, given that ethnographic artifacts functioned as collective memories of a national past, they have been essential components of historical museum collections. Thus, North American museum curators were aghast when contemporary Native groups requested the repatriation of human remains, as well sacred and objects. The Musée du quai Branly has sacred objects in its collection, including items that are perceived as alive. They may have also been objects that were historically protected from outsiders by the tribes. These spiritual beliefs are as alive today among many Native Americans as they were historically. That is why a number of Indian leaders consider the depiction of a colonized past that disregards the spiritual integrity of objects as offensive (De Jong 2009; 2011; 2013). Given their objections it is understandable why co-curating, in a multidisciplinary group with indigenous representatives, is essential. Moreover, tribal ownership of artifacts is also important. Ethnographic museums in Europe have changed from 'cabinets of curiosity' to places of educational representations and dialogue. The key inquiry of the representation of tribal social and spiritual legacies is how to appreciate their ways of life and spiritual convictions. These goals are achieved by ideally relying on different layers of co-constructed traditions of knowledge in a museum setting. Museums ought to reconsider their roles as conservators and intermediaries of indigenous material.

In the USA there is a heightened awareness regarding indigenous objects and consultations with tribal leaders are becoming common practice. Nationally, Native American leaders have lobbied for laws permitting them to recover ownership and responsibility over human remains, as well as related funeral objects. Native activists and museums worked through many issues in developing a law in 1990 that recognized both perspectives, the Native American Graves Protection and Repatriation Act (NAGPRA). They came to an acceptable compromise regarding their respective obligations and rights (Anderson 2004). Fleming commented on the Native Americans rights under this law as follows: "the Native American Graves Protection and Repatriation Act (NAGPRA) permits tribes to repatriate the skeletal remains of known ancestors that are housed in museums and other repositories for proper reburial" (2003:284). Anderson (2004) explains the dialogues leading to NAGPRA as bringing together two contradictory worldviews on the issues of who was to administer the repatriation of indigenous remains, as well as who were the legitimate owners of the collections. At the point when an object is taken from an exhibition under NAGPRA rules or because of transactions with tribal delegates, this choice is a story to be told a wider audience, voicing the views of the museum and the native groups involved.

In Europe, repatriation and co-curation were not issues until 2004 when the United Kingdom passed the Human Tissue Act. As Jenkins observed, "the Human Tissue Act 2004 was passed, amending the 1963 British Museum Act, and consequently permitted, and encouraged, the removal of human remains material from specific (and previously resistant) museums" (2012:2). In European museums the opinion of the tribes should also be included in determining the stewardship of collections. They should be consulted as to whether objects should remain in the museum or be lent to tribes for ceremonies. Another option is to remove objects or the collection to a place more fitting and respectful of indigenous peoples. Even though a place outside the museum setting does not fit most museums' mission, whether human remains and sacred objects should be in museums at all is still open for discussion. The tribes should have the final and definitive say about their stewardship.

Jenkins believes that the debate between museums and indigenous peoples is the manifestation of a crisis in cultural authority, brought about by the persistent questioning of the purpose of museums. A number of theorists regard museums as facilitators of the cohesion and reproduction of a capitalistic market system, thus reinforcing dominant ideologies. There is still an issue of whether museums serve this function when those in the museum sector question and disown their authority (Jenkins 2012:1).

This issue is even more complex in the context of globalization as demonstrated by Anderson when he moves the discussion outside the museum walls. He argues that merely recognizing that the stewardship of objects has changed is a misrepresentation. He argues that identity, cultural awareness, care for the environment, and other issues outside the scope of a single museum have yielded another set of criteria and perspectives for those managing museums such as the co-creation and consulting with Native groups. According to Anderson, Native groups, activists, and the public, now, more than ever, understand their rights regarding the care of resources related to their heritage as well as the earth (2004:266).

How Native groups view their material culture is an extremely important aspect of this new paradigm in museology. As Rosoff rightly states, museum staff need to research how Native people respect and treat their objects and then incorporate these traditional practices into the standard practices of museum conservation and curation (2003:78-79). The difficulties of incorporating traditional Native practices and stewardship in museums with respect to tourism and entertainment should also be addressed. Gilles Deleuze and Félix Guattari (1994) argue that these philosophical issues go beyond everyday practices. In cases where philosophy and art meet, Deleuze and Guattari find that they "pass into each other in a becoming that sweeps them both up in an intensity which co-determines them" (1994:66). A philosophical reconsideration of museum dynamics where ethnographic collections and indigenous concerns meet would yield further insights. Deleuze and Guattari's theorizations of de- and reterritorialization are especially helpful in moving past simple concepts of representation. In their philosophy, deterritorialization and reterritorialization movements are relative, always connected and caught up in one another (1987:10). Their concept suggests that objects in museums can be seen as 'assemblages', a gathering of heterogeneous connections that function together until they change direction and turn into something else. Objects relocated across cultures and continents take on multitude of meanings. Some have solid ties to their original tribal connection, while others address the specific characteristics of education, research and amusement or other means of signification. The concepts of Deleuze and Guattari are an intrinsic part of this case study and the perspective from which it was written.

The Plains Indians, Artists of Earth and Sky: a Case Study at the Musée du quai Branly

The Musée du quai Branly

Almost next to the Eiffel Tower the Musée du quai Branly exhibits 3,500 works of art from Africa, the Americas, Asia, and Oceania. This important collection makes it an unquestionable seat of non-western cultures and arts (Musée Quai Branly n.d.). This collection creates a remarkable identity for the Musée du quai Branly; visitors are presented with a plethora of exhibits that combine art and heritage from the non-European world. "The museum's original and imposing architecture, designed by Jean Nouvel, as well as its wild garden, created by the landscaper Gilles Clément, make it a pleasant and unique place. The museum is the fourth largest museum in Paris" (Tripadvisor n.d.). The mission of the museum is "To showcase non-Western artwork; and to open the eyes of the public" (Lewaltparis n.d.). Since its conception the Musée du quai Branly has aimed to fully integrate research and higher teaching into the life of the institution (Musée Quai Branly n.d.). The museum conveys a message of 'art', 'dialogue' and 'sustainability' that promotes environmental protection, stronger economy, and social progress thus reflecting the needs of museum guests the Musée du quai Branly is also dedicated to collection safeguarding and quality displays (Sustainable development report 2011).

Many scholars are highly critical of the Musée du quai Branly, characterizing exhibits as stereotyped and dismissive of the perceptions, attitudes, and beliefs of indigenous peoples. They claim that the museum exhibitions have been influenced by the overly asserted relations between museum directors and their personal and national political agendas (Price 2010). These critics argue that the exhibits should present France's colonizing past more fully (ibid), rather than a watered down version of historical events, legacies and distortions. These representations require input from the source communities rather than only from a few museum professionals (ibid). The struggle between art, history, geography, and formal sciences cannot continue if a museum is going to exclusively represent the here and now. The museum should include 21st century exhibits as well as those that define the lifestyles and related histories that comprise a museum's original purposes (Clifford 1999). Ruiz-Gómez indicates that unfortunately, the Musée du quai Branly's displays and exhibited artifacts invite a one-sided reading that combines colonialism and primitivism with a modern indulgence. According to Price "visitors to the MQB are rarely invited to step outside of a 1950's-style ethnographic present, rarely given the opportunity to venture beyond an exoticizing vision of non-European cultures that has long since been surpassed in both anthropological and art historical writing. Computers on the multimedia mezzanine, for example, offer information under such categories as shamanism, hunting and gathering, totemism, kinship, sacrifice, initiation, age groups, and cannibalism, but one searches in vain for any mention of (for example) colonialism, collecting, slavery, or tourism" (2007:174). Moreover, the institution has been criticized by Montebello for the use of the trendy notion of museum-as-entertainment and its Disneyfied design (quoted in Levin 2014).

The Plains Indians: Artists of Earth and Sky

Julián Zugazagoitia, Director & CEO of the Nelson-Atkins museum, called "The Plains Indians: Artists of Earth and Sky" at the Musée du quai Branly "a defining moment in the understanding of Native American art" (quoted in: Nelson-Atkins 2014). He also stated that "The works on view convey the continuum of hundreds of years of artistic tradition" (ibid). Stephane Martin, President of the Musée du quai Branly wrote: "The exhibition was designed by Mr. Gaylord Torrence, Merrill Senior Curator of American Indian Art at the Nelson-Atkins Museum of Kansas City, and Fine Arts Professor Emeritus at Drake University in Iowa" (2014:Preface) in a collaboration with three museums: The Musée du quai Branly in Paris, The Nelson-Atkins Museum of Art in Kansas City and The Metropolitan Museum of Art in New York." (Nelson-Atkins 2014). The exhibit was at the Musée du Quai Branly in Paris from April to July 2014, then travelled to the Nelson-Atkins in Kansas City from Sept. 2014 to Jan. 2015, and finally moved to The Metropolitan Museum of Art in New York from March to May 2015 (Nixon 2013). The exhibition of indigenous craftsmanship and art was based on Torrence's scholarship in the field of Plains Indians and his longstanding ties with Native American communities (Nelson-Atkins 2014). According to Torrence, the Musée du quai Branly exhibit captured the aesthetic qualities and spiritual reverberation of Plains Indian art. Moreover, he believed that the objects encapsulated both the creative splendor of their individual creators and the significance of cultural- and spiritual traditions (Nelson-Atkins 2014).

The Nelson-Atkins Museum of Art commented regarding the exhibit that "More than 130 works of art from 57 European, Canadian, and American institutions and private collections will be displayed in an unprecedented continuum from pre-contact to the present-day. Featured works include numbers of the great early Plains Indian robes, and other masterworks" (2014). The show displays an important collection of Native American works, including some exceptional bison robes with painted decorations. Furthermore it connects the often-contentious gap between the field of anthropology and art history, which facilitates dialogue among visitors about issues of viewing the exhibit as either 'art' or 'culture' or both. Most significant is that the exhibition tells stories of lives and souls encompassing hundreds of years and materials vital to contemporary Native artists (Kansas City Star 2014). One newspaper article praises the museum's president, Stéphane Martin, for telling French and European visitors that the Plains Indians objects were very recent so that people stood in long lines to see the exhibition. According to the president the visitors had been more used to art from the Northwest coast of North America; contemporary Plains Indians art had hardly ever been presented before on the European continent. For Martin it was striking to see that [contemporary] Native art is very much alive and creating superb 'stuff' (Spencer 2014).

Oak Shield

Although this exhibition contains many excellent examples of de- and reterritorialization, it is outside of the scope of the current study to examine each. So rather than focus on the overall exhibition, a particular object will be used as an example of the processes of de- and reterritorialization. An object labeled "Shield, ca. 1780; Northern Cheyenne Artist, Wyoming" is particularly esthetically pleasing but also has a complex significance. In the exhibition catalogue Peter Powell, Episcopal minister, independent scholar and a member of the Chief's Society of the Northern Cheyenne People, explains how "Cheyenne sacred shields are living, holy beings, forged in Sun's likeness, radiating supernatural power for protection" (Powell 2014:86), thus referring to the spiritual and sacred qualities of the shield. He states in the catalogue: "A Cheyenne warrior named Oak first possessed this shield; Oak's shield is among the holiest of sacred shields and is most intimately related to Cheyenne suffering" (2014:86). In this way Powell includes the spiritual qualities of the shield, as well as its historical and cultural significance to the Cheyenne. The shield originated in the following way: "Dreamed and made by Oak around 1780 when the Cheyenne lived together in the Black Hills country, the shield was presented by Oak to his son of the same name, who gave it to his son Great Eyes, born about 1818. Great Eyes carried the shield throughout his warrior years and guarded it to his death" (2014:86).

The catalog describes the spiritual significance of the object in detail. It states that Oaks' shield is distinguished for both its supernatural power and beauty" (Powell 2014:86). It also observes "Sun's immense power blessed the bearers of Oak's shield both day and night" (ibid 86); the catalogue also notes that "Grizzly-bear claws protrude from the shield's face, with two paws incised on the back. The grizzly possesses tremendous strength and is difficult to kill. The shield bearer was blessed with the same great powers that flowed from the grizzly claws on the shield's face and thus turned those claws toward the enemy in battle to destroy him" (ibid 86). Also that the owl feathers on the shield "blessed the shield bearer with power to swoop swiftly and smoothly through the night, able to see and destroy his foes in the darkness, as an owl does his prey" (ibid 86). The catalogue additionally mentions that "A buffalo hide trailer flows down the shield's face, bringing the blessing upon the shield bearer of Esevone the Sacred Buffalo Hat (referring to a herd of female bison), that greatest spiritual treasure of the Cheyenne people" (ibid 86). Another spiritual feature pointed out in the observation that "Four rows – the sacred number – of golden-eagle tail feathers fall from the trailer, bringing the blessing and protection of that holiest, most powerful of warrior birds to the shield bearer" (ibid 86). Powell tells the story of Great Eyes, who in 1878-1879, a member of a band of Cheyennes led by Morning Star and Little Wolf. After a battle with U.S. soldiers they were taken prisoner and left to starve at Fort Robinson (ibid 86). Finally, one evening the other members of the band decided to break out, but Great Eyes, knew he was to oold to join them. Great Eyes decided to give his revered Oak shield to his 13 year old, Red Bird, to carry, protect and save the Cheyenne people in the future (ibid 86). Great Eyes stroked the feathers of the shield and thanked it for "protecting him and his people for so long" (ibid 86). After much hardship Red Bird and other survivors of the Northern Cheyenne were moved to a reservation in their own homeland "Red Bird guarded Oak's shield until 1900" (ibid 88), after which he gave it away. According to Powell: "By that time, the warfare ended, the shield's protecting power was no longer vital to the life of the people" and the shield came into the care of the anthropologist, author and conservationist George Bird Grinnell, an expert on Cheyenne culture (ibid 88).

According to Powell "Oak's shield is a spirit-filled being of enduring supernatural power" (2014:88). When Grinnel obtained the Oak shield's spiritual significance was disrupted and it became deterritorialized as it entered the world of (museum) collections. The shield is in the care of the American Museum of Natural History, Division of Anthropology. Currently, the shield is lent to museums in Paris, Kansas City and New York. The shield had undergone significant reterritorializing into an object of conservation and curation with aesthetic and historical meaning. Moreover, it has become part of a tourist attraction people are wiling to wait hours to see. As demonstrated by the history of Great Eyes and the shield it has many sacred and spiritual meanings, as well as bestowing blessings and protections on its bearer. Yet, neither the display labels nor the exhibition catalogue states how – if at all – the Musée du quai Branly deals with these spiritual artifacts in its role of cultural stewardship. There are no protocols or procedures for handling and exhibiting sacred objects. Neither do the labels and catalogue indicate whether Native cultural and spiritual owners of the Oak shield were consulted regarding its exhibition.

Reflections on Native exhibitions, museums and tourism

One of the primary difficulties ethnographic museums face concerning the stewardship of culturally sensitive artifacts is to become aware of the variety of elucidations that can be made in the collaborations with tribal delegates, source communities, exhibition staff and a wide diversity of visitors. Deleuzian and Guattarian's philosophical reflections encourage new ways of thinking about how museum objects interact with the complex global world of tourists and museums; not only do tourists travel, but the objects move through different cultures as well. These theories provide conceptual tools and language that ethnographic museums could use to reexamine themselves. It is essential that European museums understand that countries around the world (especially North America, Canada, Australia and New Zealand) are acquiring knowledge and experience regarding dialogues with tribal delegates. Laws have been passed addressing these issues. Different approaches to museum practice and culturally sensitive objects have been instituted. However, as demonstrated by the "Plains Indians: Artists of Earth and Sky" exhibition at the Musée du quai Branly these changes have not been executed to the fullest, especially regarding spiritual objects as well as collaborative co-curations when a Deleuzian-Guattarian inspired philosophical language creates an awareness and bridge between the different perspectives of museums, visitors and represented Native communities thus creating innovative ways to obtain 'true' dialogue as well as representing difference. To make a philosophical reflection about objects, museums and visitors, inspired by Deleuze and Guattari's (1987) ideas, one might say: In spite of widely held convictions, a museum is not an image of the world. It forms a rhizome with museum visitors, both locals and tourists, and the world. There is a disruptive development (making and unmaking) of the museum and the world. The museum deterritorializes the world, but the world reterritorializes the museum, which then deterritorializes itself (if it is capable, if it can)[1]. In the processes of de- and reterritorialization, many different assemblages lose and gain connections. When mapping these processes one can look at the culturally sensitive object in its original context of having spiritual and communal connotations. In the same light, the tourist can be viewed from his or her 'home' context. However, when the tourist leaves the home country or an object is displaced, new connections and thus assemblages are made and re-made. It could be said that the tourist becomes a visitor, one of many in the long lines waiting to enter the exhibition. Who is a local and who is a tourist becomes obscure. In turn the object becomes translated into the museum environment as well. In this instance, the institutionalized view on '*arts premiers*', the view of the Musée du quai Branly on indigenous objects. In the processes of interaction between Native object(s), institution(s) and visitor(s), new connections, intensities and assemblages are continuously being created and undone. It is important to co-construct exhibitions that create an inspiring place for locals, tourists and represented communities alike, without harming the integrity of the objects and their spiritual histories.

---

1 Contrary to a deeply rooted belief, the book is not an image of the world. It forms a rhizome with the world, there is an aparallel evolution of the book and the world; the book assures the deterritorialization of the world, but the world effects a reterritorialization of the book, which in turn deterritorializes itself in the world (if it is capable, if it can) (Deleuze and Guattari 1987:11).

References

Anderson, G. (2004), The Role of the Object: The Obligation of Stewardship and Cultural Responsibility; in: Anderson, G. (ed.) *Reinventing the Museum: Historical and Contemporary Perspectives on the Paradigm Shift*: 265-267. Walnut Creek, CA: Alta Mira Press.

Clifford, J. (1999), Museums as Contact Zones; in: Clifford, J., *Routes: Travel and Translation in the Late Twentieth Century*: 188-219. Cambridge, MS: Harvard University Press.

Clifford, J. (2007), Quai Branly in Process; October 12, 2007: 3-23. 14 June 2015. Webpage: http://www.mitpressjournals.org/doi/abs/10.1162/octo.2007.120.1.3#.VX3cDs4xH-Y.

Daily Dawn (2008), Quai Branly Museum: Article Published in Daily Dawn.; Queuing up at the Museum. N.d. 4 Nov. 2008. Web. 31 Jan. 2015. Webpage: http://www.ambafrance-pk.org/QuaiQuai-Branly-Museum-article.

De Jong, M. (2009), The Museum as Visitor Experience: Displaying Sacred Native American Objects; in: R. K. Isaac, V. Platenkamp, & A. Portegies, eds., *Voices in Tourism Management: Creating Spaces for Tacit Knowledge and Innovation*:72-85. Breda, Netherlands: NHTV.

De Jong, M. (2011), The Museum as a Visitor Experience: Displaying Sacred Haitian Vodou Objects; *International Journal of Business and Globalisation* 7 (1): 29-39.

De Jong, M. (2013), The Future of European Ethnographic Museums, in: A. Postma & I. Yeoman, eds., *The Future of European Tourism*: 194-214. Leeuwarden, Netherlands: ETFI.

Deleuze, Gilles & Félix Guattari (1987), *A Thousand Plateaus: Capitalism and Schizophrenia*. Minneapolis, MN: University of Minnesota, 1987.

Deleuze, Gilles & Félix Guattari (1994), *What Is Philosophy?* New York: Columbia University Press.

Gilmore, J. & Pine, J. (1999), *The Experience Economy: Work is Theatre and Every Business a Stage*. Boston, MS: Harvard Business School.

Gilmore, J. & Pine, J. (1998), Welcome to the Experience Economy; *Harvard Business Review*, 1 July 1998. Webpage: https://hbr.org/1998/07/welcome-to-the-experience-economy.

Gurian, E.H. (2004), What is the Object of This Exercise?; in: Anderson, G., ed., *Reinventing the Museum: Historical and Contemporary Perspectives on the Paradigm Shift*: 269-283. Walnut Creek, CA: Alta Mira Press.

Jenkins, T. (2012), Who are We to Decide? Internal Challenges to Cultural Authority in the Contestation over Human Remains in British Museums; *Cultural Sociology* 6 (3): 455-470.

Kansas City Star (2014), New Exhibit at Kansas City's Nelson-Atkins Presents the Astounding Art of the Plains Indians; in: Kansas City Star, 17 Sept. 2014. Webpage: http://www.kansascity.com/opinion/editorials/article2143220.html.

Kirshenblatt-Gimblett, B. (1998), *Destination Culture: Tourism, Museums, and Heritage*. Berkeley, CA: University of California Press.

Kratz, Corinne & Karp, Ivan (2006), Introduction; in: I. Karp, C.A. Kratz, L. Szwaja & T. Ybarra-Frausto, eds., *Museum Frictions: Public Cultures, Global Transformations*: 1-34. Durham, NC: Duke University Press.

Kreps, C.F. (2003), *Liberating Culture: Cross-Cultural Perspectives on Museums, Curation, and Heritage Preservation*. London: Routledge.

Levin, Ann (2014), Critic & Museum Director on Encounters with Art; in: U-T San Diego, 30 Sept. 2014. Webpage: http://www.utsandiego.com/news/2014/sep/30/critic-museum-director-on-encounters-with-art/.

MacDonald, S. (2004), Enchantment and its Dilemmas: The Museum as a Ritual Site; in: M. Bouquet & N. Porto, eds., *Science, Magic, and Religion the Ritual Process of Museum Magic*: 209-228. New York: Berghahn Books.

Macgregor Wise, J. (2005), Assemblage; in: Charles J. Stivale, ed., *Gilles Deleuze: Key Concepts*: 77-87. Montreal: McGill-Queen's University Press.

Musée Du Quai Branly (n.d.), Musée Du Quai Branly: Foreign Visitors; in: Musée Du Quai Branly: Foreign Visitors; webpage: http://www.quaibranly.fr/en/accueil/acces-rapide-haut/foreign-visitors.html.

Musée Du Quai Branly (2015a), Musée Du Quai Branly: Research and Teaching Department; 31 Jan. 2015; webpage: http://www.quaibranly.fr/en/enseignement/research-and-teaching-department.html.

Musée Du Quai Branly (2015b), Musée Du Quai Branly: Sustainable Development; *Musée Du Quai Branly: Sustainable Development*; 28 July 2015; webpage: http://www.quaibranly.fr/en/the-public-institution/sustainable-development.html.

Nason, James D. (2000), Our" Indians: The Unidimensional Indian in the Disembodied Local Past; in: NMAI, ed., *The Changing Presentation of the American Indian: Museums and Native Cultures*: 29-46. Washington, D.C.: National Museum of the American Indian, 2000.

Nelson-Atkins Museum of Art (2014), Major Plains Indian Exhibition Opens in Paris, Propels Nelson-Atkins Into International Arena; 25 Mar. 2014; webpage: http://www.nelson-atkins.org/images/PDF/press/2014%20 03%2025%20Plains%20Paris%20opening%20FINAL.pd.

Nixon, L. (2015), War Horse ... Show Horse; in: Capital Journal, 31 Jan. 2015; webpage: http://www.capjournal.com/news/war-horse-show-horse/article_ e10a21ea-3a11-11e3-99e8-0019bb2963f4.html.

Page, S. & Connell, J. (2009), *Tourism: A Modern Synthesis*. Andover, UK: South-Western Cengage Learning.

Parr, Adrian (2005), Deterritorialisation / Reterritorialisation; in: A. Parr, ed., *The Deleuze Dictionary*: 66-69. New York: Columbia University Press.

Peers, L.L. & Brown, A. K. (2003), *Museums and Source Communities*. London: Routledge.

Powell, Peter J. (2014), Shield; in: Gaylord Torrence, ed., *The Plains Indians: Artists of Earth and Sky*: 86-88. N.p.: Skira, 2014.

Price, Sally (2007), *Paris Primitive: Jacques Chirac's Museum on the Quai Branly*. Chicago, IL: University of Chicago Press, 2007.

Rosoff, N.B. (2003), Integrating Native Views into Museum Procedures: Hope and Practice at the National Museum of the American Indian; in: L.L. Peers & A.K. Brown, eds., *Museums and Source Communities*: 72-79. London: Routledge.

Sleeper-Smith, S. (2009), *Contesting Knowledge: Museums and Indigenous Perspectives*. Lincoln, NE: University of Nebraska Press.

Spencer, Laura (2014), Three Museum Directors On The New Plains Indians Art Exhibit At The Nelson; 17 Sept. 2014; webpage: http://kcur.org/post/ three-museum-directors-new-plains-indians-art-exhibit-nelson.

Le Walt Paris (n.d.), The Quai Branly Museum near the Boutique Hotel Le Walt in Paris; webpage: http://lewaltparis.com/en/quai-branly-paris.

Torrence, Gaylord (2014), *The Plains Indians: Artists of Earth and Sky*. N.p.: Skira, 2014.

Tripadvisor (n.d.), Musée Du Quai Branly, Paris; on: TripAdvisor: Hours, Address, Tickets & Tours, Reviews; webpage: http://www.tripadvisor.com/ Attraction_Review-g187147-d500272-Reviews-Musee_du_quai_Branly-Paris_Ile_de_France.html.

Rosoff, N.B. (2003), Integrating Native Views into Museum Procedures: Hope and Practice at the National Museum of the American Indian; in: Peers, L. L. and Brown, A.K., eds. *Museums and Source Communities*:72-99. London: Routledge.

Witz, Leslie (2006), Transforming Museums on Postapartheid Tourist Routes; in: I. Karp, C.A. Kratz, L. Szwaja & T. Ybarra-Frausto, eds., *Museum Frictions: Public Cultures, Global Transformations*: 107-134. Durham, NC: Duke University Press.

The Contributors

Bruce Bernstein (1953) is executive director of the Ralph T. Coe Foundation for the Arts in Santa Fe, NM, and serves as executive director of the Continuous Pathways Foundation and Tribal Historic Preservation Officer for the Pueblo of Pojoaque. He previously served as director of research and collections at the National Museum of the American Indian, Smithsonian Institution (Washington, DC), director and chief curator of the Museum of Indian Arts and Cultures/ Laboratory of Anthropology (Santa Fe, NM), and director of the Southwestern Association of Indian Arts (Santa Fe, NM). He published extensively on Indian art, notably basketry and Pueblo pottery, and on contemporary museum issues. E-mail:bernsteinbruce@gmail.com.

Susanne Berthier-Foglar (1953) holds a Ph.D. in Native American Studies from the University of Grenoble (France). From 2007-2012 she was on the staff of the Université de Savoie. Since 2012 she is Professor at the University of Grenoble and specializes in Native American history and identities. She has published articles on uranium mining in the American Southwest, a monograph on Pueblo history (2010) and (co)edited books on the French colonial period in North America (2009), power and conflict in mountain areas (2011), and biomapping of indigenous peoples (2012). E-mail: susanne.berthier-foglar@u-grenoble3.fr.

Birgit Däwes (1973) recently moved to Europa University in Flensburg, Germany where she serves as Professor and Chair of American Studies. She was previously Professor of American Studies and Director of the Center of Canadian Studies at the University of Vienna, Austria, and held teaching positions at the Universities of Mainz and Würzburg, and at National Sun Yat-sen University in Kaohsiung, Taiwan. Her research specialized in Native American and First Nations Studies, especially drama and performance and contemporary Native literature and art, as well as contemporary American novels, television series, and issues of terrorism and surveillance. She published on Native North American drama and theater, and an award-winning study on 9/11 fiction as a mode of cultural memory. With Karsten Fitz and Sabine N. Meyer she co-edits the international book series Routledge Research in Transnational Indigenous Perspectives. E-mail: birgit.daewes@uni-flensburg.de.

Maaike de Jong (1969) is a Senior Lecturer at Stenden University of Applied Sciences' School of Leisure and Tourism. She received an MA in European Leisure Studies from Tilburg University (1994), an MA cum laude in Religious Studies from the University of Amsterdam (2008) and a Ph.D. in Governance at Utrecht University (2014). Her thesis addressed the applied use of concepts from the French philosophers Gilles Deleuze and Félix Guattari in qualitative research and social studies. She specializes in Tourism, Museums and Religion with special interest in issues of interpretation of indigenous sacred objects, the representation of spirituality to widely diverse audiences, and local community involvement in museums. Research was carried out at the Museum of the Rockies in Bozeman, Montana, and she studied Middle-Eastern museum collections in the context of cultural history, memory and identity. Results were presented at international conferences throughout Europe, and in several publications. E-mail: Jonggrit@hotmail.com.

Eloïse Galliard (1986) studied History of Art and Collections at the École du Louvre in Paris, France. For her Ph.D. she studied the history of the collections of Native artifacts from the Southwest and California curated in French museums. She worked as co-curator for an exhibition about aboriginal peoples from the Southwest and California "Les Fils du Soleil" at the New World Museum in La Rochelle, France. She is currently in charge of the Archives at the Fairground Art Museum in Paris, but still engaged in studies of Native American collections from the Southwest, and Native-French relations in North America since the 1850's. E-mail: eloise.j.galliard@gmail.com.

Alexander Grit (1970) is a research lecturer at Stenden University of Applied Sciences and a senior research fellow at Leicester University, United Kingdom. He teaches courses on leisure studies, tourism development, urban development, hospitality and retail concept development. He also does research with students and colleagues regarding the art of facilitating serendipity in spaces of hospitality. His research interests focus on the health of interactional spaces, network organizations, art and hospitality, serendipitous processes and Deleuzian philosophy. He has contributed articles to academic journal articles and written book chapters on art, retail concepts, home exchanges and museums. E-mail: Alexander.grit@gmail.com.

Mette van der Hooft (1983) studied Archaeology and History of Native American Peoples at Leiden University (the Netherlands). She worked on the scientific documentation of a wide range of collections and as project assistant at the National Museum of World Cultures in Leiden. She contributed to several permanent and temporary exhibits and co-curated "The Story of the Totem Pole" exhibition (2012-13) at the same institution. Her research interests include textile production, tourism and female collectors in the American Southwest, and published previously on Dutch tourists in that region. E-mail: amarna6@hotmail.com.

Pieter Hovens (1951) curates the North American collection at the National Museum of World Cultures in Leiden, The Netherlands. He studied cultural anthropology at Radboud University (Nijmegen, The Netherlands) and First Nations Studies at the University of British Columbia (Vancouver, Canada). Subsequently he worked for the Dutch government in ethnic minority, volunteering and citizenship education policies. His publications focus on the history of anthropology and North American Indian studies, Native American art and material culture, and the history of Indian-Dutch relations. E-mail: pieter.hovens@wereldculturen.nl.

Markus Lindner (1974) studied Cultural Anthropology, Prehistory and Politics at Goethe University Frankfurt (Germany). As a student he worked for the Hessian State Museum Darmstadt (Germany) and later at the Museum der Weltkulturen (Frankfurt). He was a guest curator at Akta Lakota Museum & Cultural Center (Chamberlain, SD). Since 2007 he has been on the staff at the Institut für Ethnologie (University Frankfurt). His doctoral thesis (2007) was about tourism on the Standing Rock Indian Reservation, based on fieldwork in the Dakotas. Other research interests include visual representations of Native Americans, self-representation, contemporary Native American art, and museum studies. He currently researches Hopi representation in Germany. E-mail: m.lindner@em.uni-frankfurt.de.

Mededelingen van het Rijksmuseum voor Volkenkunde

No. 1 J.P.B. de Josselin de Jong, *Archeological Materials from Saba and St. Eustatius, Lesser Antilles*, 1947. 54 pp. + 19 figs. + 16 p. plates.

No. 2 J.L. Swellengrebel, *Een vorstenwijding op Bali. Naar materiaal verzameld door H.J.E.F. Schwartz*, 1947. 27 pp. + 18 p. plates.

No. 3 C. Nooteboom, *Quelques techniques de tissage des Petites Iles de la Sonde.* With *Discussion et données complémentaires à propos de l'ouvrage de M. James Hornell,* Watertransport, Origin and Early Evolution, par Pierre Paris 1948. 46 pp.+ 8 p. plates + 10 figs.

No. 4 P.J.L. Vandenhoute, *Classification stylistique de masque Dan et Guéré de la Côte d'Ivoire occidentale (A.O.F.)*, 1948. 48 pp.+ 7 p. plates, map.

No. 5 T. Volker, *Ukiyoe Quartet: Publisher, Designer, Engraver and Printer*, 1949 vi + 29 pp. ill.

No. 6/7 T. Volker, *The animal in Far Eastern Art and especially in the Art of the Japanese Netsuke, with references to Chinese origins, traditions, legends and art, 1950.* 190 pp. + 19 p. plates.

No. 8/9 P.H. Pott, *Introduction to the Tibetan Collection of the National Museum of Ethnology, Leiden*, 1951. 184 pp.+ 32 p. plates.

No. 10 J.P.B. de Josselin de Jong, *Lévi-Strauss's Theory on Kinship and Marriage*, 1952. iv + 59 pp. + figs. Reprinted 1970.

No. 11 Tijs Volker, *Porcelain and the Dutch East India Company, as recorded in the Dagh-registers of Batavia Castle, those of Hirando and Deshima and other contemporary papers, 1602-1682*, 1954. 243 pp. + 32 p. plates, maps.

No.12 Adriaan A. Gerbrands, *Art as an Element of Culture, especially in Negro-African*, 1957. x + 158 pp. + 16 p. plates. Translated from the Dutch by G.E. van Baaren-Paape.

No. 13 Tijs Volker, *The Japanse Porcelain Trade of the Dutch East India Company after 1683*, 1959. 92 pp. + 26 p. plates.

No. 14 Herman H. Frese, *Anthropology and the Public: The Role of Museums*, 1960. viii + 253 pp. +16 p. plates.

No. 15 *The Wonder of Man's Ingenuity. Being a Series of Studies in Archaeology, Material Culture, and Social Anthropology by Members of the Academic Staff of the National Museum of Ethnology, Published on the Occasion of the Museum's 125th Anniversary*, 1962. 165 pp. + 24 p. plates, map.

No. 16 Simon Kooijman, *Ornamented Bark-Cloth in Indonesia*, 1963. viii + 145 pp. + 32 p. plates and 235 drawings.

No. 17 Gert W. Nooter, *Old Kayaks in the Netherlands*, 1971. 76 pp. ill.

No. 18 Freerk C. Kamma and Simon Kooijman, Rowawa Forja, *Child of the Fire. Iron Working and the Role of Iron in West New Guinea (West Iran)*, 1973. viii + 45 pp. ill. map.

No. 19 Ger D. van Wengen, *The Cultural Inheritance of the Javanese in Surinam*, 1975. iv + 55 pp.

No. 20 Gert Nooter, *Leadership and Headship: Changing Authority of the Patterns in an East Greenland Hunting Community*, 1976. viii + 117 pp. ill.

No. 21 Simon Kooijman, *Tapa on Moce Island, Fiji: A Traditional Handicraft in a Changing Society*, 1977. x + 176 pp. ill.

No. 22 W.R. van Gullik, *Irezumi: The Pattern of Dermatography in Japan*, 1982. xviii + 308 pp. + 72 p. plates.

No. 23 Ted J.J. Leyenaar, Ulama*: The Perpetuation in Mexico of the Pre-Spanish Ball Game Ullamalitzli*, 1978. viii + 120 pp. ill.

No. 24 Simon Kooijman, *Art, Art Objects, and Ritual in the Mimika Culture*, 1984. xix + 173 pp. Translated from The Dutch by Inez Seeger.

No. 25 Pieter ter Keurs and Dirk Smidt (eds.), *The language of Things. Studies in Ethnocommunication, in Honour of Professor Adrian A. Gerbrands*, 1990. 208 pp. ill.

No. 26 Gerard W. van Bussel, Paul L. T. van Dongen and Ted J.J. Leyenaar (eds), *The Mesoamerican Ballgame. Papers presented at the International Colloquium 'The Mesoamerican Ballgame 2000 BC-AD 2000', Leiden, June 30th-July 3rd, 1988*, 1991. 300 pp.ill.

No. 27 Rita Bolland, with Rogier M.A. Bedaux and Renée Boser- Sarivaxevanis, *Tellem Textiles, Archaeological Finds from Burial Caves in Mali's Bandiagara Cliff.* Published in Cooperation with the Tropenmuseum, Royal Tropical Institute Amsterdam, 1991. 321 pp. ill.

No. 28 Dirk A.M. Smidt, Pieter ter Keurs and Albert Trouwborst (eds.), *Pacific Material Culture. Essays in Honour of Dr. Simon Kooijman, on the Occasion of his 80th birthday*, 1995. 336 pp. ill.

No. 29 Michael Prager and Pieter ter Keurs (eds.), *W.H. Rassers and the Batak Magic Staff*, 1998. 152 pp. ill.

No. 30 Reimar Schefold and Han F. Vermeulen (eds.), *Treasure Hunting? Collectors and Collections of Indonesian Artefacts*, Mededelingen van het Rijksmuseum voor Volkenkunde Leiden, no. 30 / CNWS Publications, Vol. 116, Leiden 2002, ISBN 978-90-5789-078-9, 324 pp. incl. Index out of print.

No. 31 Laura Van Broekhoven, *Conquistando Io Invencible. Fuentes históricas sobre las culturas indígenas de la region Central de Nicaragua*, 2002 ISBN 978-90-5789-083-3, 352 pp. Incl., bibl., app., index, € 36,00.

No. 32 Cunera Buijs, *Furs and Fabrics. Transformations, Clothing and Identity in East Greenland*, Mededelingen van het Rijksmuseum voor Volkenkunde Leiden, no. 36 / CNWS Publications Vol. 129, Leiden 2004, ISBN 978-90-5789-094-9, 300 pp. Incl. photogr.,figs., app., index, out of print.

No. 33 R. Bedaux, J. Polet, K. Sanogo & A. Schmidt (éds), *Recherches archéologiques à Dia dans le Delta intérieur du Niger (Mali): bilan des saisons de fouilles 1998-2003*, Mededelingen van het Rijksmuseum voor Volkenkunde Leiden, no. 33/ CNWS Publications Vol. 144, Leiden 2005, ISBN 978-90-5789-107-6, 560 pp., richly ill,. Incl. figs., bibl., annexes, € 48,00.

No. 34 Pieter ter Keurs, *Condensed Reality. A study of material culture. Case studies from Siassi (Papua New Guinea) and Enggano (Indonesia)*, Mededelingen van het Rijksmuseum voor Volkenkunde Leiden, no. 34 / CNWS Publication Vol. 148, ISBN 978-90-5789-112-0, 240 pp. Ill., incl.,append., bibl., index, € 36,00

No. 35 Joost Willink, *Stages in Civilisation, Dutch museums in quest of West Central African collections (1856-1889)*, Mededelingen van het Rijksmuseum voor Volkenkunde Leiden, no. 35 / CNWS Publicaties, € 49,95.

No. 36 Pieter ter Keurs (ed.), *Colonial Collections Revisisted*, Mededelingen van het Rijksmuseum voor Volkenkunde Leiden, no. 36 / CNWS Publications Vol. 152, Leiden 2007, ISBN 978-90-5789-152-6, 270 pp. Ill. € 36,00.

No. 37 Rudolf Effert, *Royal Cabinets and Auxiliary Branches. Origins of the National Museum of Ethnology 1816-1883*, Mededelingen van het Rijksmuseum voor Volkenkunde Leiden, no. 37 / CNWS Publications No. 159, Leiden 2008, ISBN 978-90-5789-159-5 340 pp. € 45,00.

No. 38 Véronique Degroot, *Candi, Space and Landscape. A study on the distribution, orientation and spatial organization of Central Javanese temple remains.* Mededelingen van het Rijksmuseum voor Volkenkunde Leiden, no. 38, Leiden 2009, ISBN 978-90-8890-039-6, 497 pp. Ill., Incl. bibl., index, € 49,95.

No. 39 Laura Van Broekhoven, Cunera Buijs & Pieter Hovens (eds), *Sharing Knowledge & Cultural Heritage: First Nations of the Americas. Studies in Collaboration with Indigenous Peoples from Greenland, North and South America*. Mededelingen van het Rijksmuseum voor Volkenkunde Leiden, no. 39, 2010, ISBN 978-90-8890-066-2, 250 pp. Ill., Incl. bibl., € 29,95.

No. 40 Karen Jacobs, *Collecting Kamoro. Objects, encounters and representation on the southwest coast of Papua*. Mededelingen van het Rijksmuseum voor Volkenkunde Leiden, no. 40, Leiden 2011, ISBN 978-90-8890-088-4, 288 pp. Ill., Incl. bibl., index, € 29,95.

No. 41 Jimmy Mans, *Amotopoan Trails, A recent archaeology of Trio movements*. Mededelingen van het Rijksmuseum voor Volkenkunde Leiden, no. 41, Leiden 2012, ISBN 978-90-8890-098-3, 332 pp. Ill., Incl. bibl., € 34,95.

No. 42 Alexander Geurds & Laura Van Broekhoven (eds), *Creating Authenticity. Authentication Processes in Ethnographic Museums*. Mededelingen van het Rijksmuseum voor Volkenkunde Leiden, no. 42, 2013, ISBN 978-90-8890-205-5, 176 pp. Ill., Incl. bibl., € 29,95.

No. 43 Luitgard Mols & Marjo Buitelaar (eds), *Hajj: Global Interactions through Pilgrimage*. Mededelingen van het Rijksmuseum voor Volkenkunde Leiden, no. 43, 2014, ISBN 978-90-8890-285-7, 275 pp. Ill., Incl. bibl., € 39,95.

No. 44 Laura van Broekhoven, *Mercados de la Mixteca. Si no hay carro, no hay negocio*. Mededelingen van het Rijksmuseum voor Volkenkunde Leiden, no. 44, 2015, ISBN 978-90-8890-289-5, 284 pp. Ill., Incl. bibl., €39,95.

Mededelingen van het Rijksmuseum voor Volkenkunde is currently published by Sidestone Press: www.sidestone.com.